Newbury & Hobbes
THE UNDYING

TITAN®
COMICS

TITAN COMICS

EDITOR TOM WILLIAMS

WITH THANKS TO STEVE WHITE

Managing Editor Martin Eden
Managing & Launch Editor Andrew James
Titan Comics Editorial Jonathan Stevenson
Production Assistant Rhiannon Roy
Production Controller Peter James
Senior Production Controller Jackie Flook
Art Director Oz Browne
Sales & Circulation Manager Steve Tothill
Marketing Assistant Charlie Raspin
Senior Publicist Will O'Mullane
Publicist Imogen Harris
Senior Brand Manager Chris Thompson
Ads and Marketing Assistant Bella Hoy
Commercial Manager Michelle Fairlamb
Head of Rights Jenny Boyce
Publishing Manager Darryl Tothill
Publishing Director Chris Teather
Operations Director Leigh Baulch
Executive Director Vivian Cheung
Publisher Nick Landau

Published by Titan Comics
A division of Titan Publishing Group, Ltd.
144 Southwark St.
London, SE1 0UP

ISBN: 9781782760399

A CIP catalogue record for this title is available from the British Library.

First edition: May 2019
10 9 8 7 6 5 4 3 2 1

Printed in Spain.

For rights information contact jenny.boyce@titanemail.com

WWW.TITAN-COMICS.COM
Become a fan on Facebook.com/comicstitan
Follow us on Twitter @ComicsTitan

Newbury & Hobbes

THE UNDYING

WRITTEN BY
George Mann

ARTWORK BY
Dan Boultwood

LETTERING BY
Rob Steen

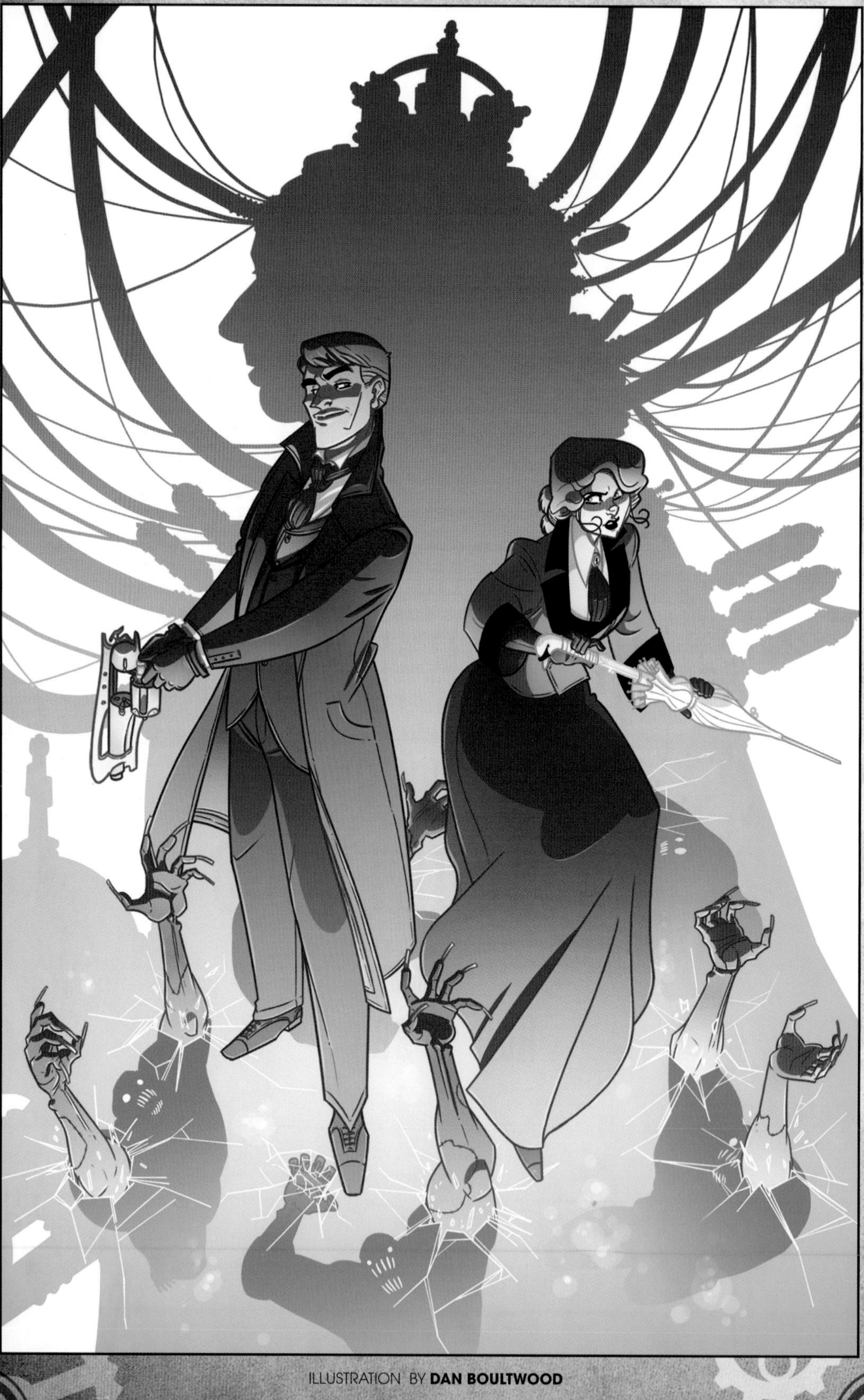

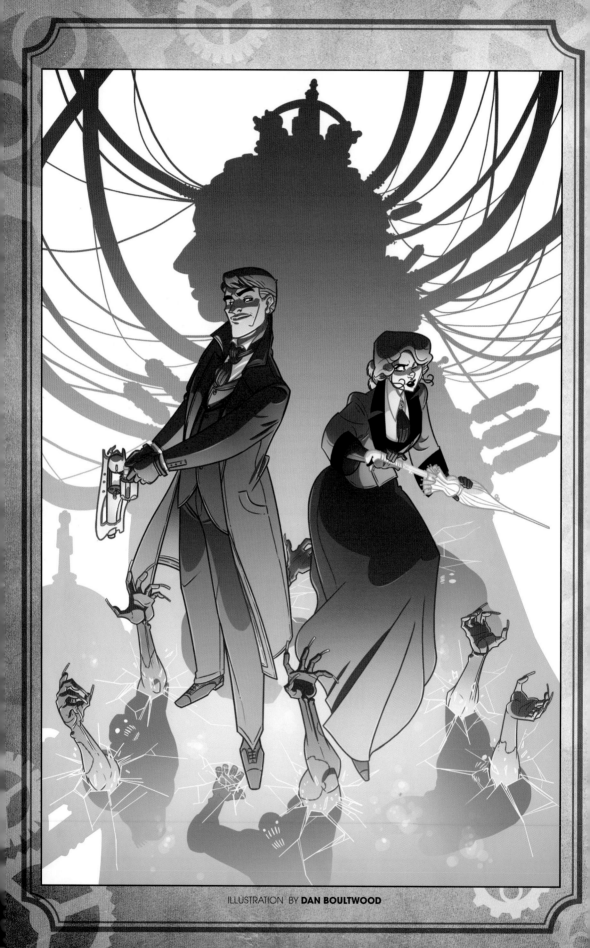

ILLUSTRATION BY **DAN BOULTWOOD**

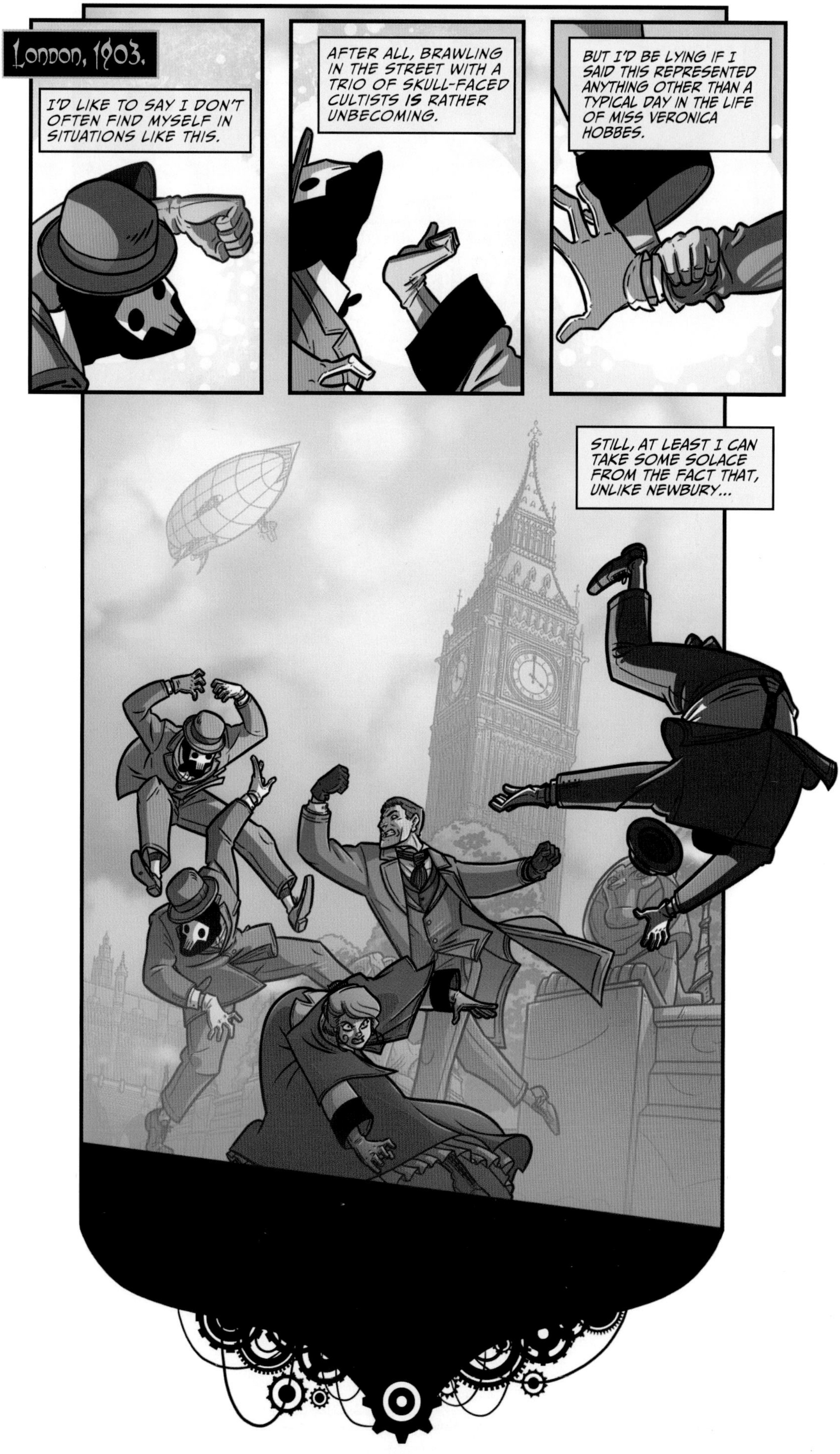
London, 1903.
I'D LIKE TO SAY I DON'T OFTEN FIND MYSELF IN SITUATIONS LIKE THIS.
AFTER ALL, BRAWLING IN THE STREET WITH A TRIO OF SKULL-FACED CULTISTS IS RATHER UNBECOMING.
BUT I'D BE LYING IF I SAID THIS REPRESENTED ANYTHING OTHER THAN A TYPICAL DAY IN THE LIFE OF MISS VERONICA HOBBES.
STILL, AT LEAST I CAN TAKE SOME SOLACE FROM THE FACT THAT, UNLIKE NEWBURY...

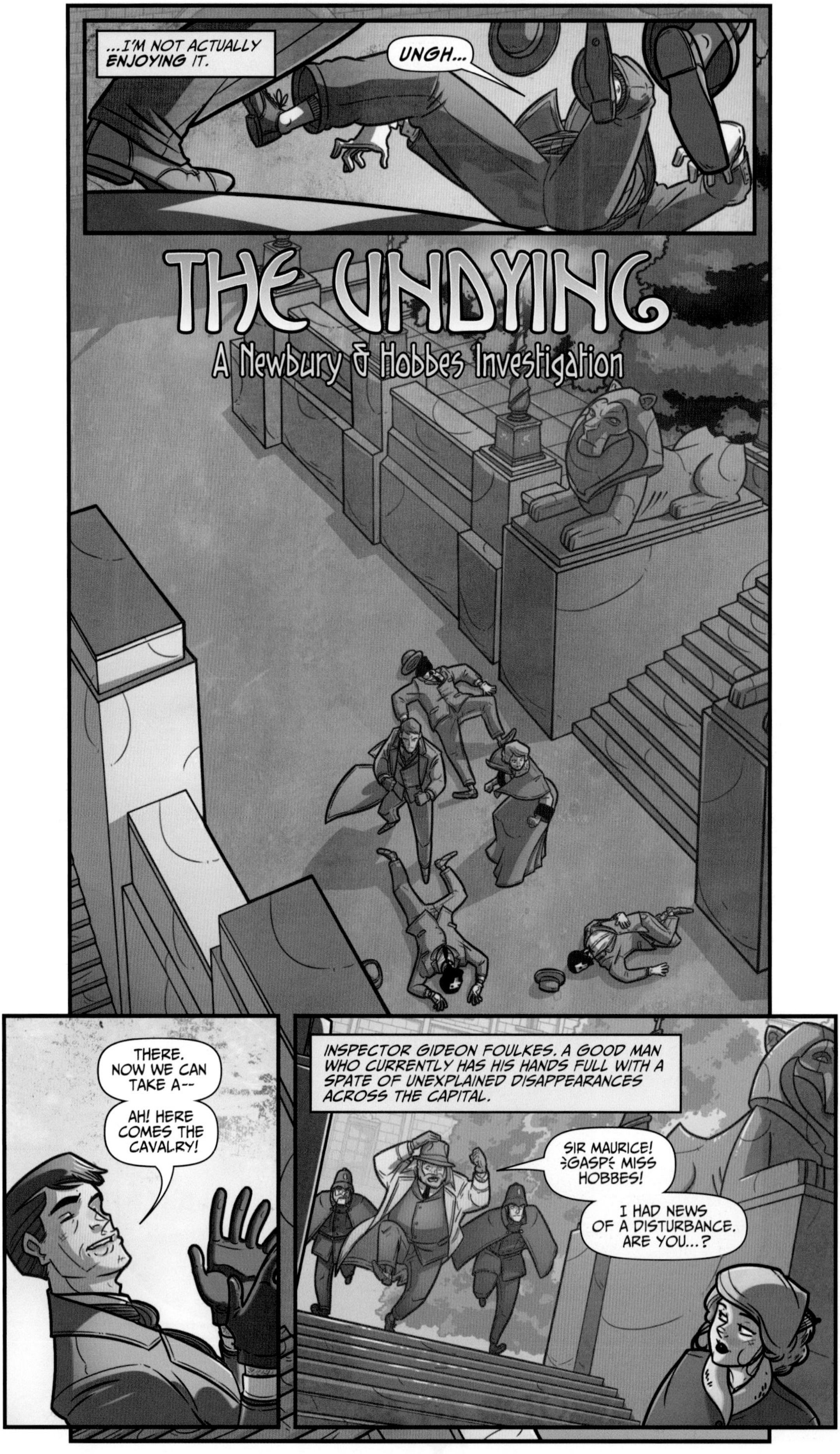
...I'M NOT ACTUALLY ENJOYING IT.
UNGH...
THE UNDYING
A Newbury & Hobbes Investigation
THERE. NOW WE CAN TAKE A--
AH! HERE COMES THE CAVALRY!
INSPECTOR GIDEON FOULKES. A GOOD MAN WHO CURRENTLY HAS HIS HANDS FULL WITH A SPATE OF UNEXPLAINED DISAPPEARANCES ACROSS THE CAPITAL.
SIR MAURICE! ⁂GASP⁂ MISS HOBBES!
I HAD NEWS OF A DISTURBANCE. ARE YOU...?

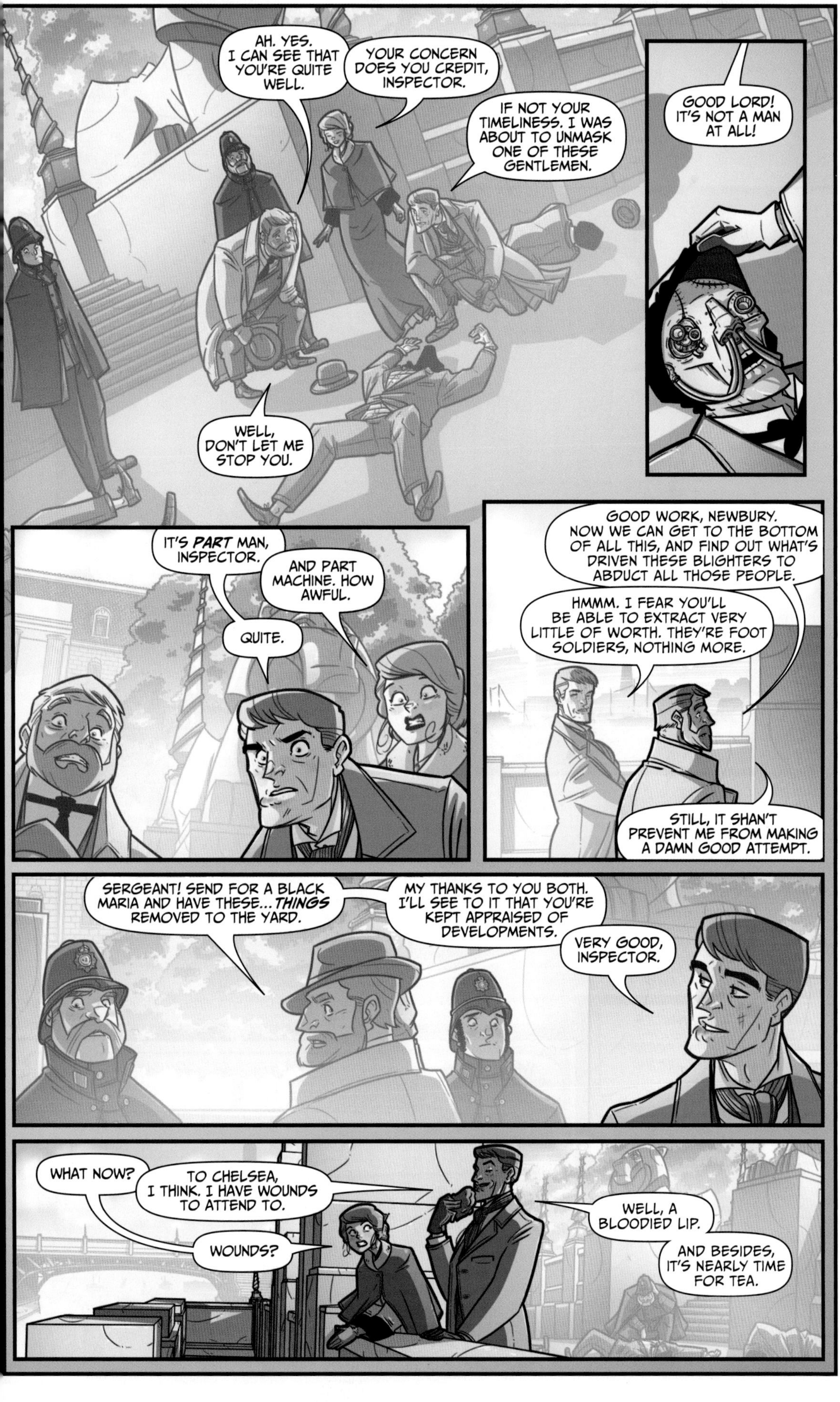
AH. YES. I CAN SEE THAT YOU'RE QUITE WELL.
YOUR CONCERN DOES YOU CREDIT, INSPECTOR.
IF NOT YOUR TIMELINESS. I WAS ABOUT TO UNMASK ONE OF THESE GENTLEMEN.
WELL, DON'T LET ME STOP YOU.
GOOD LORD! IT'S NOT A MAN AT ALL!
IT'S PART MAN, INSPECTOR.
AND PART MACHINE. HOW AWFUL.
QUITE.
GOOD WORK, NEWBURY. NOW WE CAN GET TO THE BOTTOM OF ALL THIS, AND FIND OUT WHAT'S DRIVEN THESE BLIGHTERS TO ABDUCT ALL THOSE PEOPLE.
HMMM. I FEAR YOU'LL BE ABLE TO EXTRACT VERY LITTLE OF WORTH. THEY'RE FOOT SOLDIERS, NOTHING MORE.
STILL, IT SHAN'T PREVENT ME FROM MAKING A DAMN GOOD ATTEMPT.
SERGEANT! SEND FOR A BLACK MARIA AND HAVE THESE... THINGS REMOVED TO THE YARD.
MY THANKS TO YOU BOTH. I'LL SEE TO IT THAT YOU'RE KEPT APPRAISED OF DEVELOPMENTS.
VERY GOOD, INSPECTOR.
WHAT NOW?
TO CHELSEA, I THINK. I HAVE WOUNDS TO ATTEND TO.
WOUNDS?
WELL, A BLOODIED LIP.
AND BESIDES, IT'S NEARLY TIME FOR TEA.

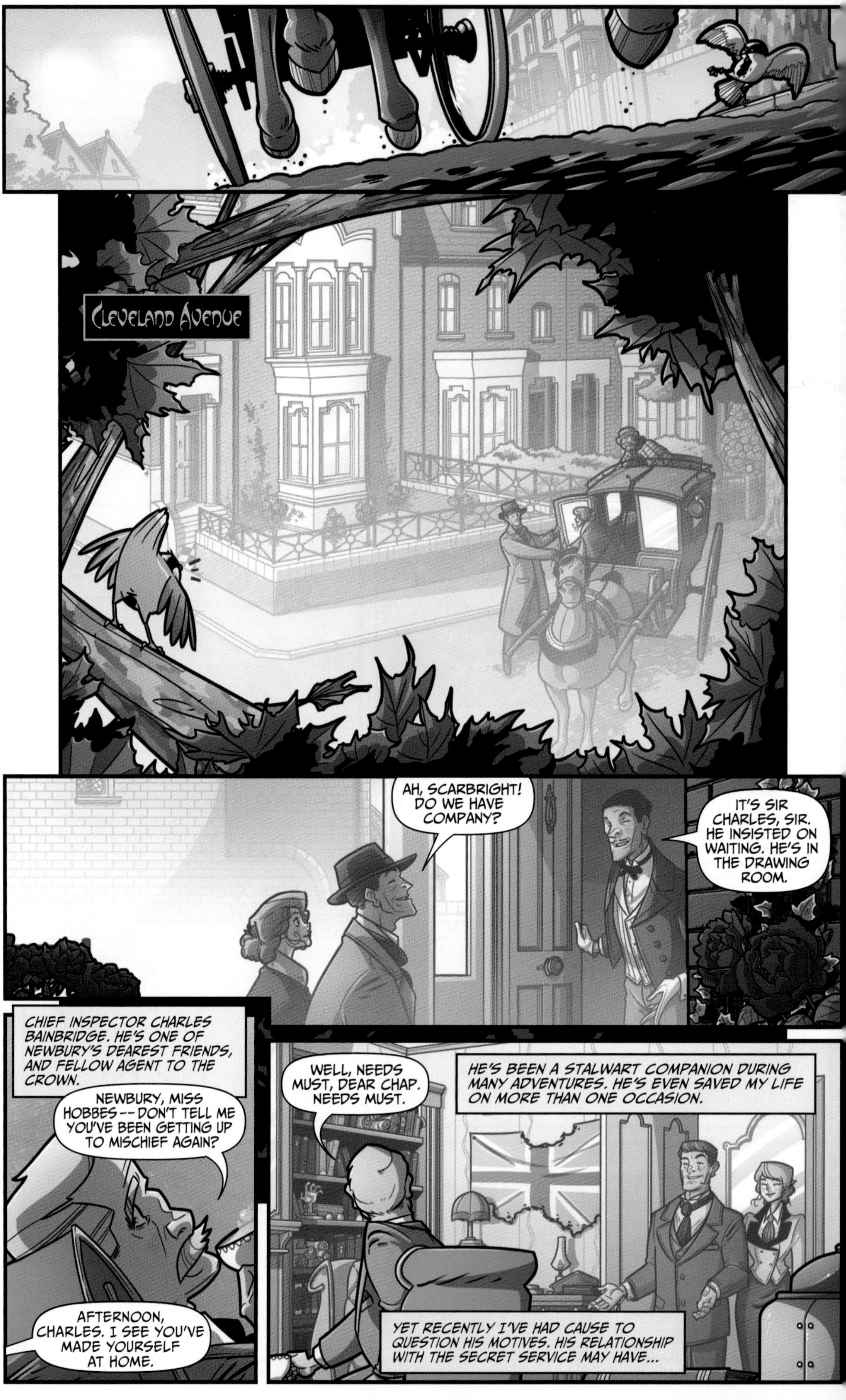

CLEVELAND AVENUE
AH, SCARBRIGHT! DO WE HAVE COMPANY?
IT'S SIR CHARLES, SIR. HE INSISTED ON WAITING. HE'S IN THE DRAWING ROOM.
CHIEF INSPECTOR CHARLES BAINBRIDGE. HE'S ONE OF NEWBURY'S DEAREST FRIENDS, AND FELLOW AGENT TO THE CROWN.
NEWBURY, MISS HOBBES-- DON'T TELL ME YOU'VE BEEN GETTING UP TO MISCHIEF AGAIN?
AFTERNOON, CHARLES. I SEE YOU'VE MADE YOURSELF AT HOME.
WELL, NEEDS MUST, DEAR CHAP. NEEDS MUST.
HE'S BEEN A STALWART COMPANION DURING MANY ADVENTURES. HE'S EVEN SAVED MY LIFE ON MORE THAN ONE OCCASION.
YET RECENTLY I'VE HAD CAUSE TO QUESTION HIS MOTIVES. HIS RELATIONSHIP WITH THE SECRET SERVICE MAY HAVE...

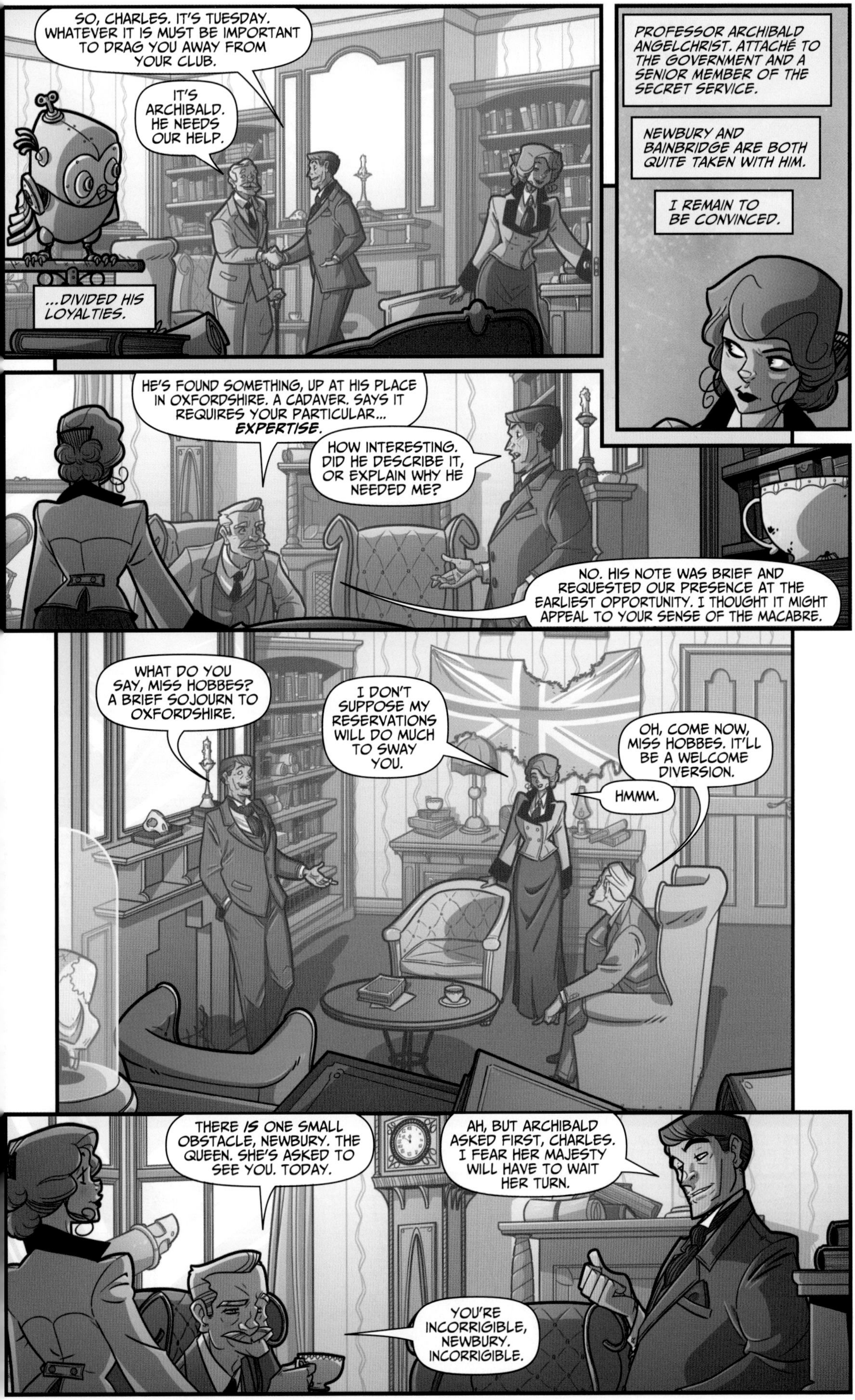
SO, CHARLES. IT'S TUESDAY. WHATEVER IT IS MUST BE IMPORTANT TO DRAG YOU AWAY FROM YOUR CLUB.
IT'S ARCHIBALD. HE NEEDS OUR HELP.
...DIVIDED HIS LOYALTIES.
PROFESSOR ARCHIBALD ANGELCHRIST. ATTACHÉ TO THE GOVERNMENT AND A SENIOR MEMBER OF THE SECRET SERVICE.
NEWBURY AND BAINBRIDGE ARE BOTH QUITE TAKEN WITH HIM.
I REMAIN TO BE CONVINCED.
HE'S FOUND SOMETHING, UP AT HIS PLACE IN OXFORDSHIRE. A CADAVER. SAYS IT REQUIRES YOUR PARTICULAR... EXPERTISE.
HOW INTERESTING. DID HE DESCRIBE IT, OR EXPLAIN WHY HE NEEDED ME?
NO. HIS NOTE WAS BRIEF AND REQUESTED OUR PRESENCE AT THE EARLIEST OPPORTUNITY. I THOUGHT IT MIGHT APPEAL TO YOUR SENSE OF THE MACABRE.
WHAT DO YOU SAY, MISS HOBBES? A BRIEF SOJOURN TO OXFORDSHIRE.
I DON'T SUPPOSE MY RESERVATIONS WILL DO MUCH TO SWAY YOU.
OH, COME NOW, MISS HOBBES. IT'LL BE A WELCOME DIVERSION.
HMMM.
THERE IS ONE SMALL OBSTACLE, NEWBURY. THE QUEEN. SHE'S ASKED TO SEE YOU. TODAY.
AH, BUT ARCHIBALD ASKED FIRST, CHARLES. I FEAR HER MAJESTY WILL HAVE TO WAIT HER TURN.
YOU'RE INCORRIGIBLE, NEWBURY. INCORRIGIBLE.

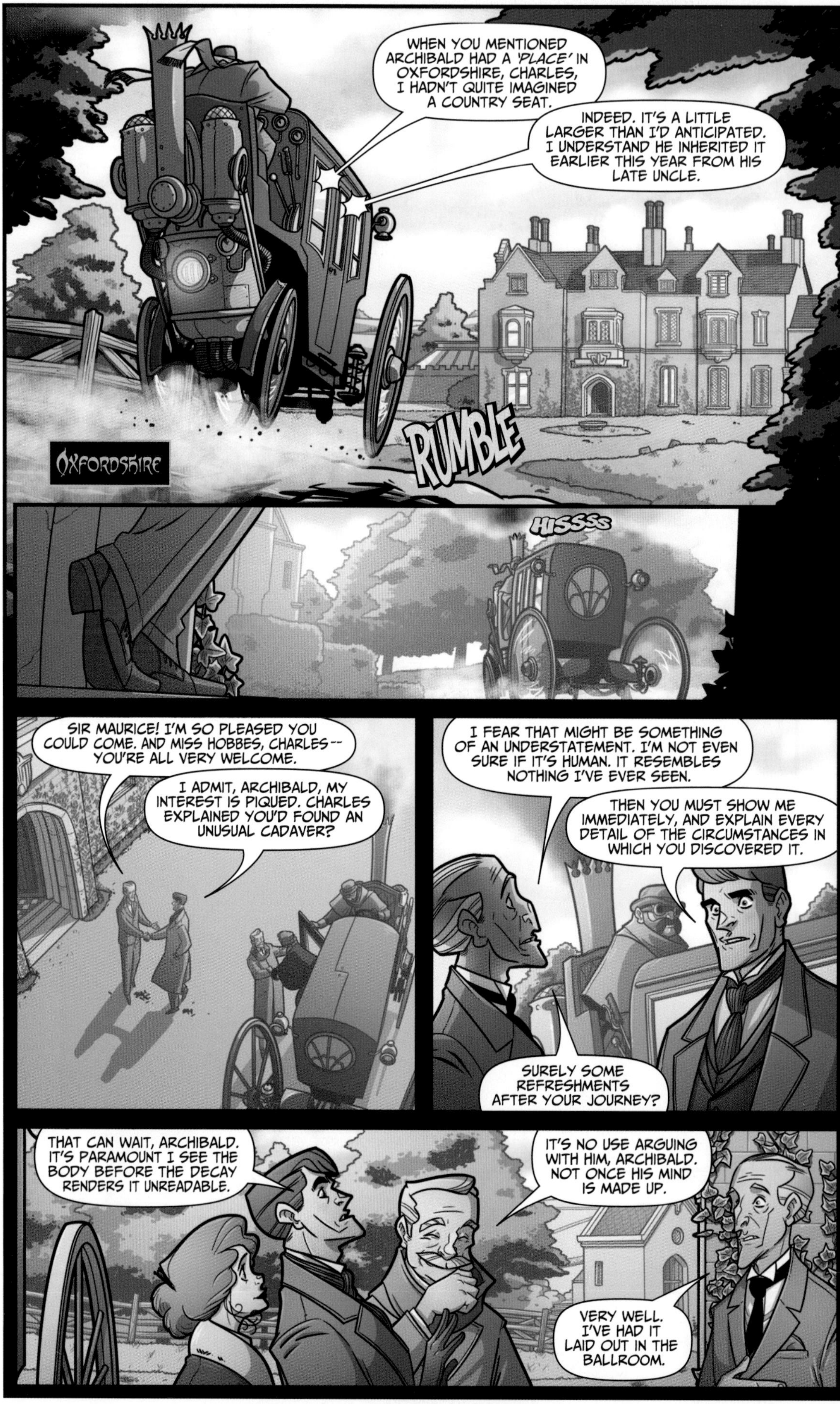
WHEN YOU MENTIONED ARCHIBALD HAD A 'PLACE' IN OXFORDSHIRE, CHARLES, I HADN'T QUITE IMAGINED A COUNTRY SEAT.
INDEED. IT'S A LITTLE LARGER THAN I'D ANTICIPATED. I UNDERSTAND HE INHERITED IT EARLIER THIS YEAR FROM HIS LATE UNCLE.
OXFORDSHIRE
RUMBLE
HISSSS
SIR MAURICE! I'M SO PLEASED YOU COULD COME. AND MISS HOBBES, CHARLES-- YOU'RE ALL VERY WELCOME.
I ADMIT, ARCHIBALD, MY INTEREST IS PIQUED. CHARLES EXPLAINED YOU'D FOUND AN UNUSUAL CADAVER?
I FEAR THAT MIGHT BE SOMETHING OF AN UNDERSTATEMENT. I'M NOT EVEN SURE IF IT'S HUMAN. IT RESEMBLES NOTHING I'VE EVER SEEN.
THEN YOU MUST SHOW ME IMMEDIATELY, AND EXPLAIN EVERY DETAIL OF THE CIRCUMSTANCES IN WHICH YOU DISCOVERED IT.
SURELY SOME REFRESHMENTS AFTER YOUR JOURNEY?
THAT CAN WAIT, ARCHIBALD. IT'S PARAMOUNT I SEE THE BODY BEFORE THE DECAY RENDERS IT UNREADABLE.
IT'S NO USE ARGUING WITH HIM, ARCHIBALD. NOT ONCE HIS MIND IS MADE UP.
VERY WELL. I'VE HAD IT LAID OUT IN THE BALLROOM.

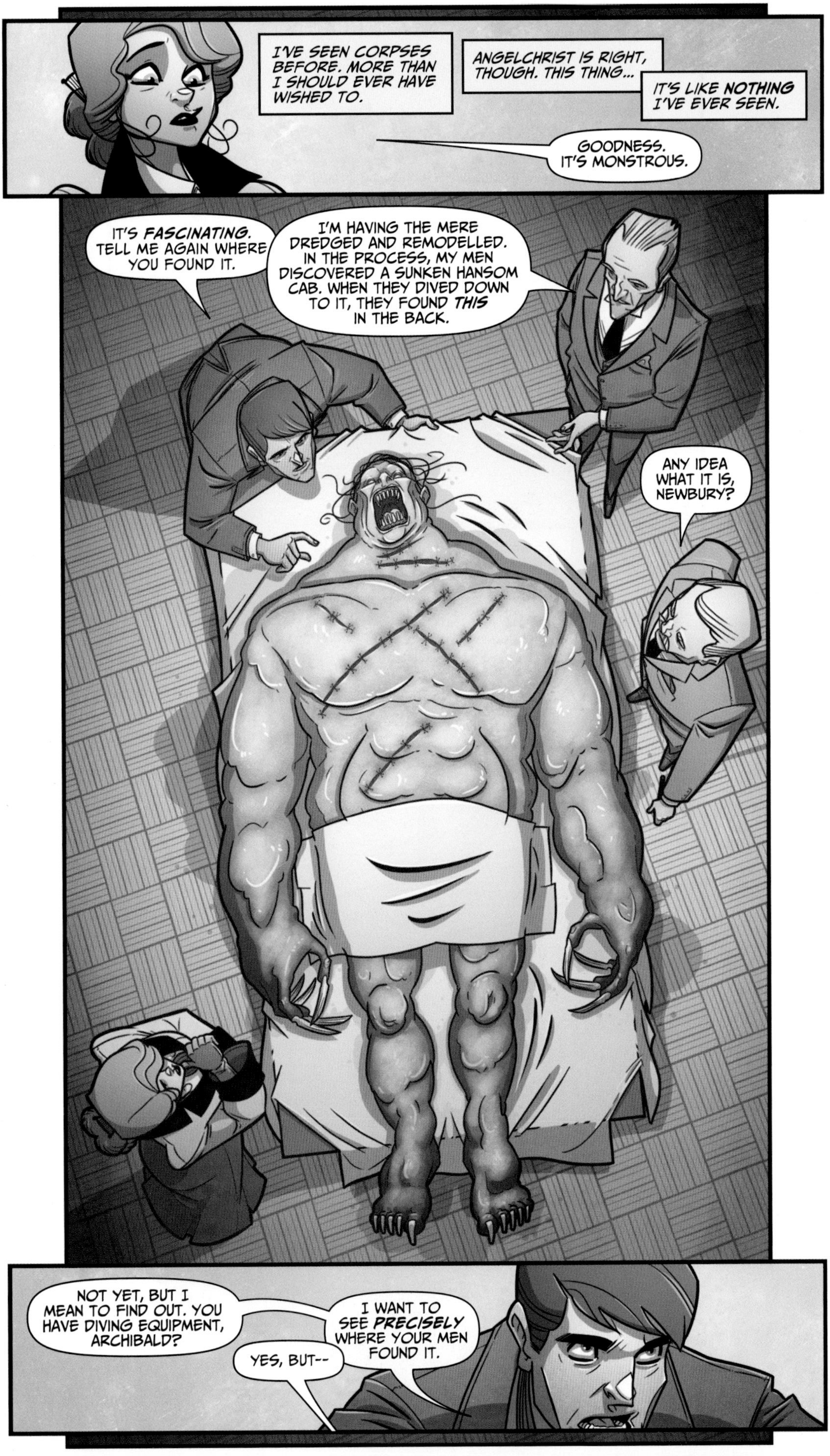
I'VE SEEN CORPSES BEFORE. MORE THAN I SHOULD EVER HAVE WISHED TO.
ANGELCHRIST IS RIGHT, THOUGH. THIS THING...
IT'S LIKE NOTHING I'VE EVER SEEN.
GOODNESS. IT'S MONSTROUS.
IT'S FASCINATING. TELL ME AGAIN WHERE YOU FOUND IT.
I'M HAVING THE MERE DREDGED AND REMODELLED. IN THE PROCESS, MY MEN DISCOVERED A SUNKEN HANSOM CAB. WHEN THEY DIVED DOWN TO IT, THEY FOUND THIS IN THE BACK.
ANY IDEA WHAT IT IS, NEWBURY?
NOT YET, BUT I MEAN TO FIND OUT. YOU HAVE DIVING EQUIPMENT, ARCHIBALD?
YES, BUT--
I WANT TO SEE PRECISELY WHERE YOUR MEN FOUND IT.

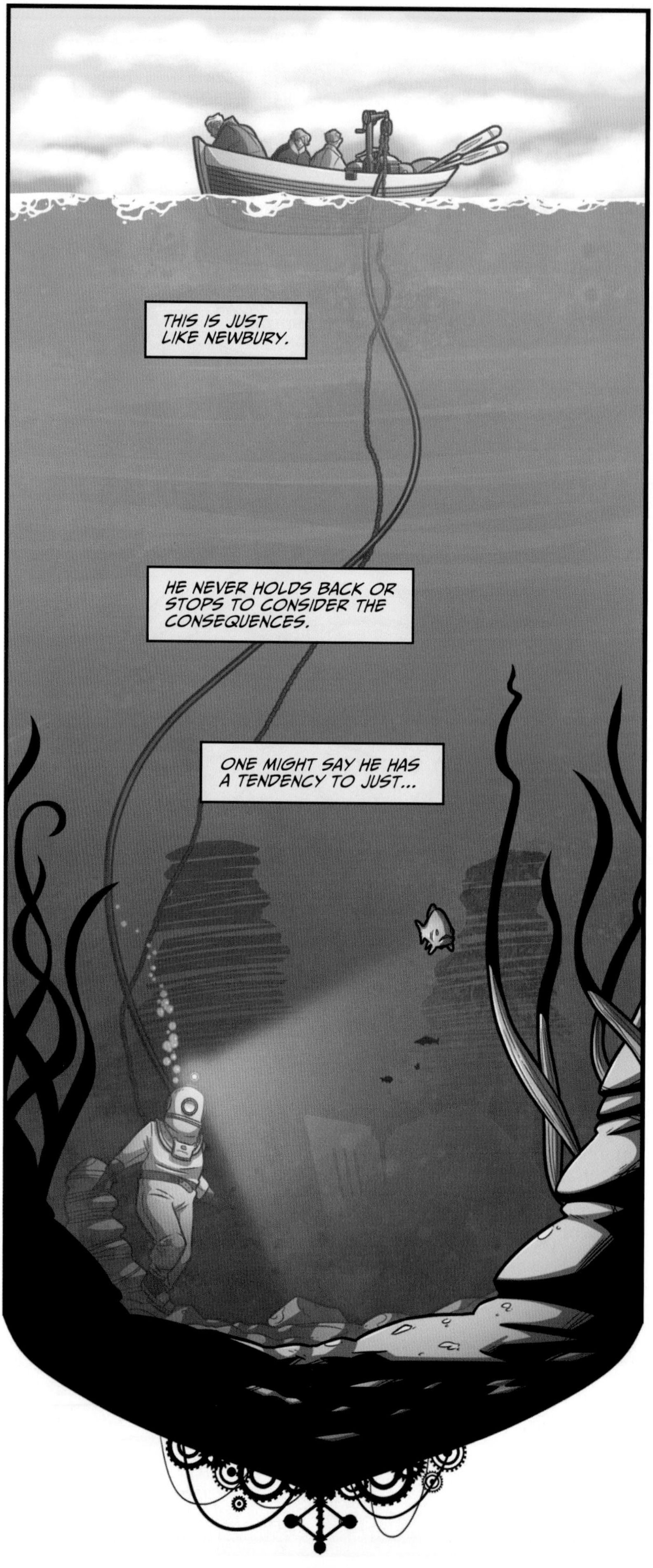
THIS IS JUST LIKE NEWBURY.
HE NEVER HOLDS BACK OR STOPS TO CONSIDER THE CONSEQUENCES.
ONE MIGHT SAY HE HAS A TENDENCY TO JUST...

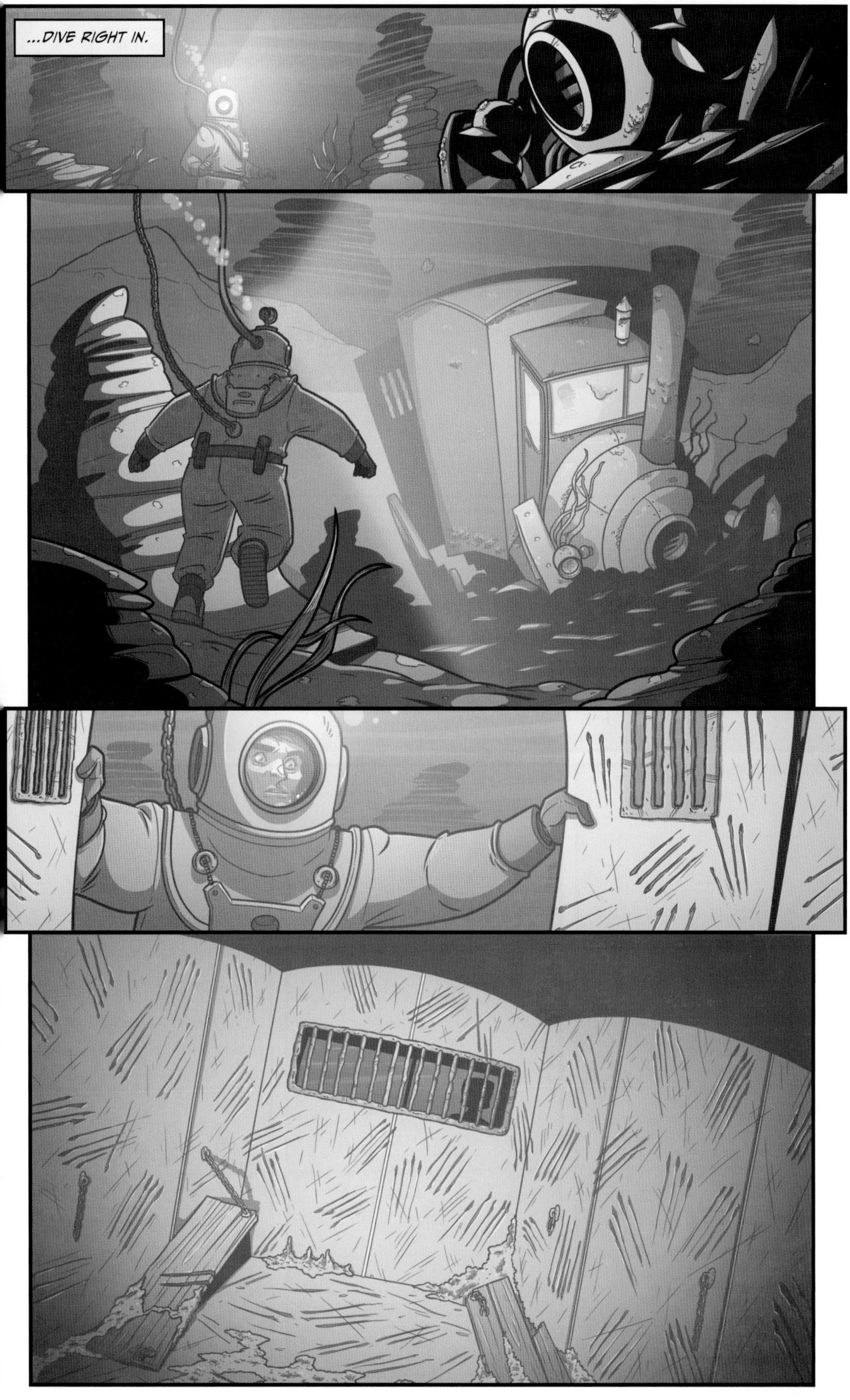
...DIVE RIGHT IN.

I ONLY HOPE THAT HE KNOWS WHAT HE'S LETTING HIMSELF IN FOR.

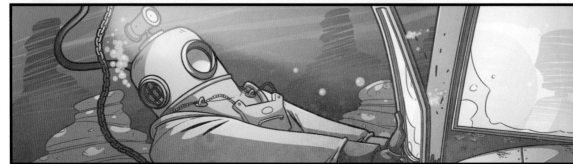

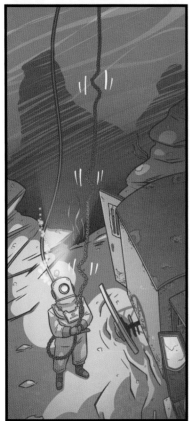

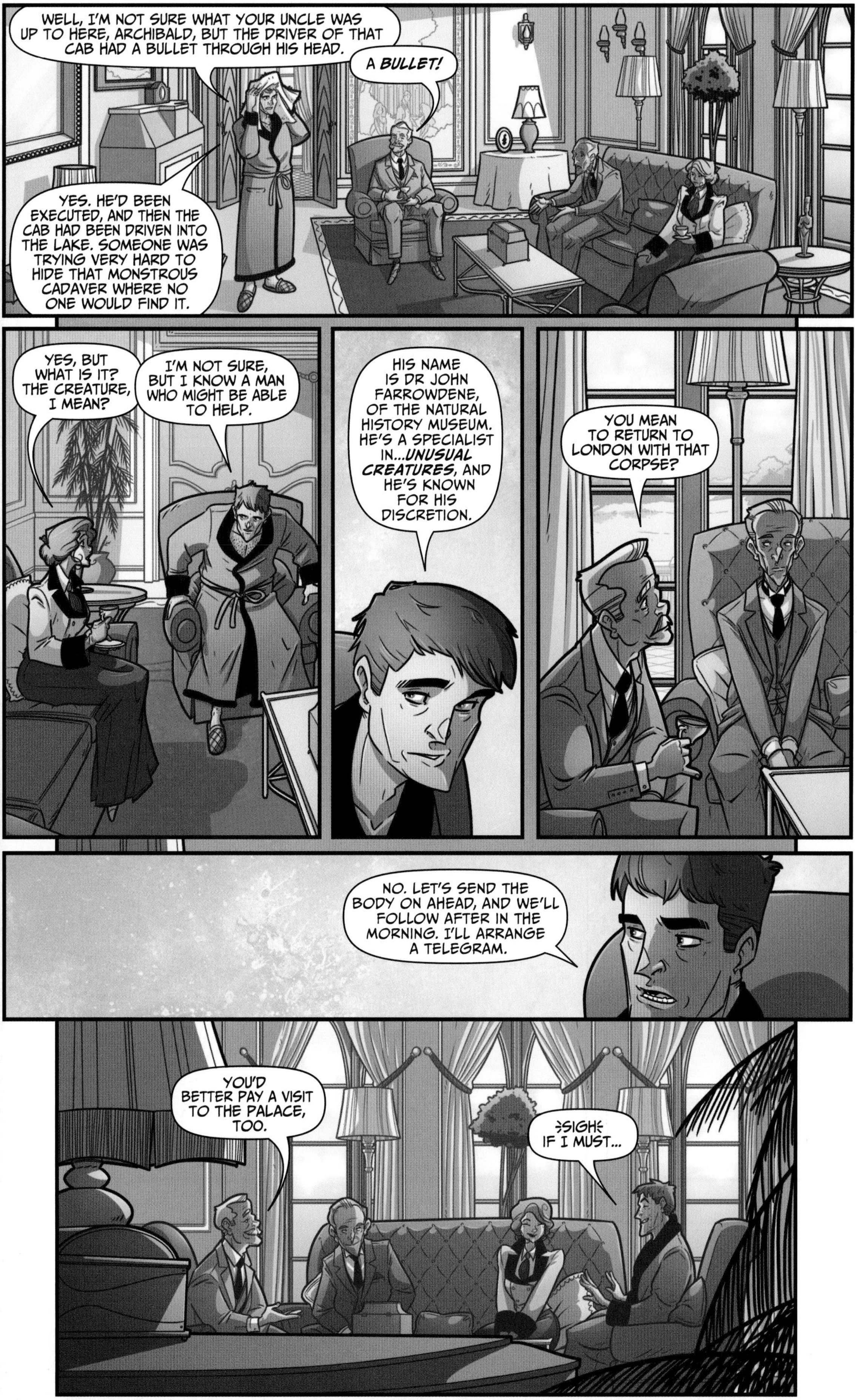
WELL, I'M NOT SURE WHAT YOUR UNCLE WAS UP TO HERE, ARCHIBALD, BUT THE DRIVER OF THAT CAB HAD A BULLET THROUGH HIS HEAD.
A *BULLET!*
YES. HE'D BEEN EXECUTED, AND THEN THE CAB HAD BEEN DRIVEN INTO THE LAKE. SOMEONE WAS TRYING VERY HARD TO HIDE THAT MONSTROUS CADAVER WHERE NO ONE WOULD FIND IT.
YES, BUT WHAT IS IT? THE CREATURE, I MEAN?
I'M NOT SURE, BUT I KNOW A MAN WHO MIGHT BE ABLE TO HELP.
HIS NAME IS DR JOHN FARROWDENE, OF THE NATURAL HISTORY MUSEUM. HE'S A SPECIALIST IN...*UNUSUAL CREATURES*, AND HE'S KNOWN FOR HIS DISCRETION.
YOU MEAN TO RETURN TO LONDON WITH THAT CORPSE?
NO. LET'S SEND THE BODY ON AHEAD, AND WE'LL FOLLOW AFTER IN THE MORNING. I'LL ARRANGE A TELEGRAM.
YOU'D BETTER PAY A VISIT TO THE PALACE, TOO.
⋟SIGH⋞ IF I MUST...

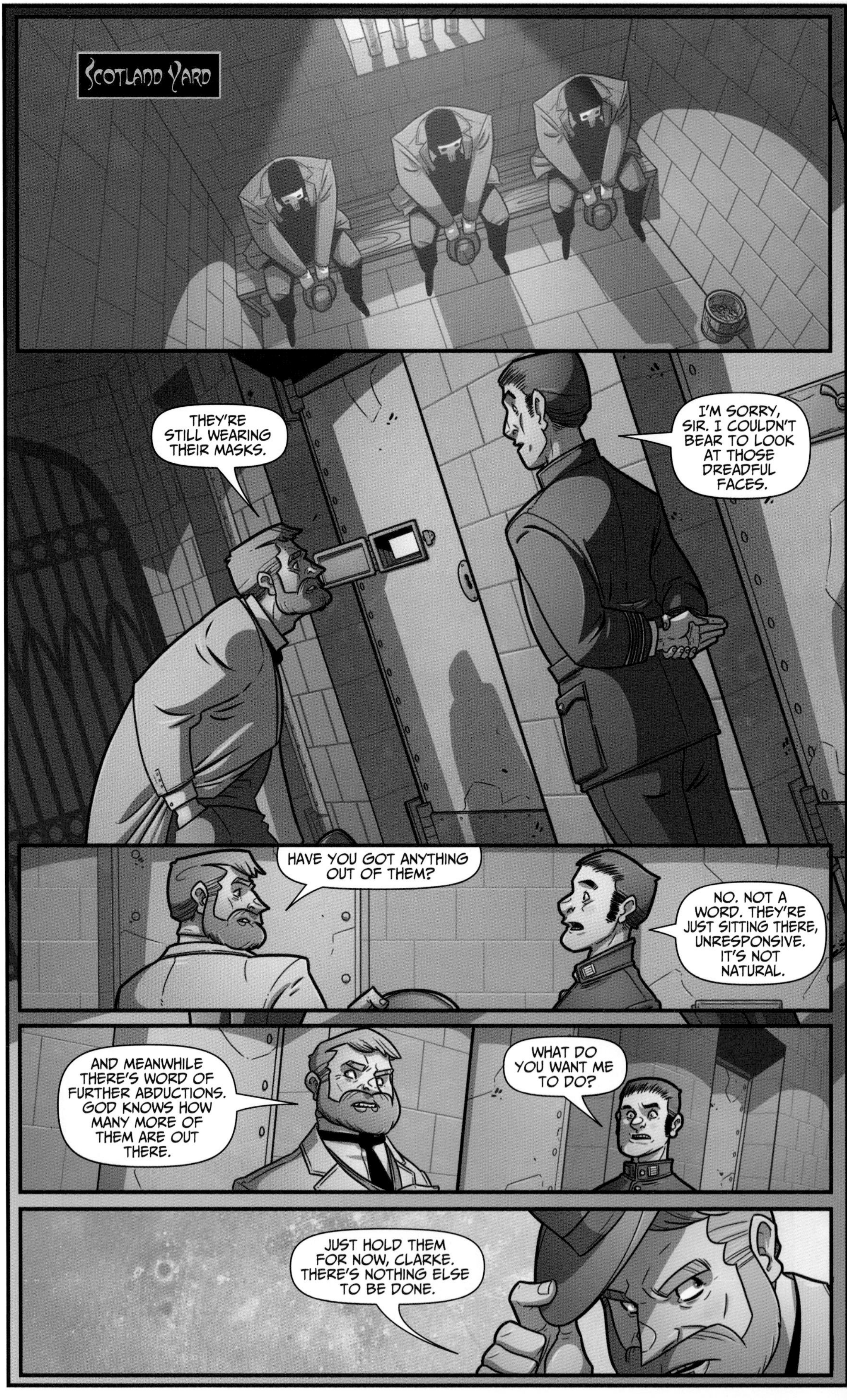
SCOTLAND YARD
THEY'RE STILL WEARING THEIR MASKS.
I'M SORRY, SIR. I COULDN'T BEAR TO LOOK AT THOSE DREADFUL FACES.
HAVE YOU GOT ANYTHING OUT OF THEM?
NO. NOT A WORD. THEY'RE JUST SITTING THERE, UNRESPONSIVE. IT'S NOT NATURAL.
AND MEANWHILE THERE'S WORD OF FURTHER ABDUCTIONS. GOD KNOWS HOW MANY MORE OF THEM ARE OUT THERE.
WHAT DO YOU WANT ME TO DO?
JUST HOLD THEM FOR NOW, CLARKE. THERE'S NOTHING ELSE TO BE DONE.

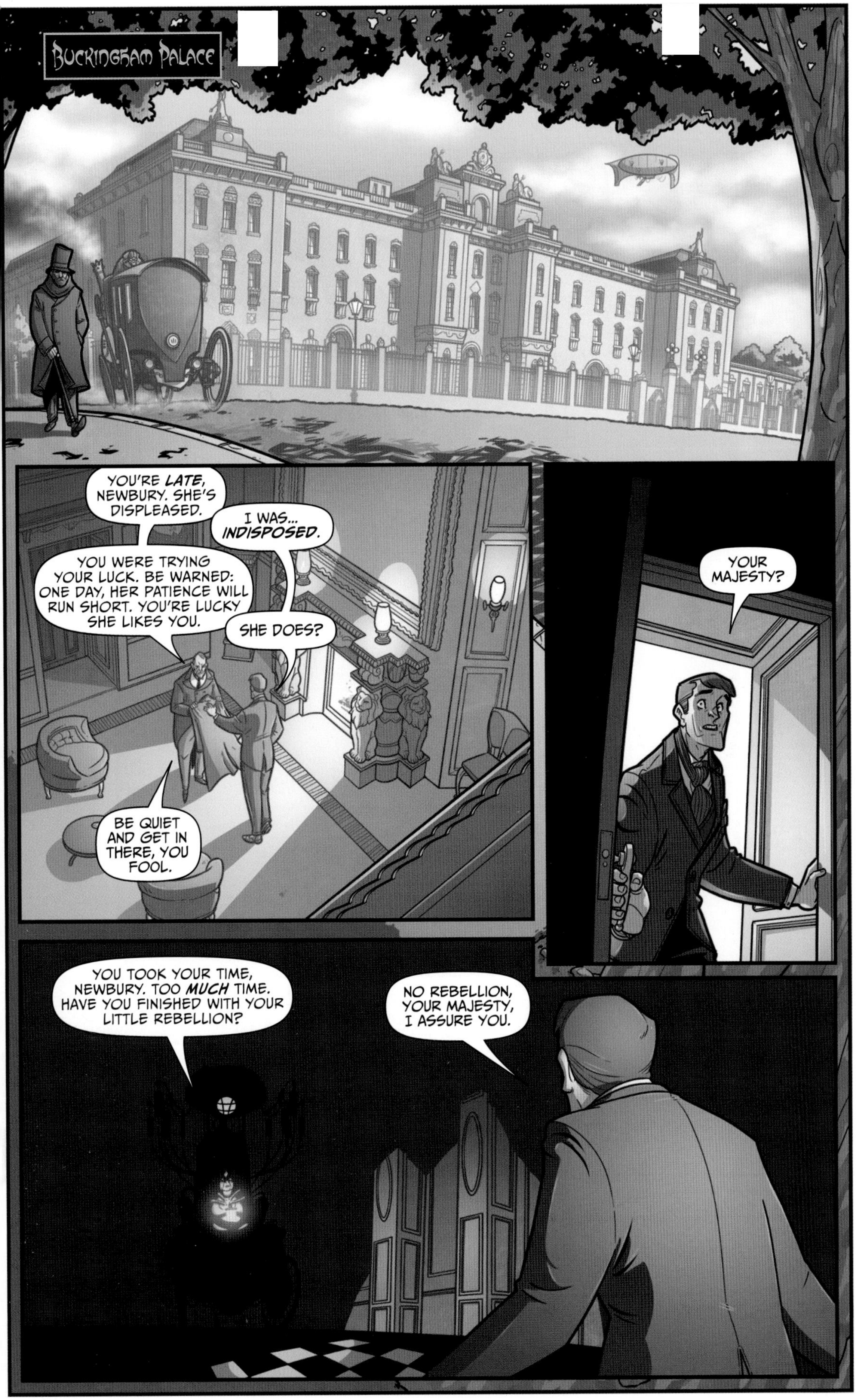
BUCKINGHAM PALACE
YOU'RE LATE, NEWBURY. SHE'S DISPLEASED.
I WAS... INDISPOSED.
YOU WERE TRYING YOUR LUCK. BE WARNED: ONE DAY, HER PATIENCE WILL RUN SHORT. YOU'RE LUCKY SHE LIKES YOU.
SHE DOES?
BE QUIET AND GET IN THERE, YOU FOOL.
YOUR MAJESTY?
YOU TOOK YOUR TIME, NEWBURY. TOO MUCH TIME. HAVE YOU FINISHED WITH YOUR LITTLE REBELLION?
NO REBELLION, YOUR MAJESTY, I ASSURE YOU.

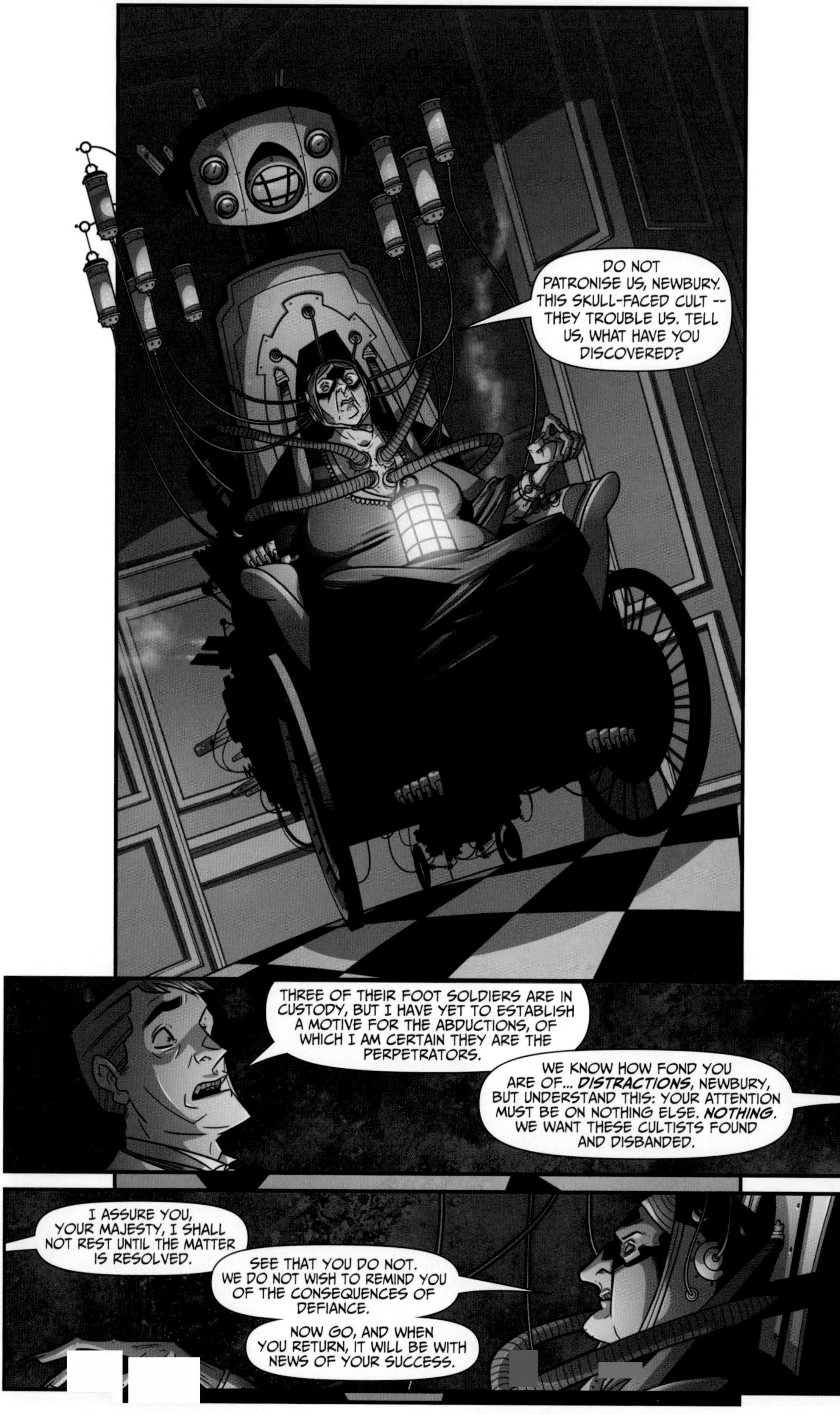
DO NOT PATRONISE US, NEWBURY. THIS SKULL-FACED CULT -- THEY TROUBLE US. TELL US, WHAT HAVE YOU DISCOVERED?
THREE OF THEIR FOOT SOLDIERS ARE IN CUSTODY, BUT I HAVE YET TO ESTABLISH A MOTIVE FOR THE ABDUCTIONS, OF WHICH I AM CERTAIN THEY ARE THE PERPETRATORS.
WE KNOW HOW FOND YOU ARE OF... *DISTRACTIONS*, NEWBURY, BUT UNDERSTAND THIS: YOUR ATTENTION MUST BE ON NOTHING ELSE. *NOTHING.* WE WANT THESE CULTISTS FOUND AND DISBANDED.
I ASSURE YOU, YOUR MAJESTY, I SHALL NOT REST UNTIL THE MATTER IS RESOLVED.
SEE THAT YOU DO NOT. WE DO NOT WISH TO REMIND YOU OF THE CONSEQUENCES OF DEFIANCE.
NOW GO, AND WHEN YOU RETURN, IT WILL BE WITH NEWS OF YOUR SUCCESS.

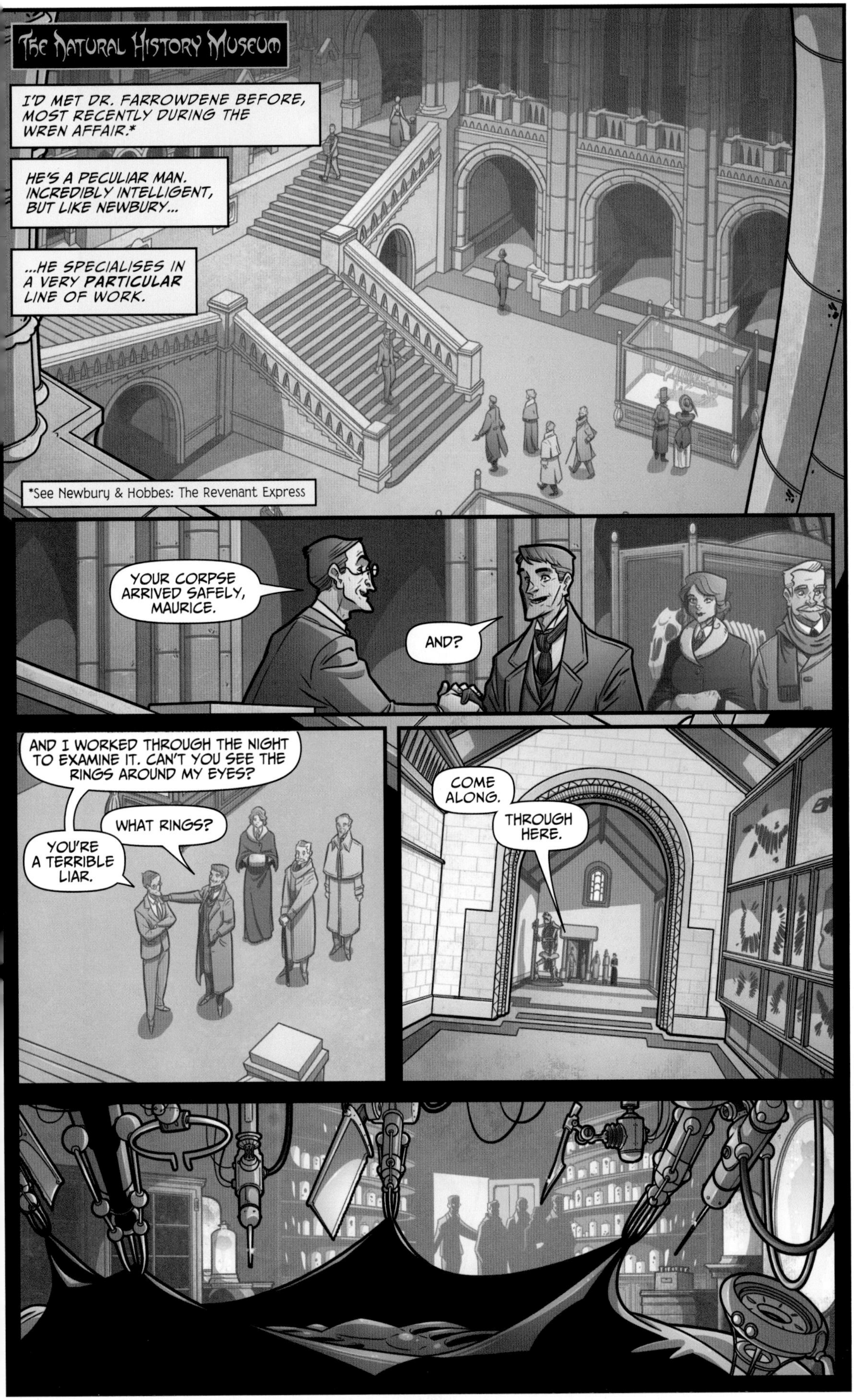
The Natural History Museum
I'D MET DR. FARROWDENE BEFORE, MOST RECENTLY DURING THE WREN AFFAIR.*
HE'S A PECULIAR MAN. INCREDIBLY INTELLIGENT, BUT LIKE NEWBURY...
...HE SPECIALISES IN A VERY PARTICULAR LINE OF WORK.
*See Newbury & Hobbes: The Revenant Express
YOUR CORPSE ARRIVED SAFELY, MAURICE.
AND?
AND I WORKED THROUGH THE NIGHT TO EXAMINE IT. CAN'T YOU SEE THE RINGS AROUND MY EYES?
WHAT RINGS?
YOU'RE A TERRIBLE LIAR.
COME ALONG.
THROUGH HERE.

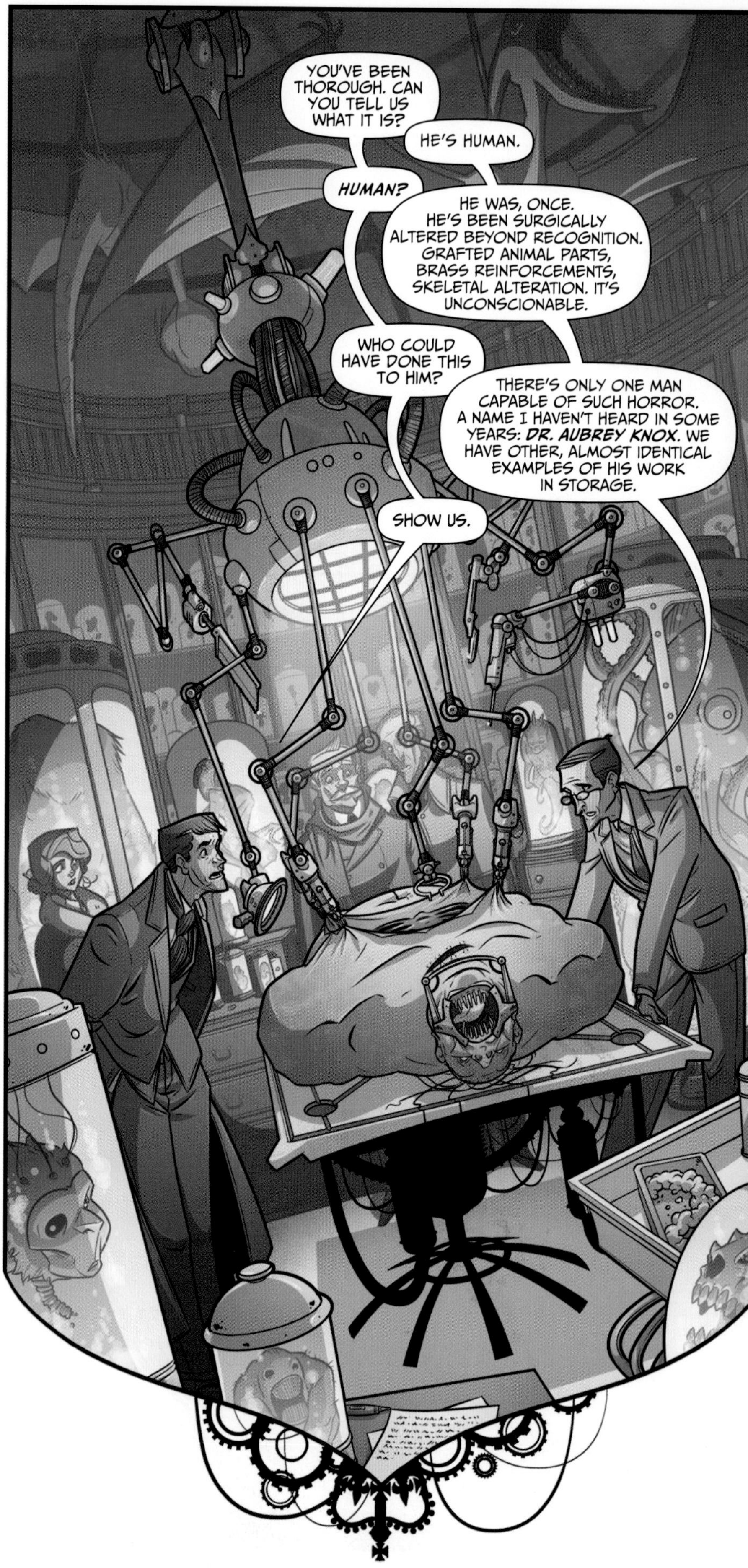
YOU'VE BEEN THOROUGH. CAN YOU TELL US WHAT IT IS?
HE'S HUMAN.
HUMAN?
HE WAS, ONCE. HE'S BEEN SURGICALLY ALTERED BEYOND RECOGNITION. GRAFTED ANIMAL PARTS, BRASS REINFORCEMENTS, SKELETAL ALTERATION. IT'S UNCONSCIONABLE.
WHO COULD HAVE DONE THIS TO HIM?
THERE'S ONLY ONE MAN CAPABLE OF SUCH HORROR. A NAME I HAVEN'T HEARD IN SOME YEARS: *DR. AUBREY KNOX*. WE HAVE OTHER, ALMOST IDENTICAL EXAMPLES OF HIS WORK IN STORAGE.
SHOW US.

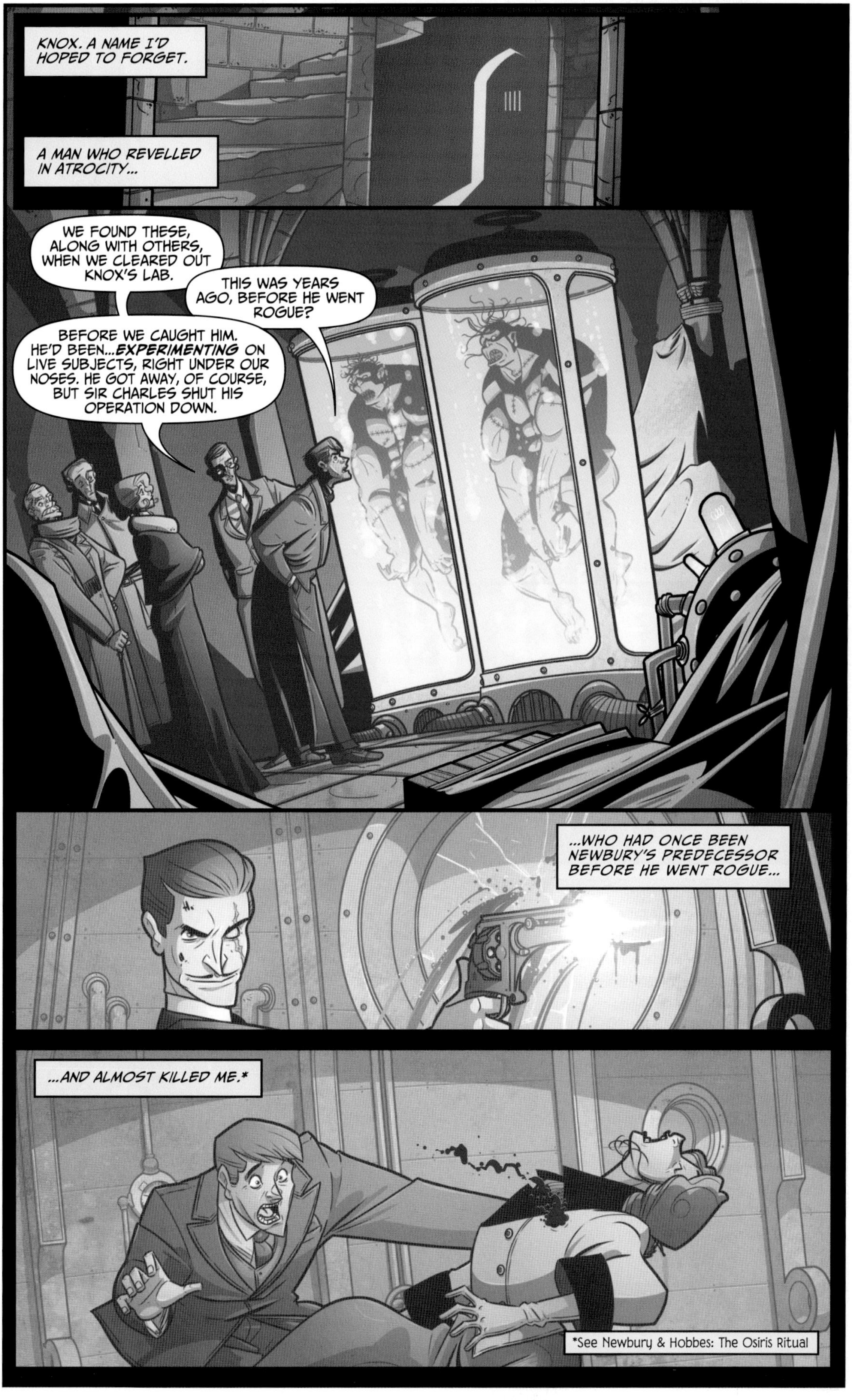

KNOX. A NAME I'D HOPED TO FORGET.
A MAN WHO REVELLED IN ATROCITY...
WE FOUND THESE, ALONG WITH OTHERS, WHEN WE CLEARED OUT KNOX'S LAB.
THIS WAS YEARS AGO, BEFORE HE WENT ROGUE?
BEFORE WE CAUGHT HIM. HE'D BEEN...EXPERIMENTING ON LIVE SUBJECTS, RIGHT UNDER OUR NOSES. HE GOT AWAY, OF COURSE, BUT SIR CHARLES SHUT HIS OPERATION DOWN.
...WHO HAD ONCE BEEN NEWBURY'S PREDECESSOR BEFORE HE WENT ROGUE...
...AND ALMOST KILLED ME.*
*See Newbury & Hobbes: The Osiris Ritual

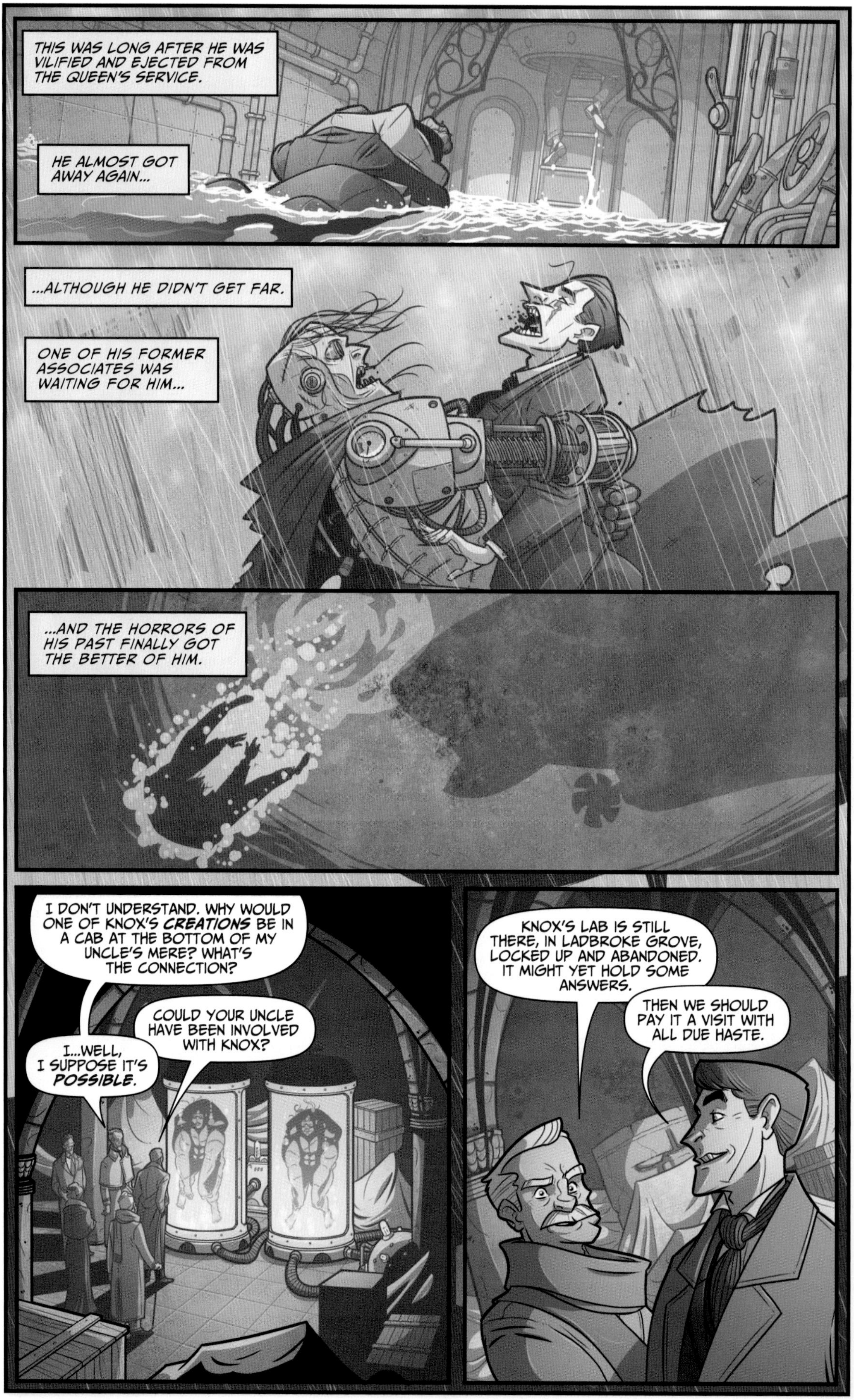

THIS WAS LONG AFTER HE WAS VILIFIED AND EJECTED FROM THE QUEEN'S SERVICE.
HE ALMOST GOT AWAY AGAIN...
...ALTHOUGH HE DIDN'T GET FAR.
ONE OF HIS FORMER ASSOCIATES WAS WAITING FOR HIM...
...AND THE HORRORS OF HIS PAST FINALLY GOT THE BETTER OF HIM.
I DON'T UNDERSTAND. WHY WOULD ONE OF KNOX'S CREATIONS BE IN A CAB AT THE BOTTOM OF MY UNCLE'S MERE? WHAT'S THE CONNECTION?
COULD YOUR UNCLE HAVE BEEN INVOLVED WITH KNOX?
I...WELL, I SUPPOSE IT'S POSSIBLE.
KNOX'S LAB IS STILL THERE, IN LADBROKE GROVE, LOCKED UP AND ABANDONED. IT MIGHT YET HOLD SOME ANSWERS.
THEN WE SHOULD PAY IT A VISIT WITH ALL DUE HASTE.

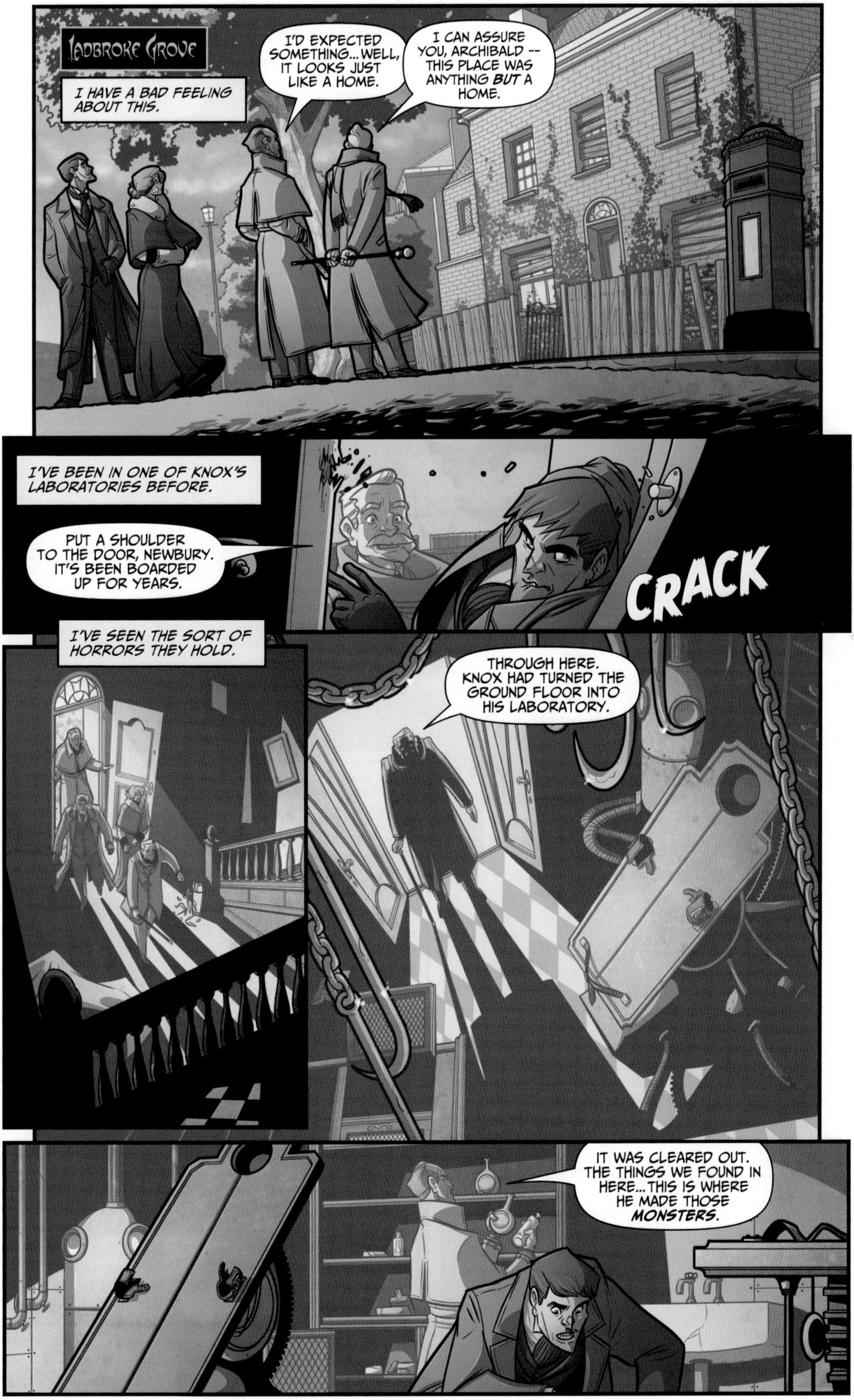
LADBROKE GROVE
I HAVE A BAD FEELING ABOUT THIS.
I'D EXPECTED SOMETHING... WELL, IT LOOKS JUST LIKE A HOME.
I CAN ASSURE YOU, ARCHIBALD -- THIS PLACE WAS ANYTHING *BUT* A HOME.
I'VE BEEN IN ONE OF KNOX'S LABORATORIES BEFORE.
PUT A SHOULDER TO THE DOOR, NEWBURY. IT'S BEEN BOARDED UP FOR YEARS.
CRACK
I'VE SEEN THE SORT OF HORRORS THEY HOLD.
THROUGH HERE. KNOX HAD TURNED THE GROUND FLOOR INTO HIS LABORATORY.
IT WAS CLEARED OUT. THE THINGS WE FOUND IN HERE... THIS IS WHERE HE MADE THOSE *MONSTERS*.

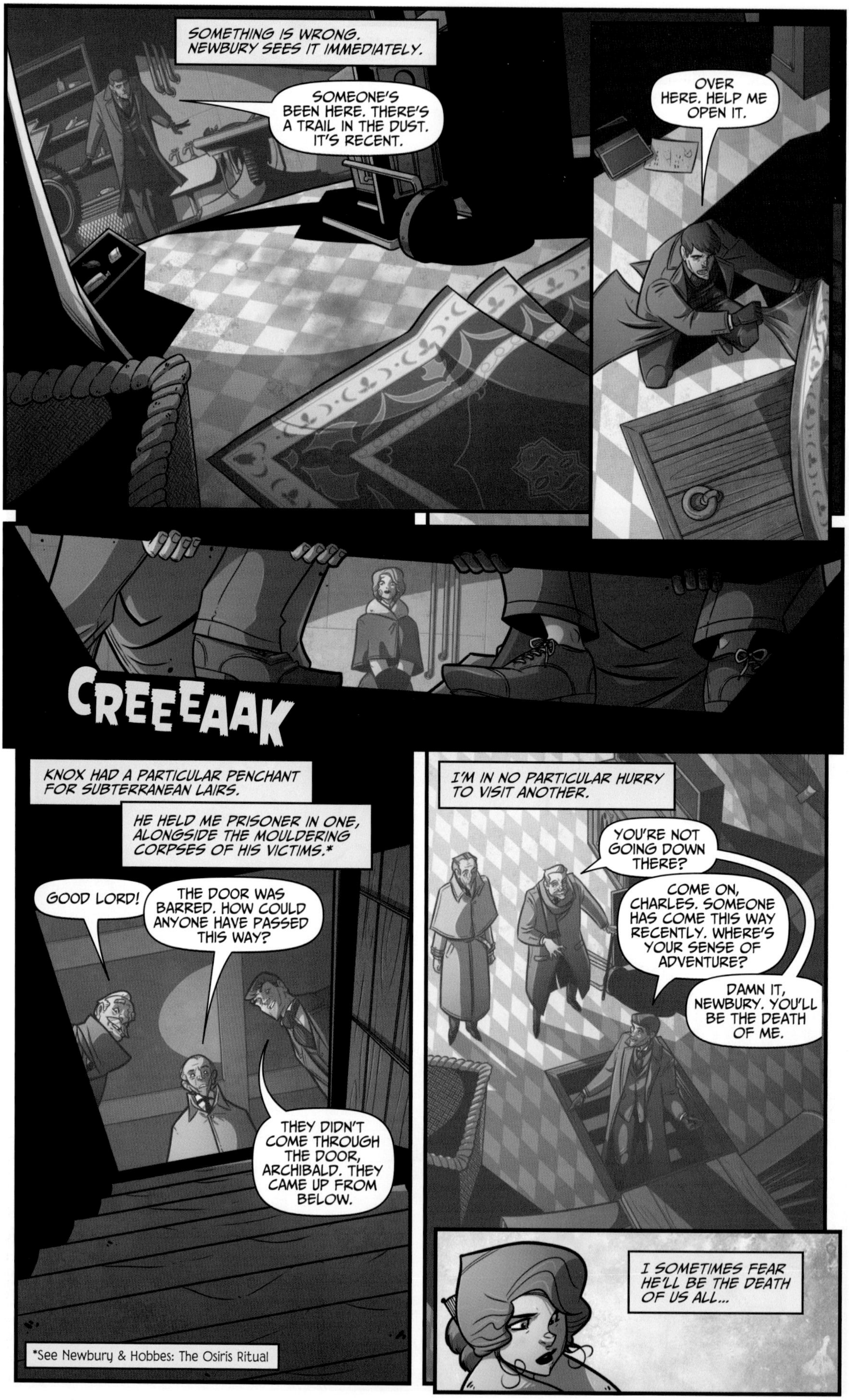
SOMETHING IS WRONG. NEWBURY SEES IT IMMEDIATELY.
SOMEONE'S BEEN HERE. THERE'S A TRAIL IN THE DUST. IT'S RECENT.
OVER HERE. HELP ME OPEN IT.
CREEEAAK
KNOX HAD A PARTICULAR PENCHANT FOR SUBTERRANEAN LAIRS.
HE HELD ME PRISONER IN ONE, ALONGSIDE THE MOULDERING CORPSES OF HIS VICTIMS.*
GOOD LORD!
THE DOOR WAS BARRED. HOW COULD ANYONE HAVE PASSED THIS WAY?
THEY DIDN'T COME THROUGH THE DOOR, ARCHIBALD. THEY CAME UP FROM BELOW.
*See Newbury & Hobbes: The Osiris Ritual
I'M IN NO PARTICULAR HURRY TO VISIT ANOTHER.
YOU'RE NOT GOING DOWN THERE?
COME ON, CHARLES. SOMEONE HAS COME THIS WAY RECENTLY. WHERE'S YOUR SENSE OF ADVENTURE?
DAMN IT, NEWBURY. YOU'LL BE THE DEATH OF ME.
I SOMETIMES FEAR HE'LL BE THE DEATH OF US ALL...

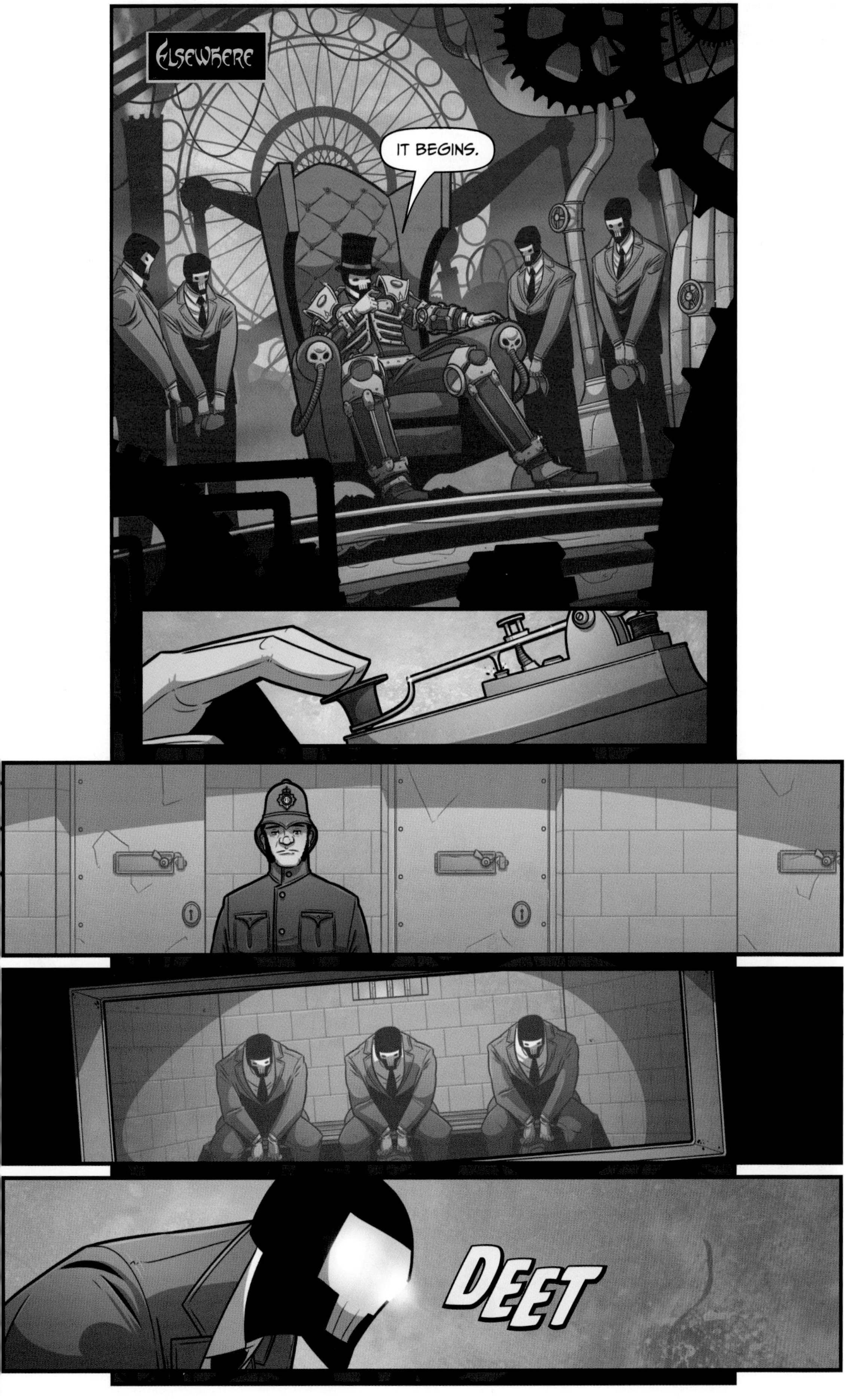
ELSEWHERE
IT BEGINS.
DEET

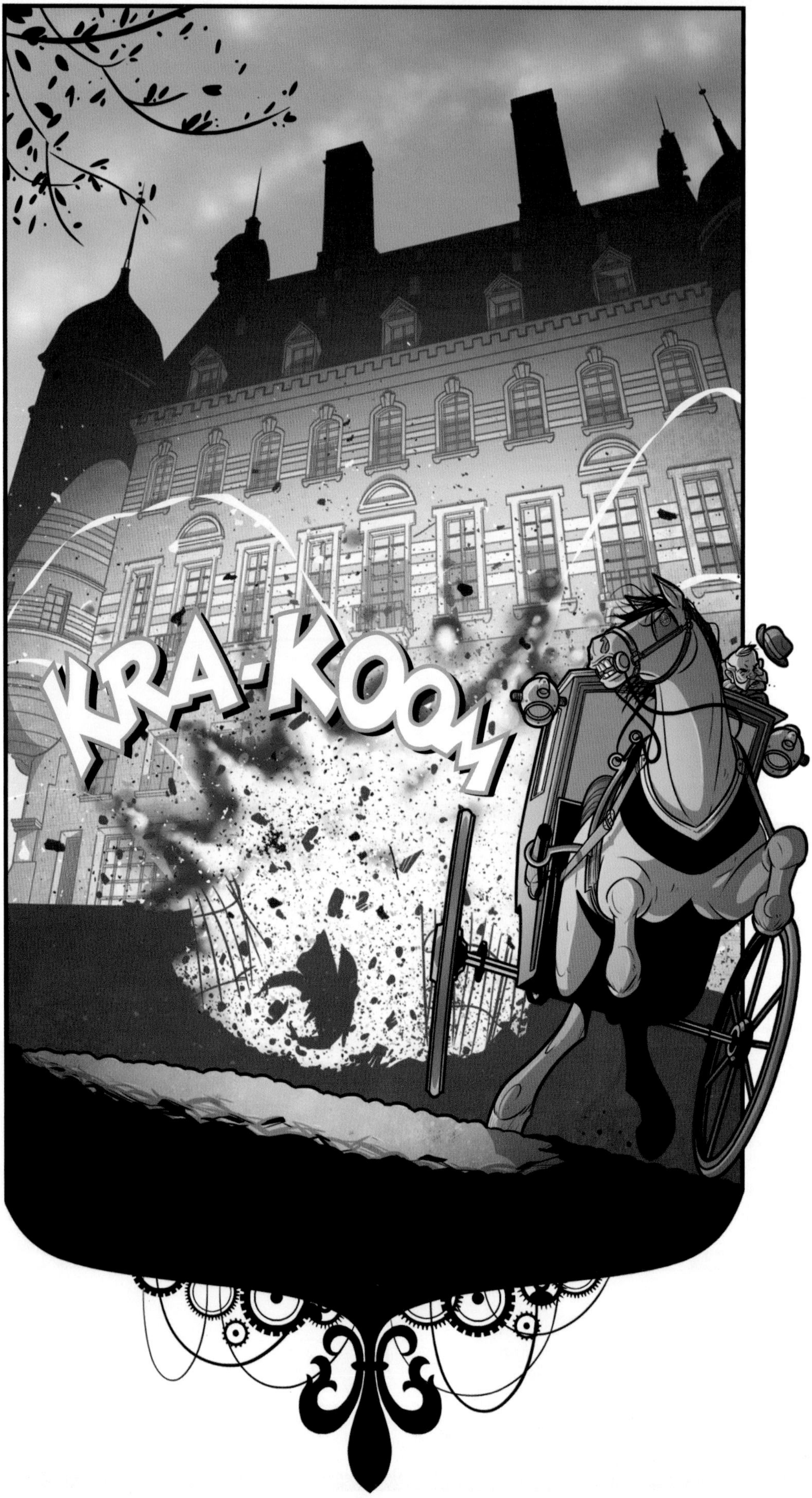
KRA-KOOM

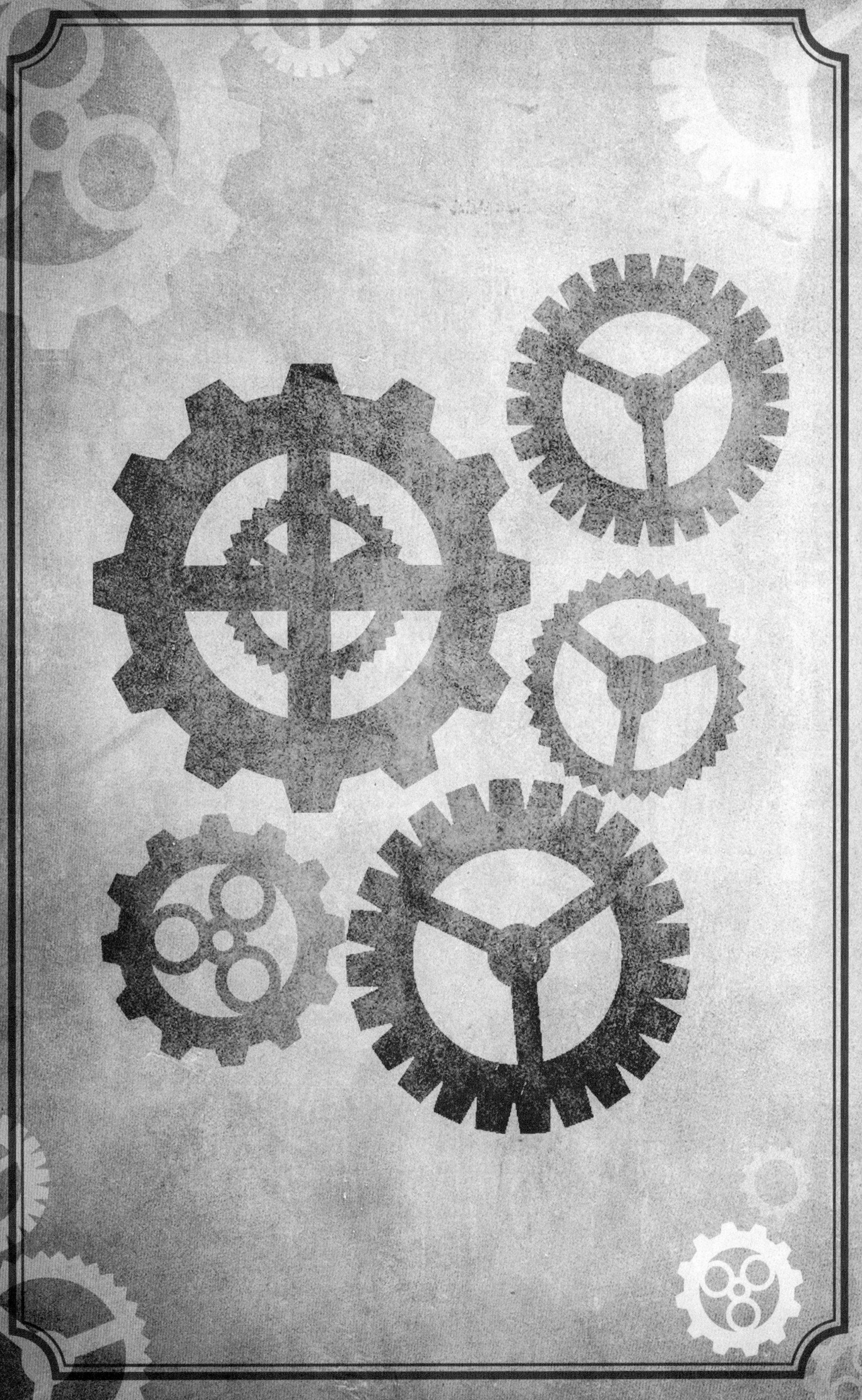

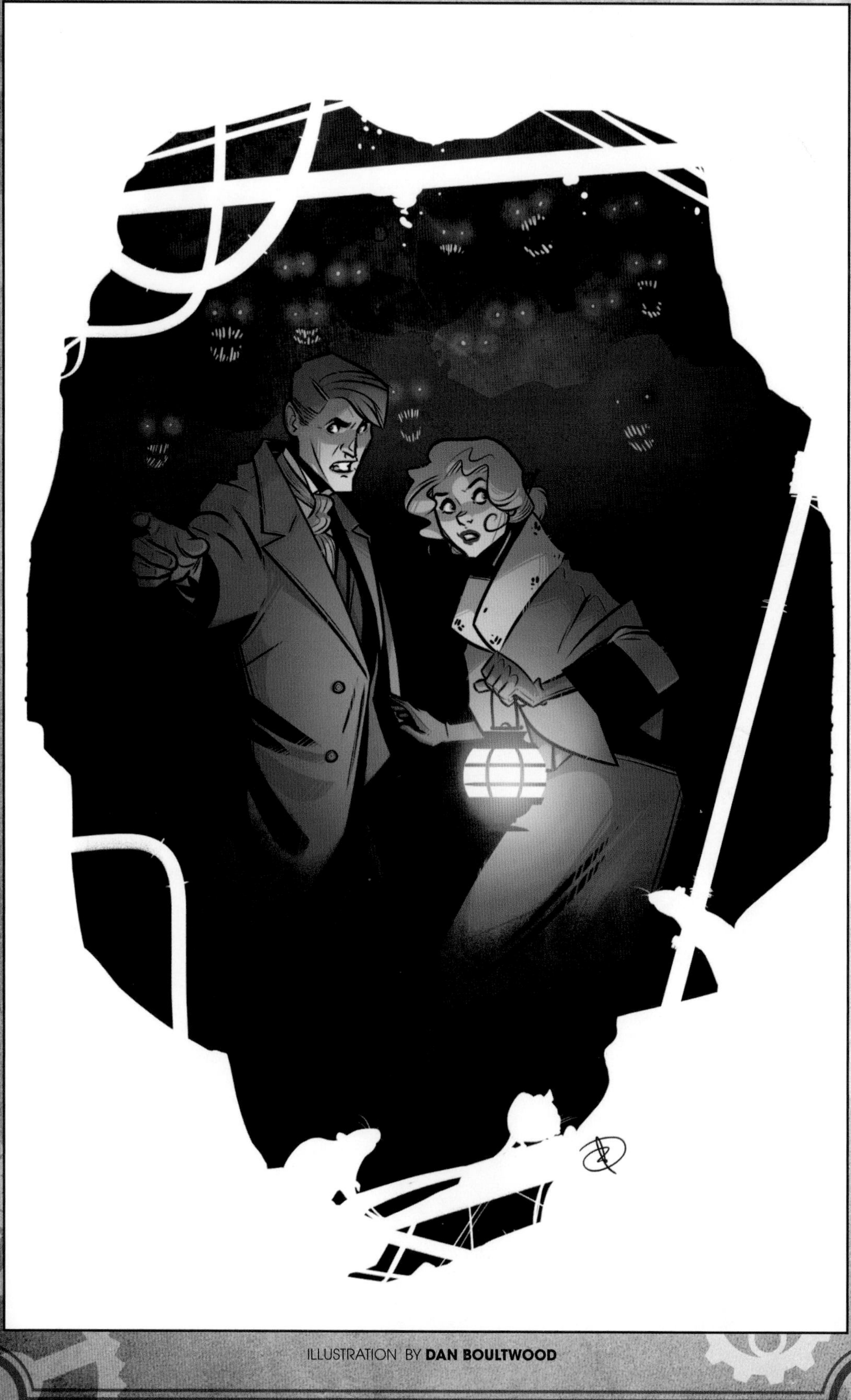

ILLUSTRATION BY **DAN BOULTWOOD**

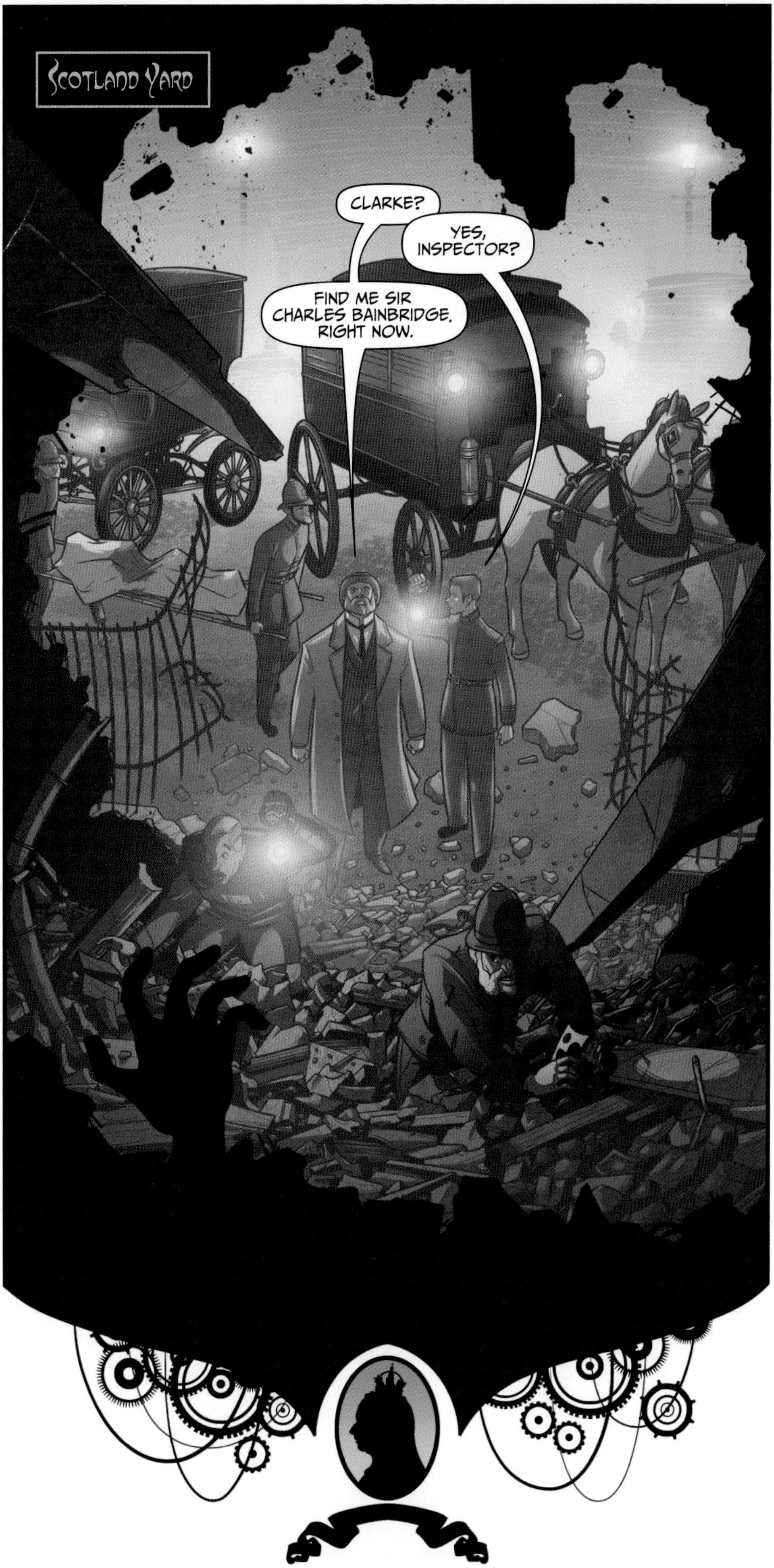
SCOTLAND YARD
CLARKE?
YES, INSPECTOR?
FIND ME SIR CHARLES BAINBRIDGE. RIGHT NOW.

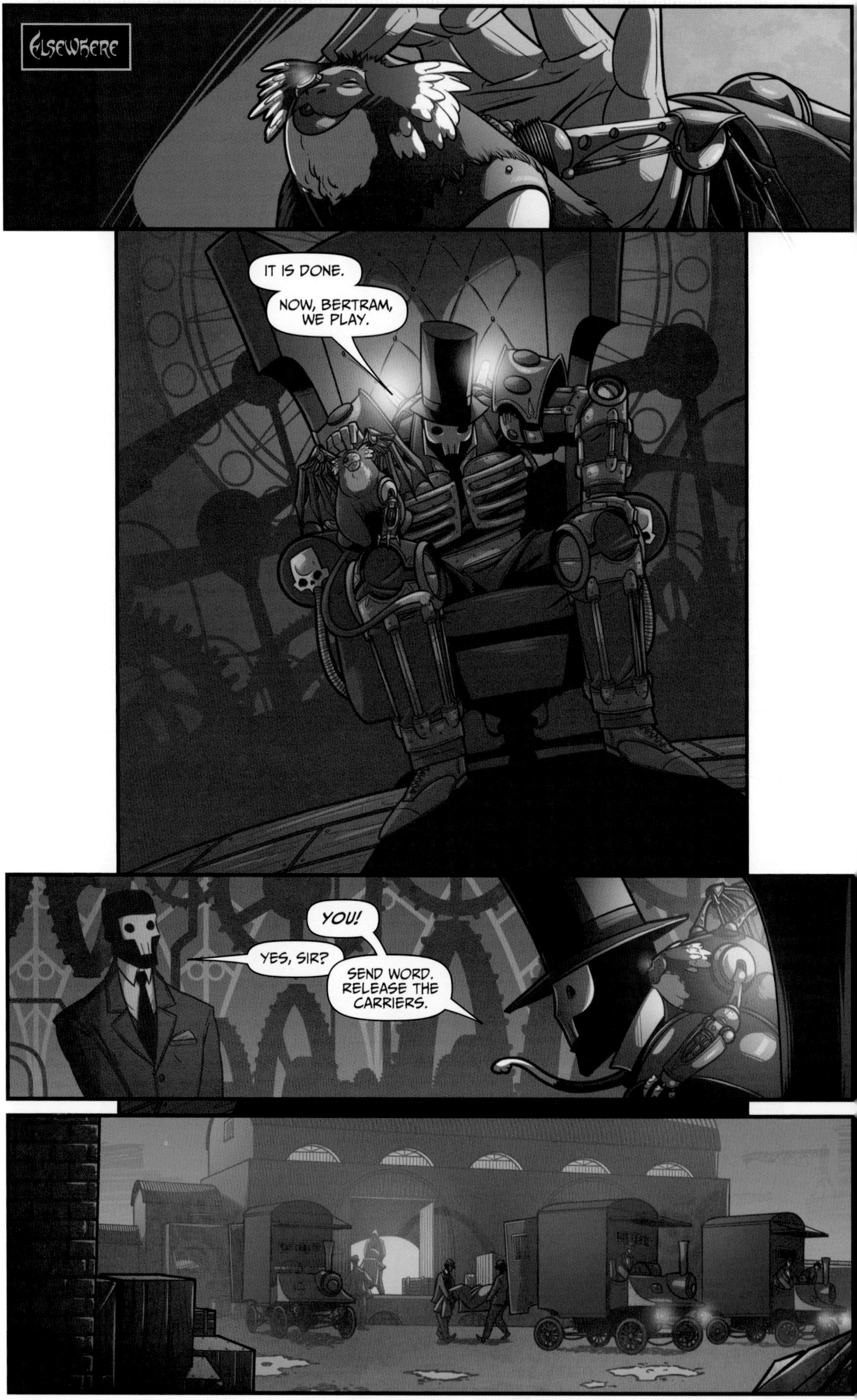
ELSEWHERE
IT IS DONE.
NOW, BERTRAM, WE PLAY.
YOU!
YES, SIR?
SEND WORD. RELEASE THE CARRIERS.

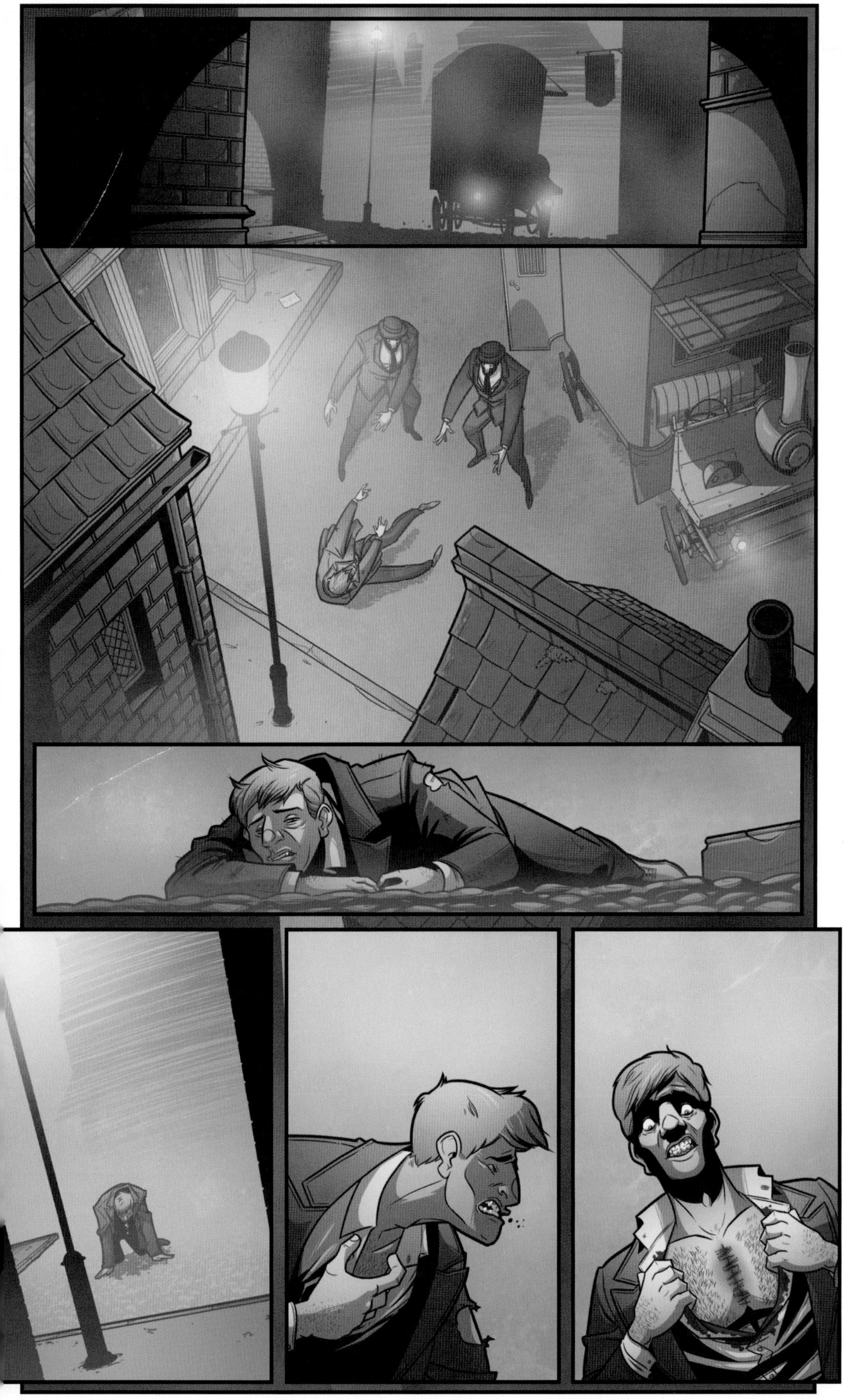

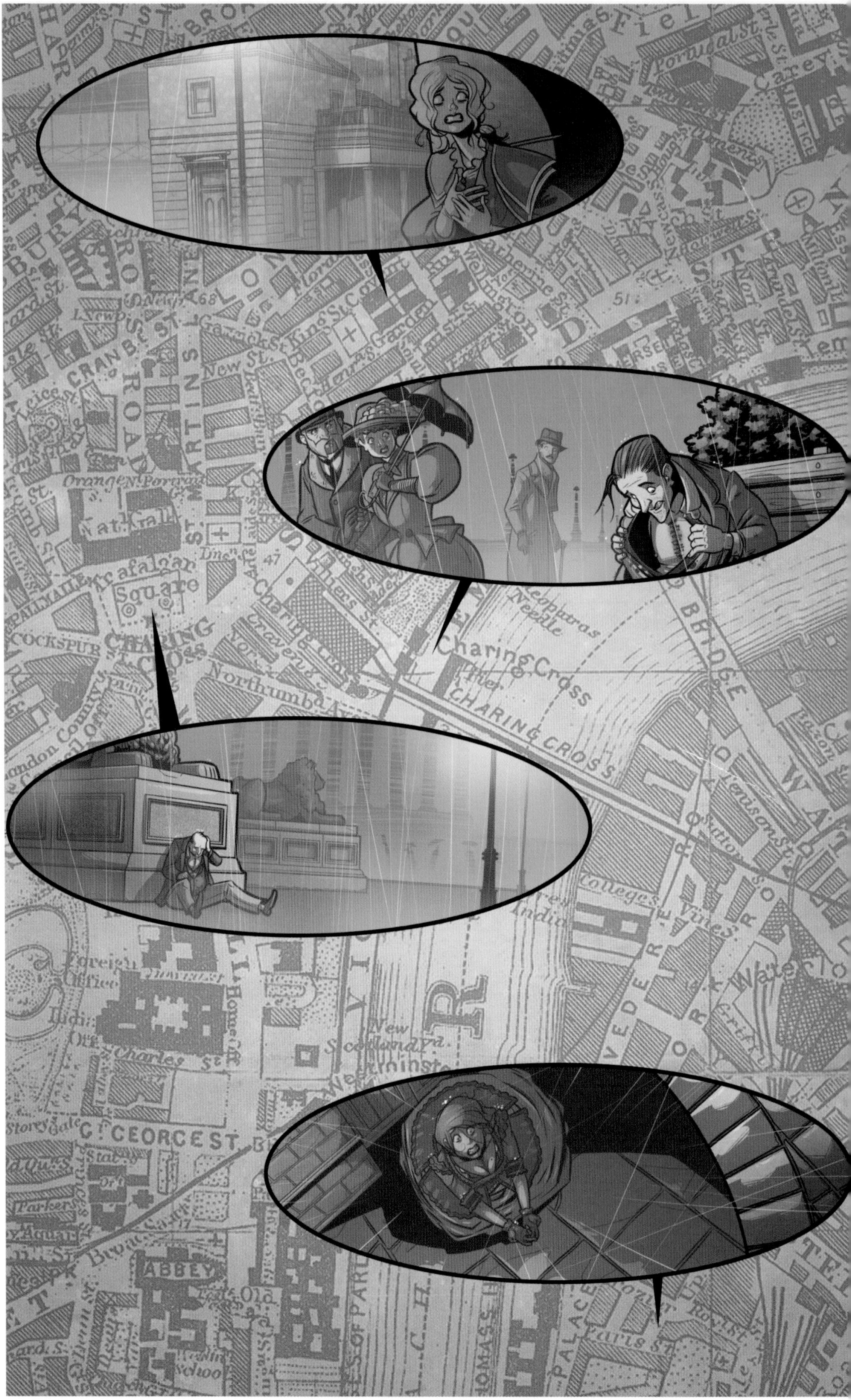
Portugal St
Wellington
Catherine St
King St
Garrick St
New St
CRAN
ST MARTINS
ROAD
Orange St
Nat. Gall.
Trafalgar Square
COCKSPUR
CHARING CROSS
Villiers St
Craven St
Northumb. Av
Cleopatras Needle
Charing Cross
CHARING CROSS
New Scotland Yd
Charles St
Gt GEORGE ST
ABBEY
Paris St

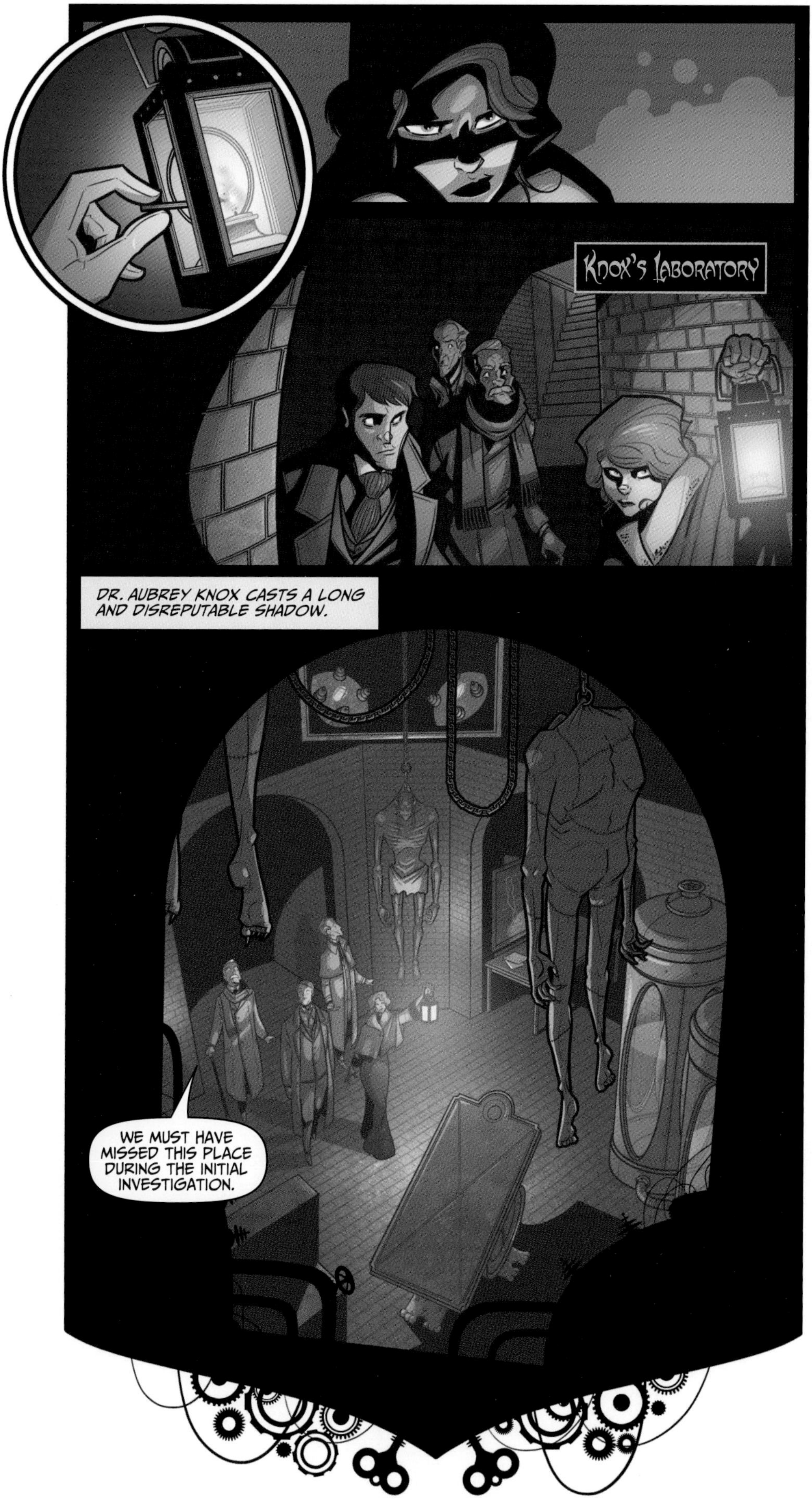

KNOX'S LABORATORY
DR. AUBREY KNOX CASTS A LONG AND DISREPUTABLE SHADOW.
WE MUST HAVE MISSED THIS PLACE DURING THE INITIAL INVESTIGATION.

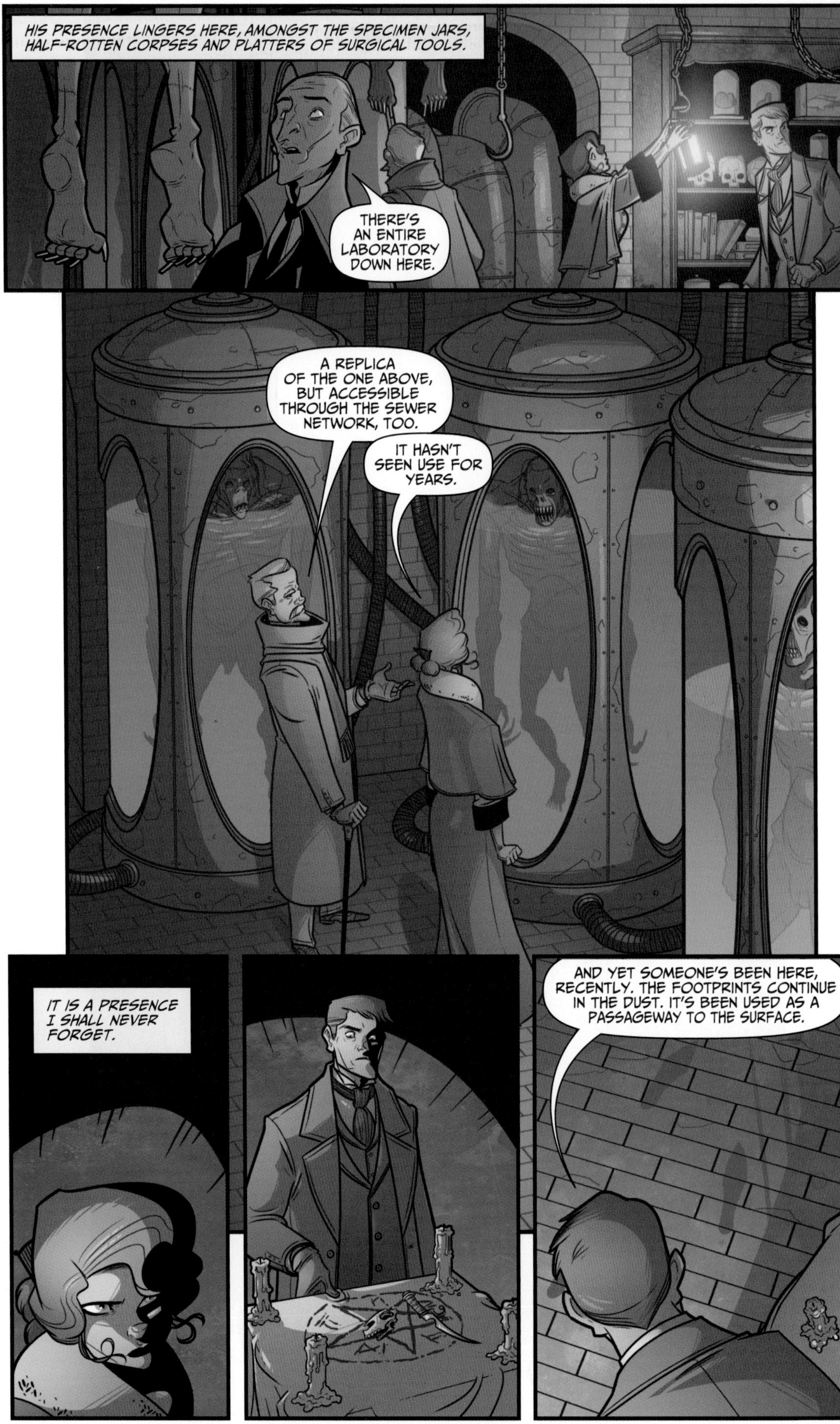
HIS PRESENCE LINGERS HERE, AMONGST THE SPECIMEN JARS, HALF-ROTTEN CORPSES AND PLATTERS OF SURGICAL TOOLS.
THERE'S AN ENTIRE LABORATORY DOWN HERE.
A REPLICA OF THE ONE ABOVE, BUT ACCESSIBLE THROUGH THE SEWER NETWORK, TOO.
IT HASN'T SEEN USE FOR YEARS.
IT IS A PRESENCE I SHALL NEVER FORGET.
AND YET SOMEONE'S BEEN HERE, RECENTLY. THE FOOTPRINTS CONTINUE IN THE DUST. IT'S BEEN USED AS A PASSAGEWAY TO THE SURFACE.

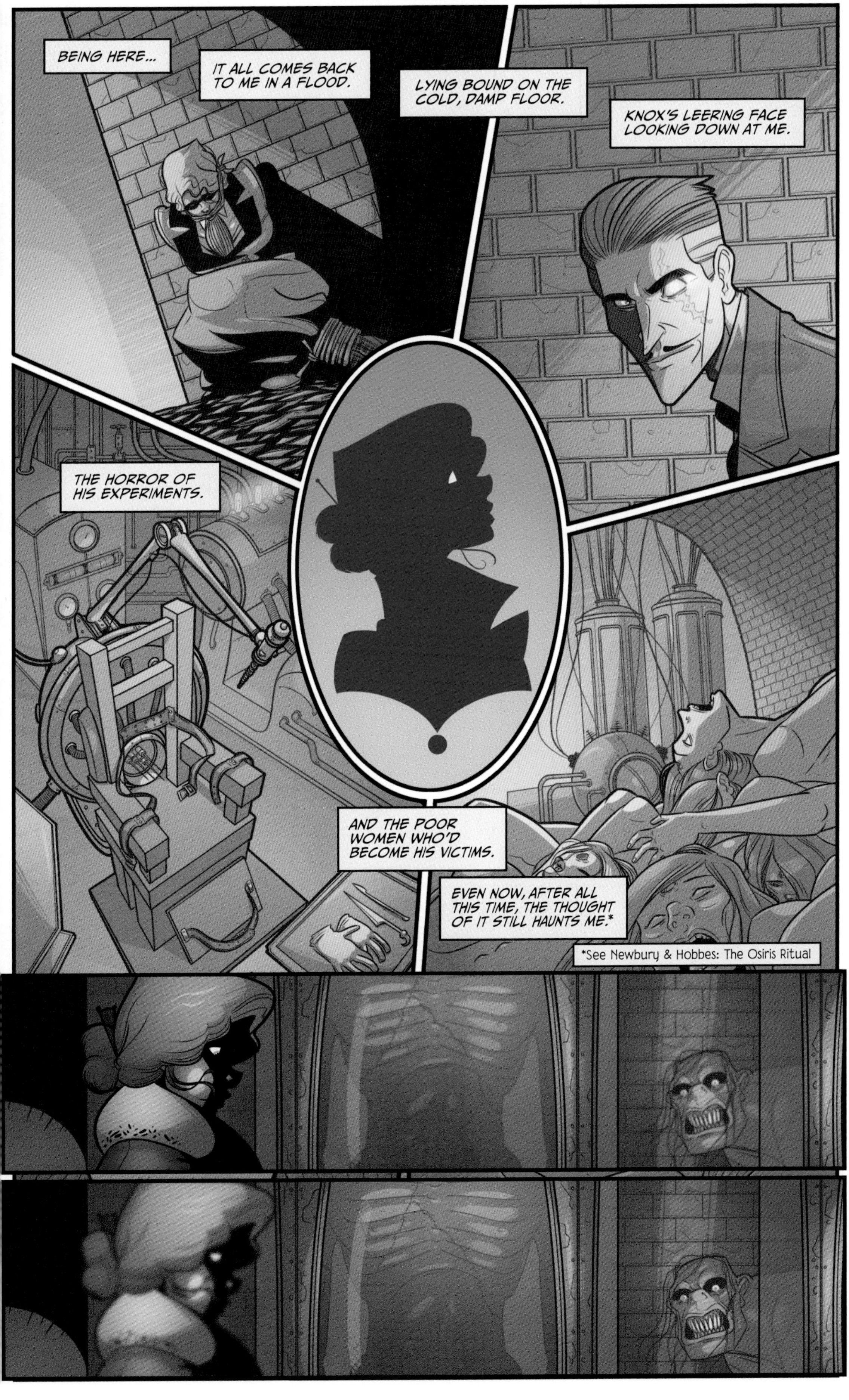
BEING HERE...
IT ALL COMES BACK TO ME IN A FLOOD.
LYING BOUND ON THE COLD, DAMP FLOOR.
KNOX'S LEERING FACE LOOKING DOWN AT ME.
THE HORROR OF HIS EXPERIMENTS.
AND THE POOR WOMEN WHO'D BECOME HIS VICTIMS.
EVEN NOW, AFTER ALL THIS TIME, THE THOUGHT OF IT STILL HAUNTS ME.*
*See Newbury & Hobbes: The Osiris Ritual

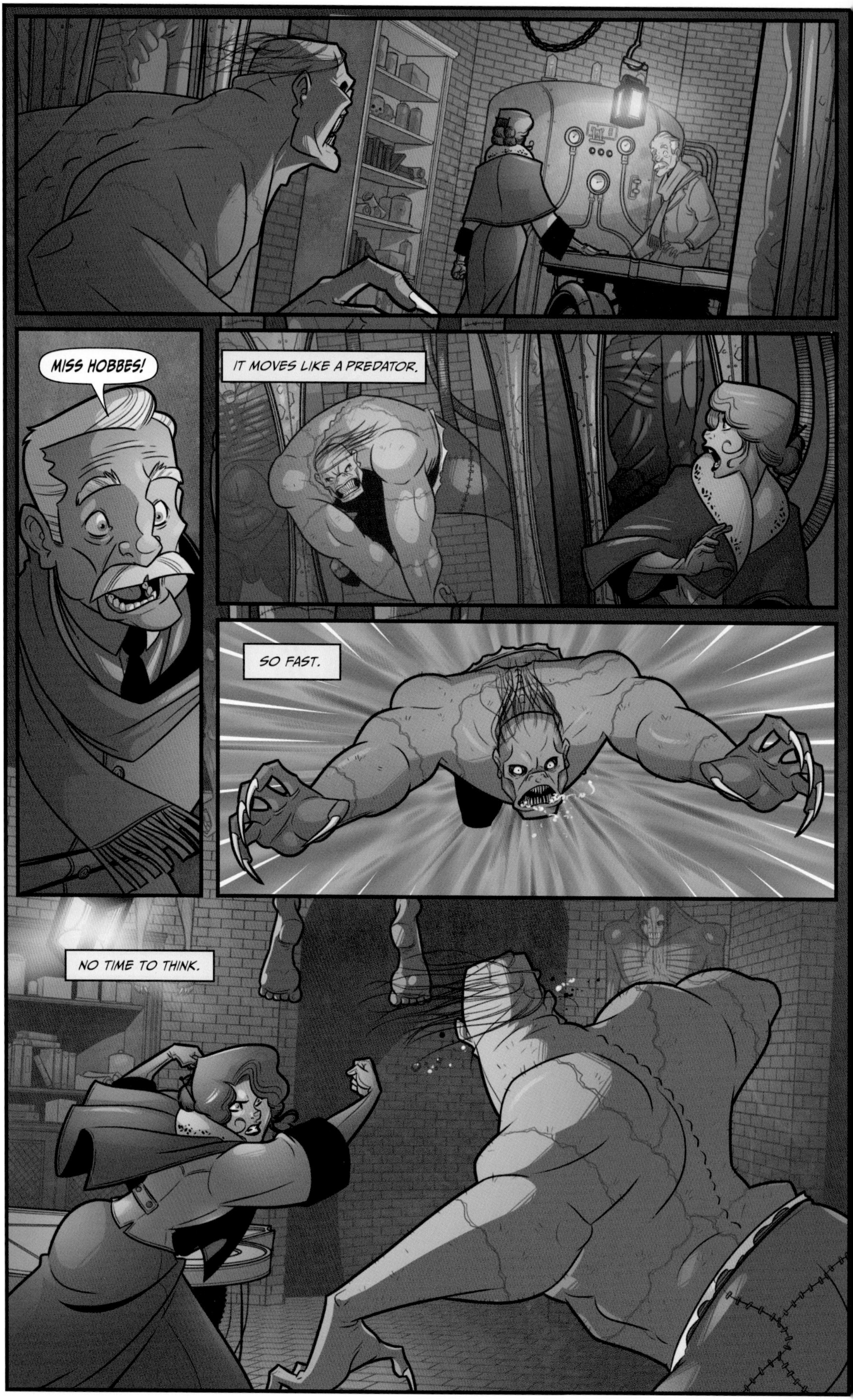
MISS HOBBES!
IT MOVES LIKE A PREDATOR.
SO FAST.
NO TIME TO THINK.

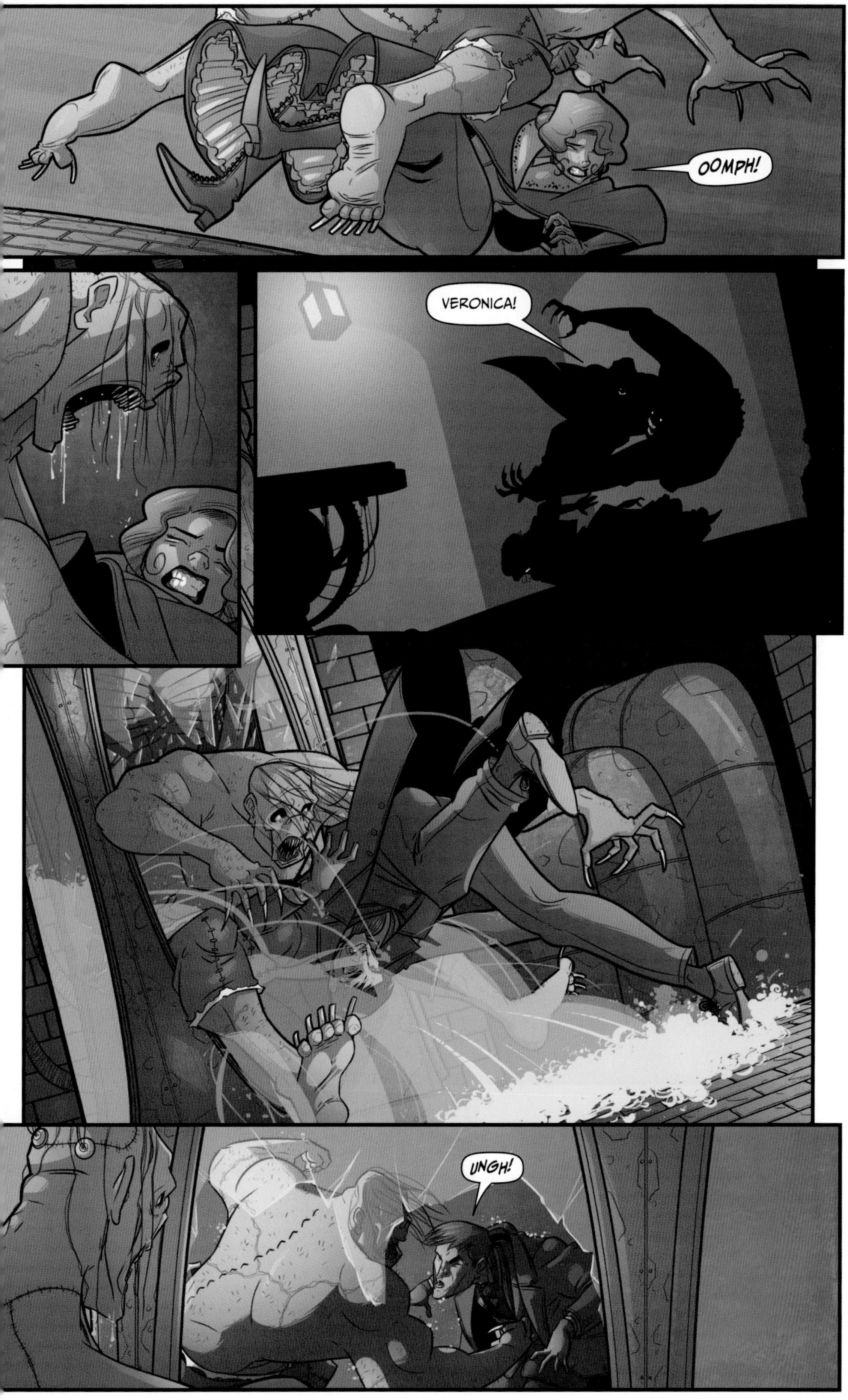
OOMPH!
VERONICA!
UNGH!

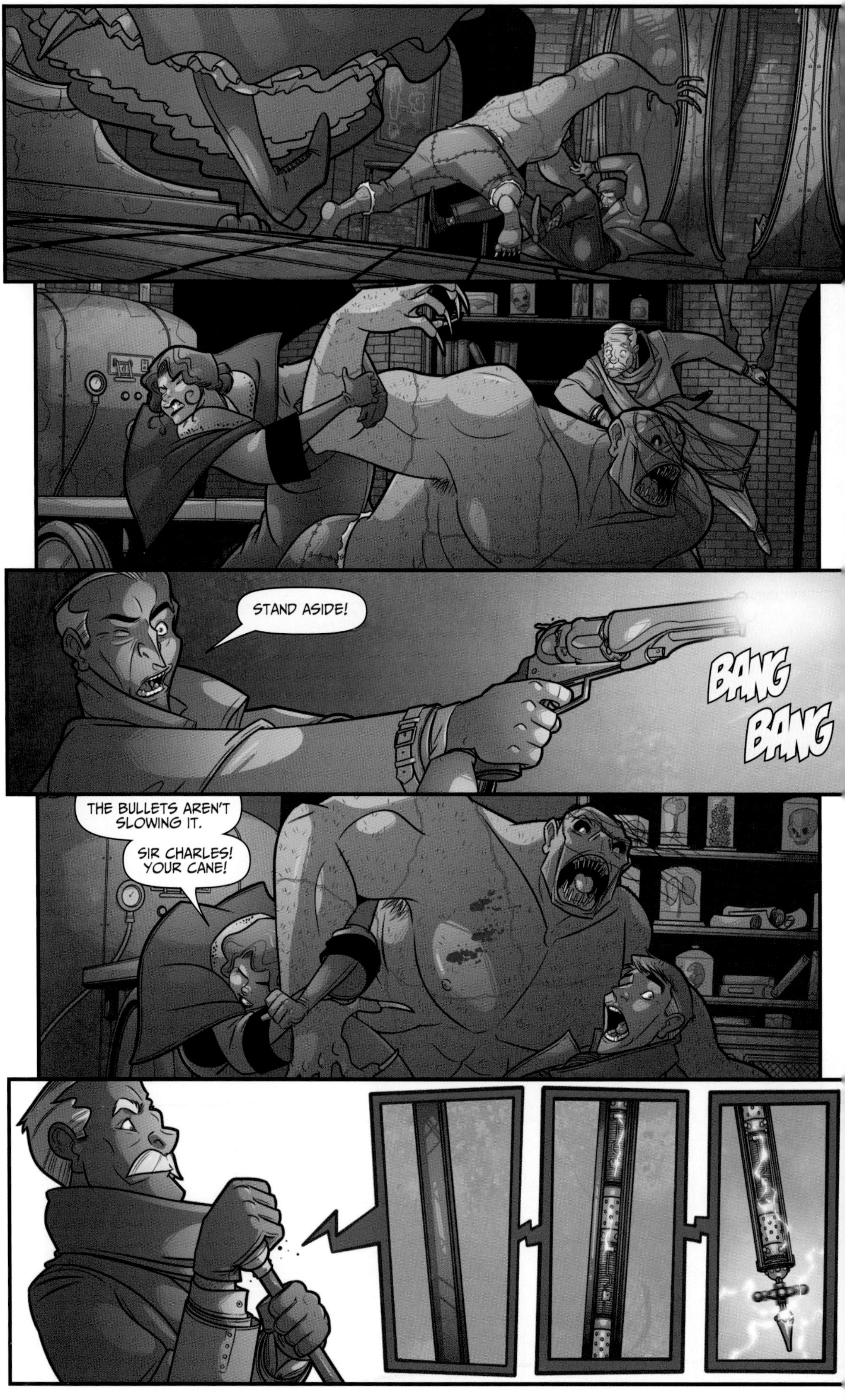
STAND ASIDE!
BANG
BANG
THE BULLETS AREN'T SLOWING IT.
SIR CHARLES! YOUR CANE!

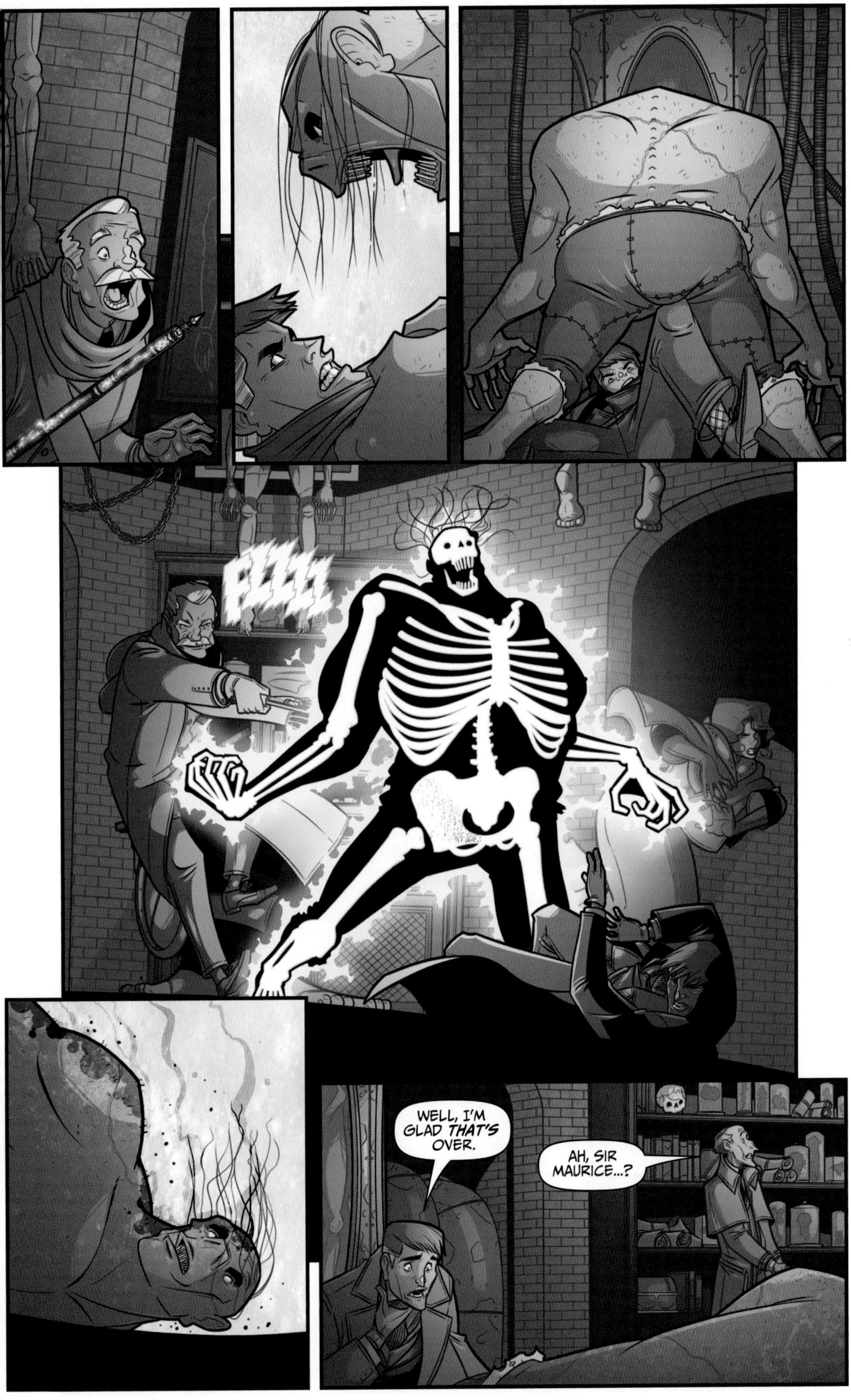
FZZZ
WELL, I'M GLAD THAT'S OVER.
AH, SIR MAURICE...?

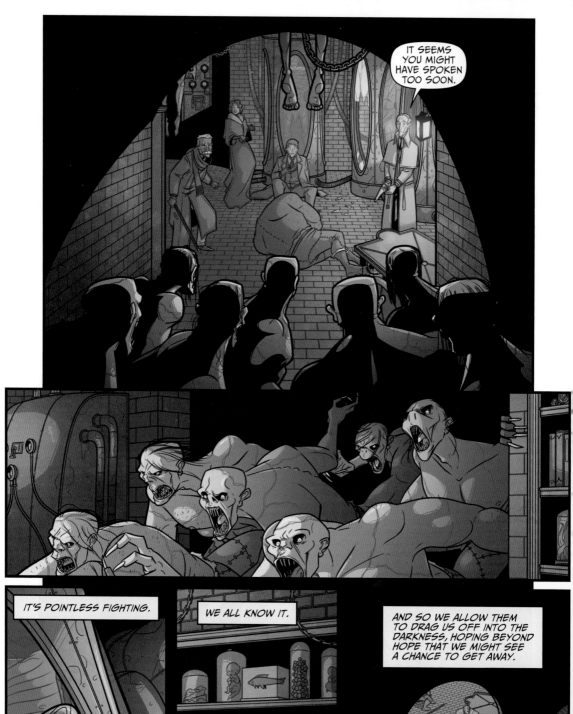

IT SEEMS YOU MIGHT HAVE SPOKEN TOO SOON.

IT'S POINTLESS FIGHTING.

WE ALL KNOW IT.

AND SO WE ALLOW THEM TO DRAG US OFF INTO THE DARKNESS, HOPING BEYOND HOPE THAT WE MIGHT SEE A CHANCE TO GET AWAY.

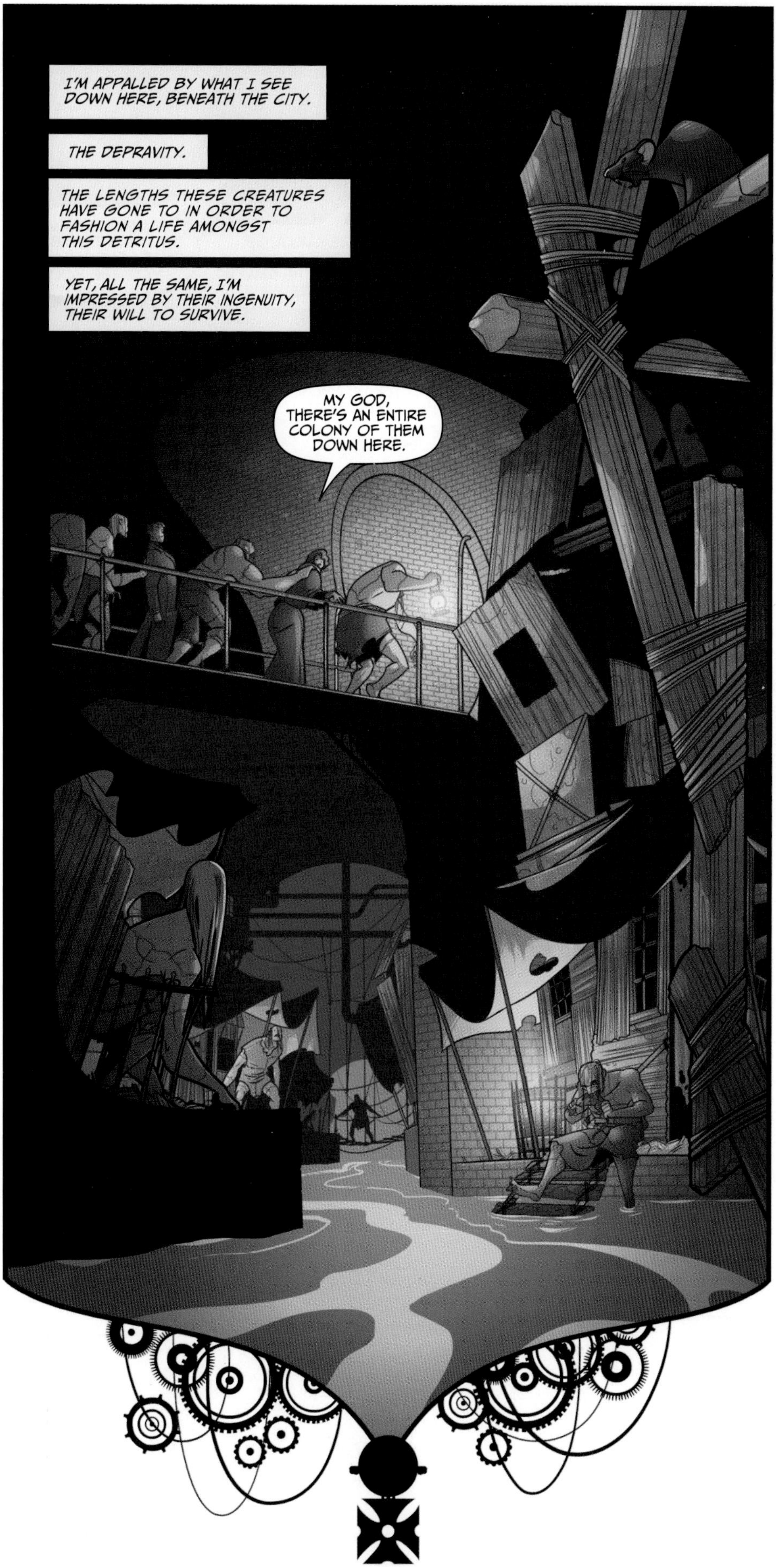
I'M APPALLED BY WHAT I SEE DOWN HERE, BENEATH THE CITY.
THE DEPRAVITY.
THE LENGTHS THESE CREATURES HAVE GONE TO IN ORDER TO FASHION A LIFE AMONGST THIS DETRITUS.
YET, ALL THE SAME, I'M IMPRESSED BY THEIR INGENUITY, THEIR WILL TO SURVIVE.
MY GOD, THERE'S AN ENTIRE COLONY OF THEM DOWN HERE.

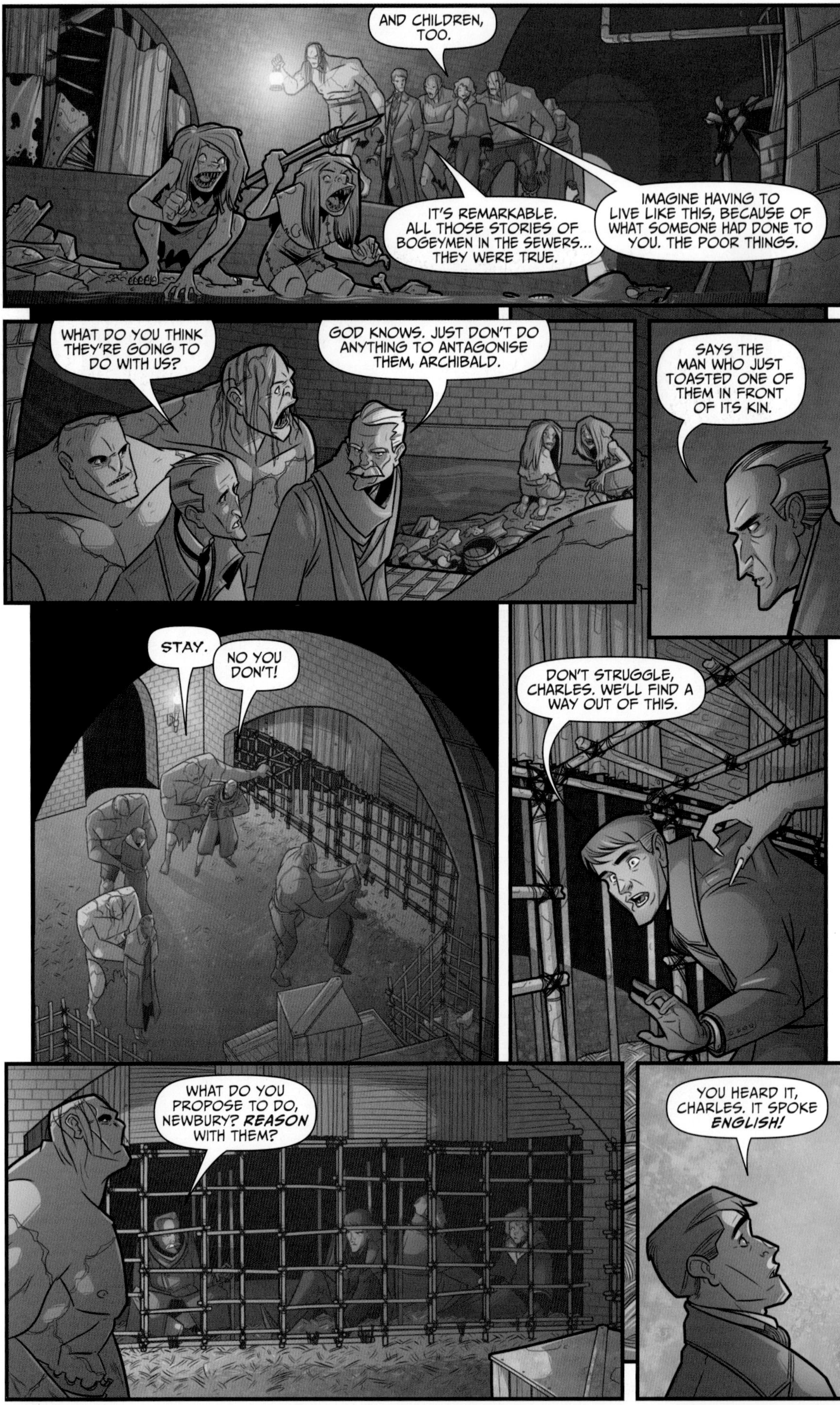
AND CHILDREN, TOO.
IT'S REMARKABLE. ALL THOSE STORIES OF BOGEYMEN IN THE SEWERS... THEY WERE TRUE.
IMAGINE HAVING TO LIVE LIKE THIS, BECAUSE OF WHAT SOMEONE HAD DONE TO YOU. THE POOR THINGS.
WHAT DO YOU THINK THEY'RE GOING TO DO WITH US?
GOD KNOWS. JUST DON'T DO ANYTHING TO ANTAGONISE THEM, ARCHIBALD.
SAYS THE MAN WHO JUST TOASTED ONE OF THEM IN FRONT OF ITS KIN.
STAY.
NO YOU DON'T!
DON'T STRUGGLE, CHARLES. WE'LL FIND A WAY OUT OF THIS.
WHAT DO YOU PROPOSE TO DO, NEWBURY? *REASON* WITH THEM?
YOU HEARD IT, CHARLES. IT SPOKE *ENGLISH!*

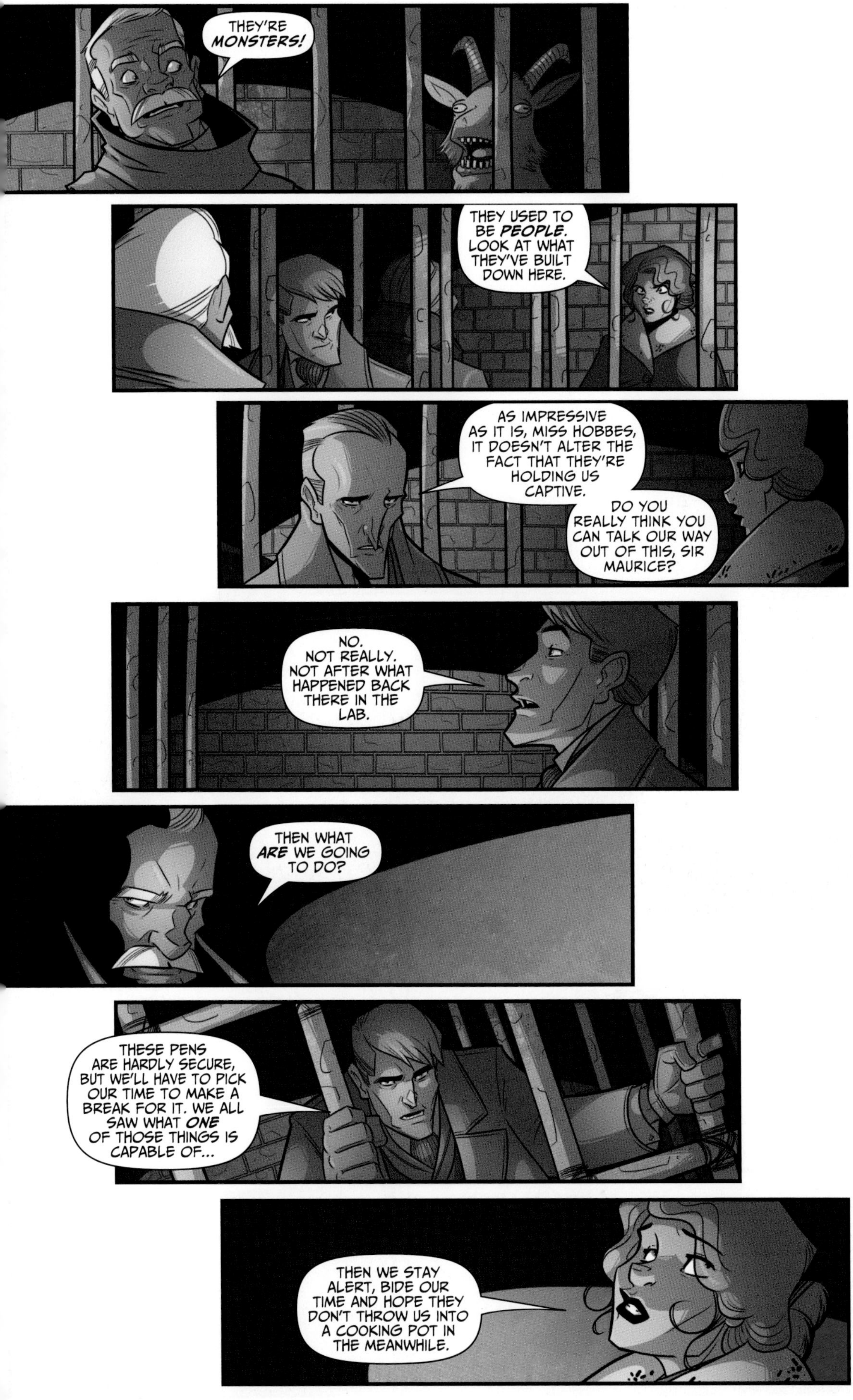
THEY'RE MONSTERS!
THEY USED TO BE PEOPLE. LOOK AT WHAT THEY'VE BUILT DOWN HERE.
AS IMPRESSIVE AS IT IS, MISS HOBBES, IT DOESN'T ALTER THE FACT THAT THEY'RE HOLDING US CAPTIVE.
DO YOU REALLY THINK YOU CAN TALK OUR WAY OUT OF THIS, SIR MAURICE?
NO. NOT REALLY. NOT AFTER WHAT HAPPENED BACK THERE IN THE LAB.
THEN WHAT ARE WE GOING TO DO?
THESE PENS ARE HARDLY SECURE, BUT WE'LL HAVE TO PICK OUR TIME TO MAKE A BREAK FOR IT. WE ALL SAW WHAT ONE OF THOSE THINGS IS CAPABLE OF...
THEN WE STAY ALERT, BIDE OUR TIME AND HOPE THEY DON'T THROW US INTO A COOKING POT IN THE MEANWHILE.

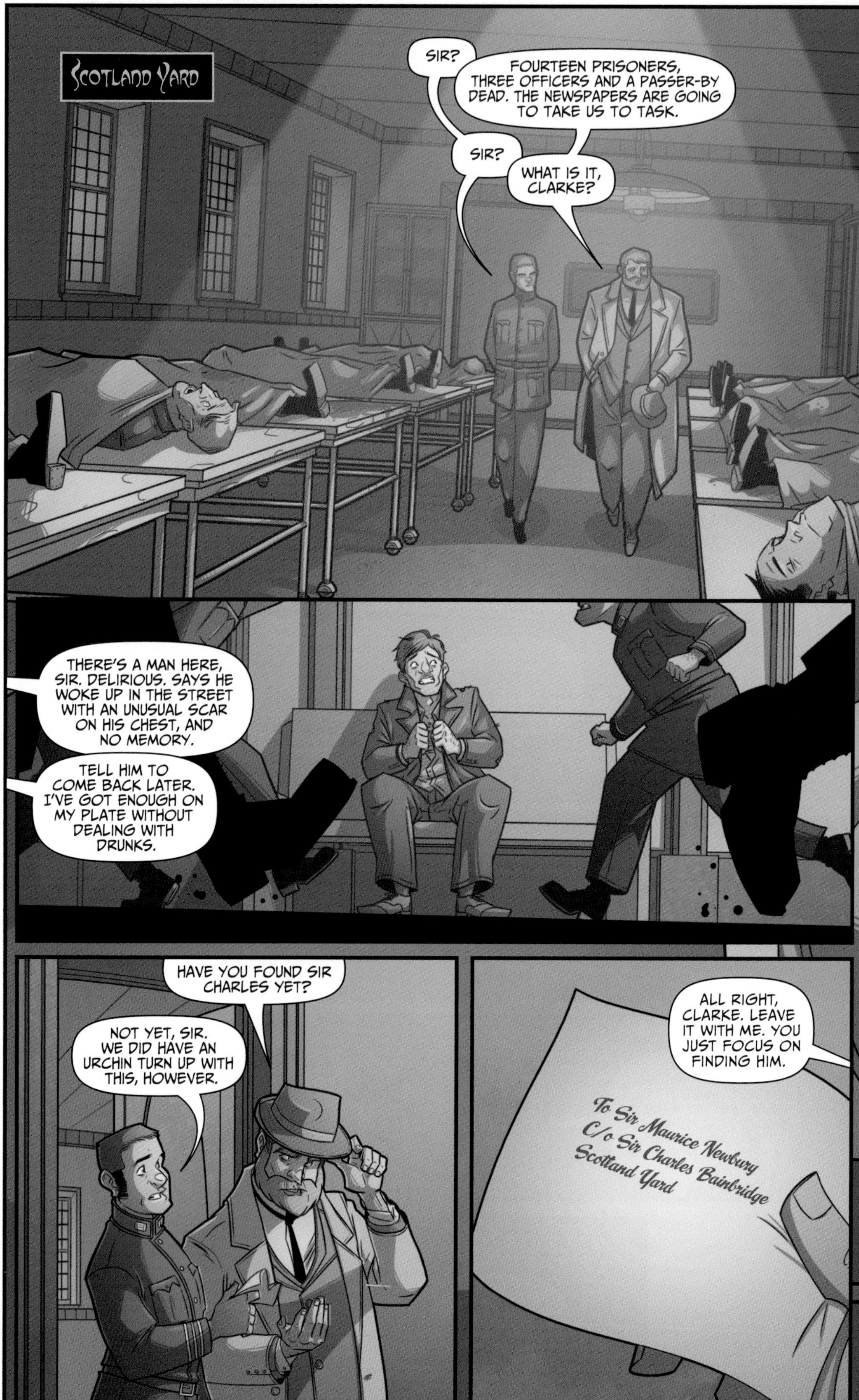
SCOTLAND YARD
SIR?
FOURTEEN PRISONERS, THREE OFFICERS AND A PASSER-BY DEAD. THE NEWSPAPERS ARE GOING TO TAKE US TO TASK.
SIR?
WHAT IS IT, CLARKE?
THERE'S A MAN HERE, SIR. DELIRIOUS. SAYS HE WOKE UP IN THE STREET WITH AN UNUSUAL SCAR ON HIS CHEST, AND NO MEMORY.
TELL HIM TO COME BACK LATER. I'VE GOT ENOUGH ON MY PLATE WITHOUT DEALING WITH DRUNKS.
HAVE YOU FOUND SIR CHARLES YET?
NOT YET, SIR. WE DID HAVE AN URCHIN TURN UP WITH THIS, HOWEVER.
ALL RIGHT, CLARKE. LEAVE IT WITH ME. YOU JUST FOCUS ON FINDING HIM.
To Sir Maurice Newbury
C/o Sir Charles Bainbridge
Scotland Yard

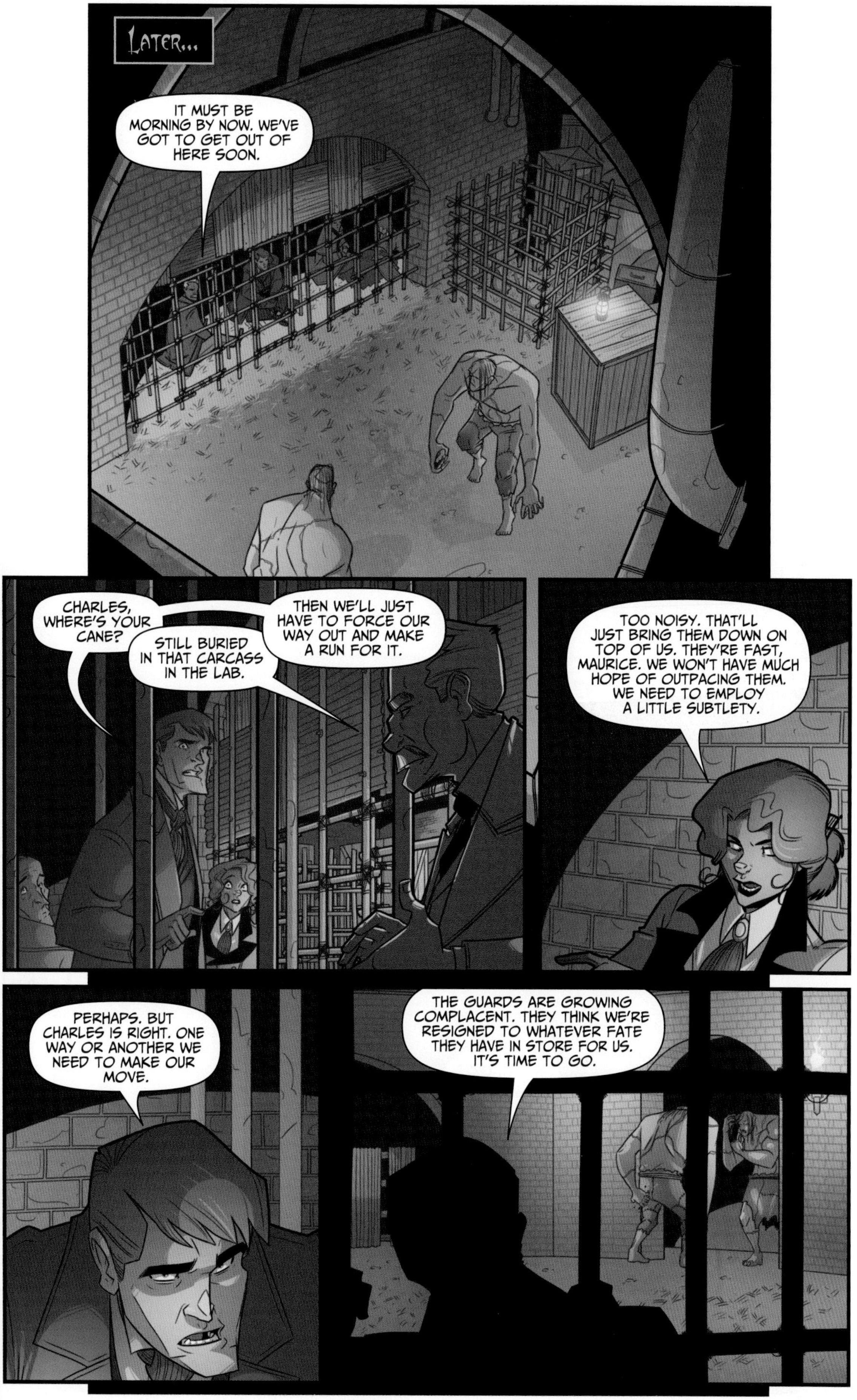
LATER...
IT MUST BE MORNING BY NOW. WE'VE GOT TO GET OUT OF HERE SOON.
CHARLES, WHERE'S YOUR CANE?
STILL BURIED IN THAT CARCASS IN THE LAB.
THEN WE'LL JUST HAVE TO FORCE OUR WAY OUT AND MAKE A RUN FOR IT.
TOO NOISY. THAT'LL JUST BRING THEM DOWN ON TOP OF US. THEY'RE FAST, MAURICE. WE WON'T HAVE MUCH HOPE OF OUTPACING THEM. WE NEED TO EMPLOY A LITTLE SUBTLETY.
PERHAPS. BUT CHARLES IS RIGHT. ONE WAY OR ANOTHER WE NEED TO MAKE OUR MOVE.
THE GUARDS ARE GROWING COMPLACENT. THEY THINK WE'RE RESIGNED TO WHATEVER FATE THEY HAVE IN STORE FOR US. IT'S TIME TO GO.

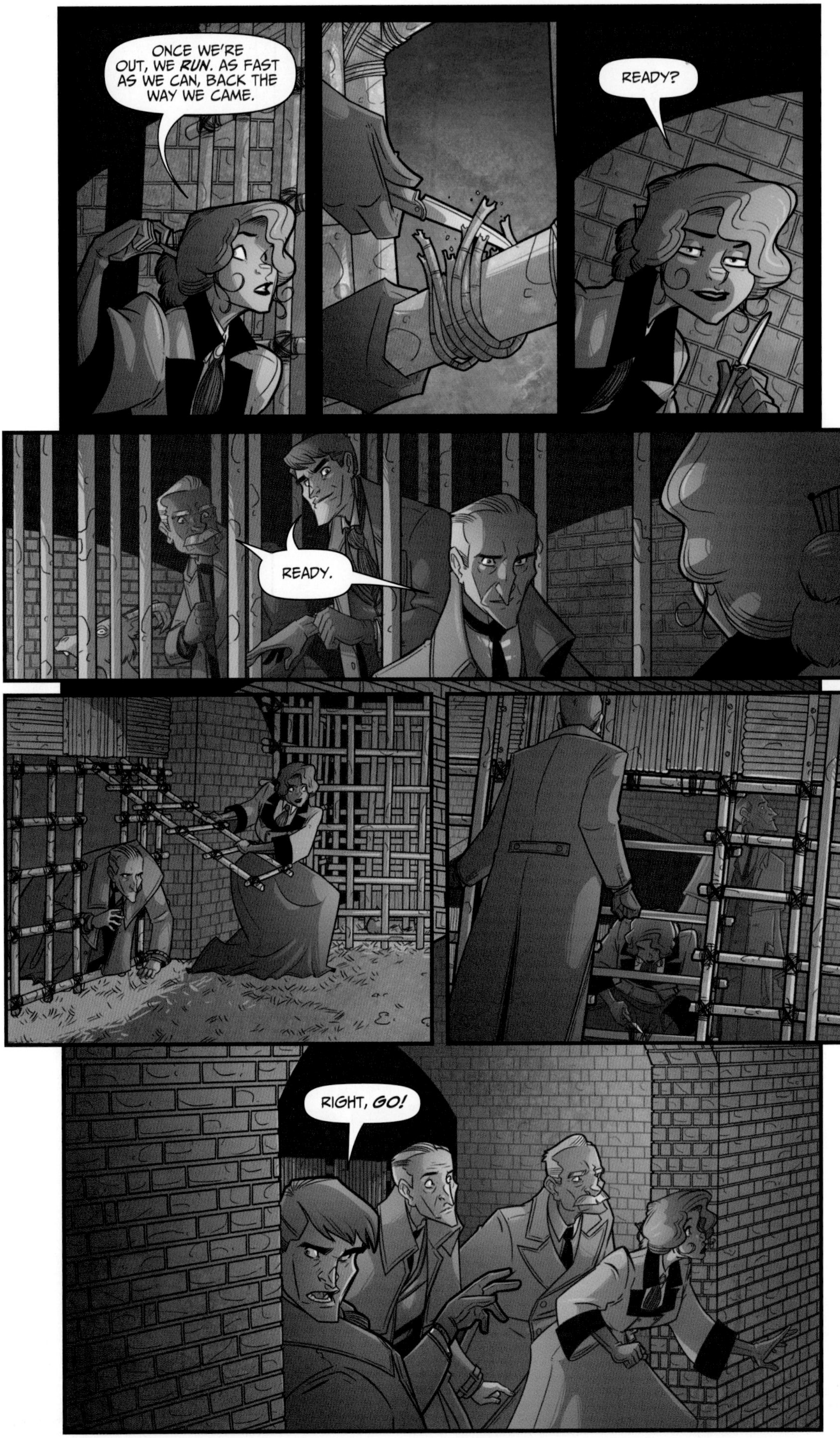
ONCE WE'RE OUT, WE *RUN*. AS FAST AS WE CAN, BACK THE WAY WE CAME.
READY?
READY.
RIGHT, *GO!*

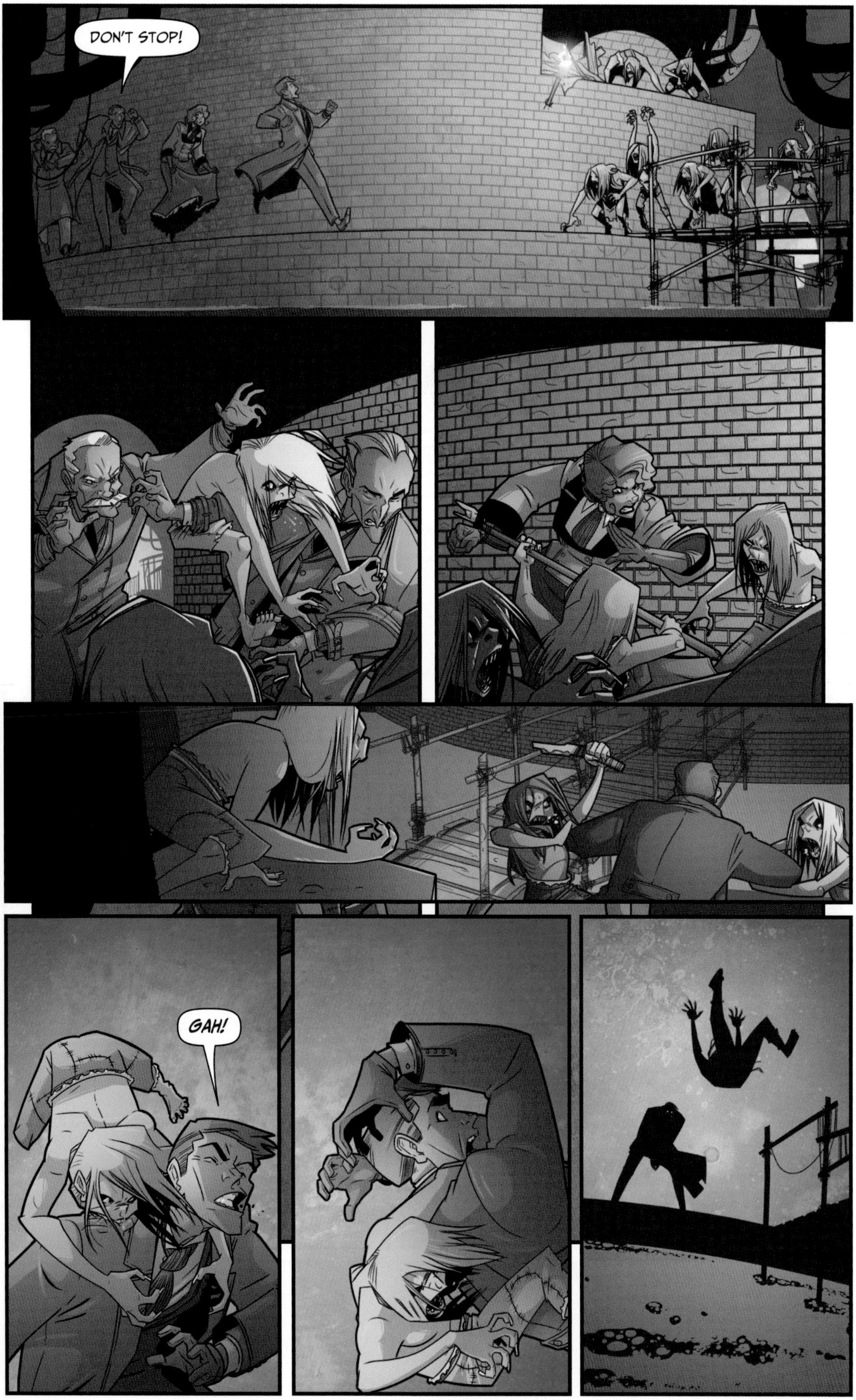
DON'T STOP!
GAH!

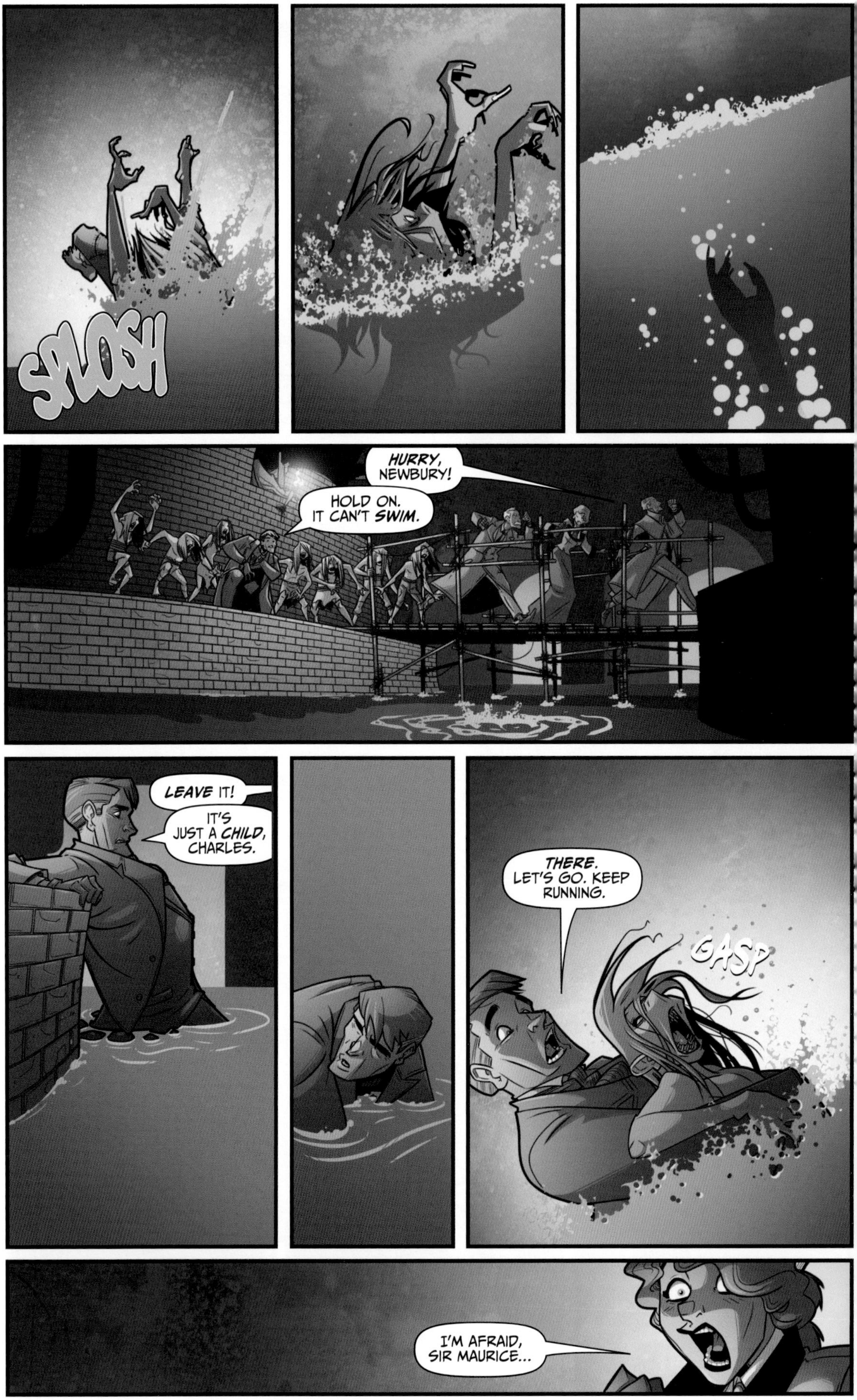
SPLOSH
HURRY, NEWBURY!
HOLD ON. IT CAN'T SWIM.
LEAVE IT!
IT'S JUST A CHILD, CHARLES.
THERE. LET'S GO. KEEP RUNNING.
GASP
I'M AFRAID, SIR MAURICE...

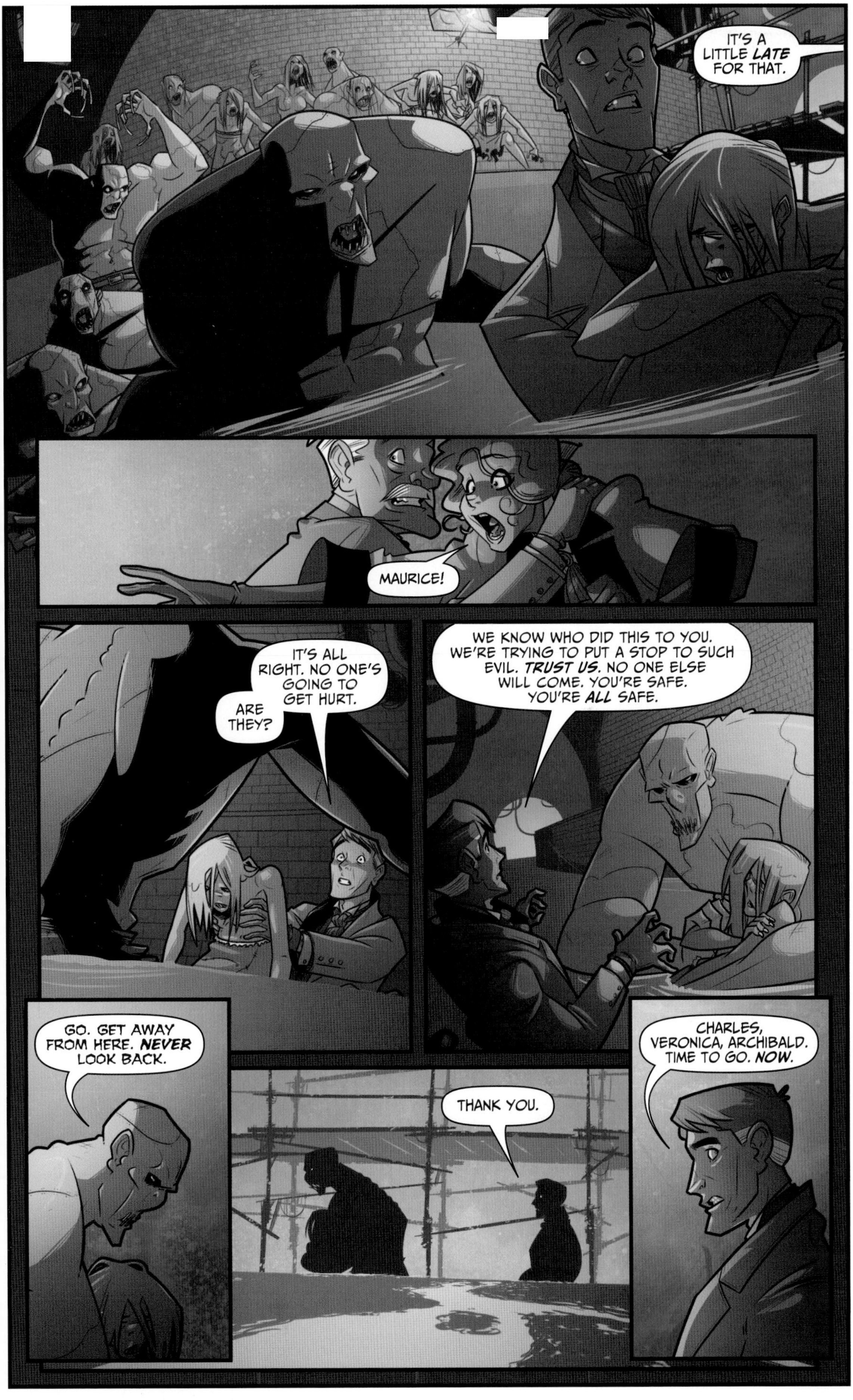
IT'S A LITTLE LATE FOR THAT.
MAURICE!
IT'S ALL RIGHT. NO ONE'S GOING TO GET HURT.
ARE THEY?
WE KNOW WHO DID THIS TO YOU. WE'RE TRYING TO PUT A STOP TO SUCH EVIL. TRUST US. NO ONE ELSE WILL COME. YOU'RE SAFE. YOU'RE ALL SAFE.
GO. GET AWAY FROM HERE. NEVER LOOK BACK.
THANK YOU.
CHARLES, VERONICA, ARCHIBALD. TIME TO GO. NOW.

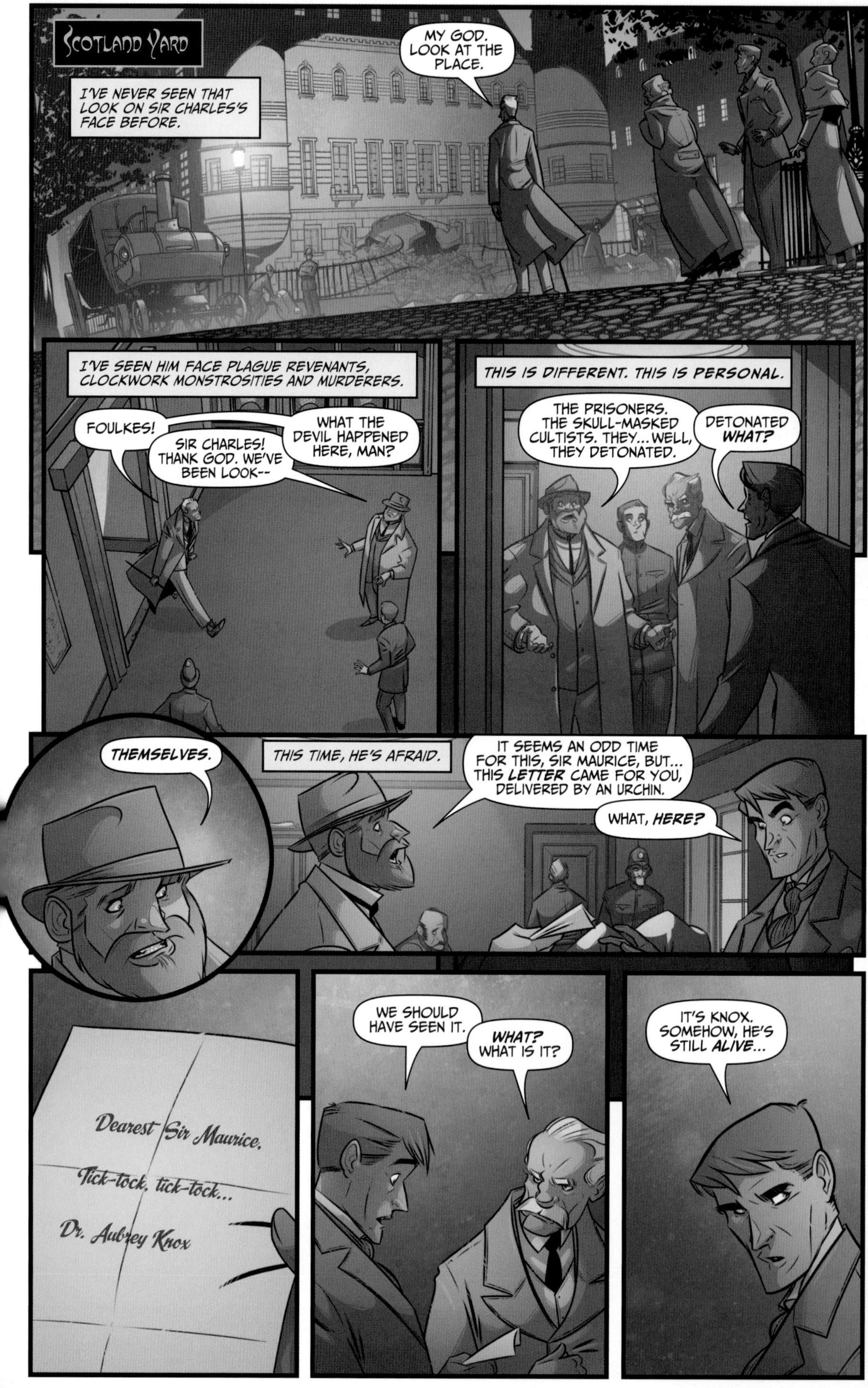
Scotland Yard
I'VE NEVER SEEN THAT LOOK ON SIR CHARLES'S FACE BEFORE.
MY GOD. LOOK AT THE PLACE.
I'VE SEEN HIM FACE PLAGUE REVENANTS, CLOCKWORK MONSTROSITIES AND MURDERERS.
FOULKES!
SIR CHARLES! THANK GOD. WE'VE BEEN LOOK--
WHAT THE DEVIL HAPPENED HERE, MAN?
THIS IS DIFFERENT. THIS IS PERSONAL.
THE PRISONERS. THE SKULL-MASKED CULTISTS. THEY... WELL, THEY DETONATED.
DETONATED WHAT?
THEMSELVES.
THIS TIME, HE'S AFRAID.
IT SEEMS AN ODD TIME FOR THIS, SIR MAURICE, BUT... THIS LETTER CAME FOR YOU, DELIVERED BY AN URCHIN.
WHAT, HERE?
Dearest Sir Maurice,
Tick-tock, tick-tock...
Dr. Aubrey Knox
WE SHOULD HAVE SEEN IT.
WHAT? WHAT IS IT?
IT'S KNOX. SOMEHOW, HE'S STILL ALIVE...

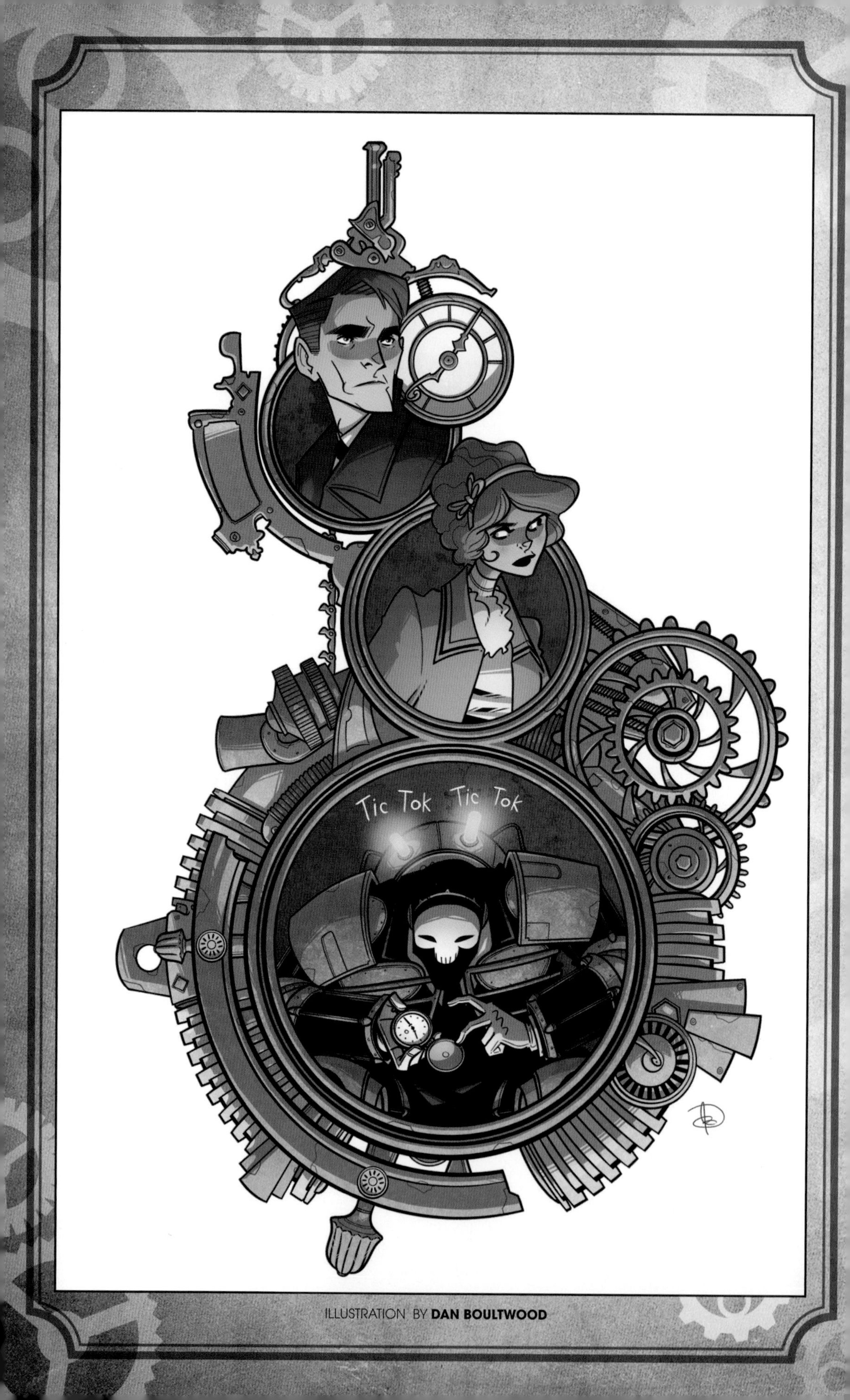
Tic Tok Tic Tok

ILLUSTRATION BY **DAN BOULTWOOD**

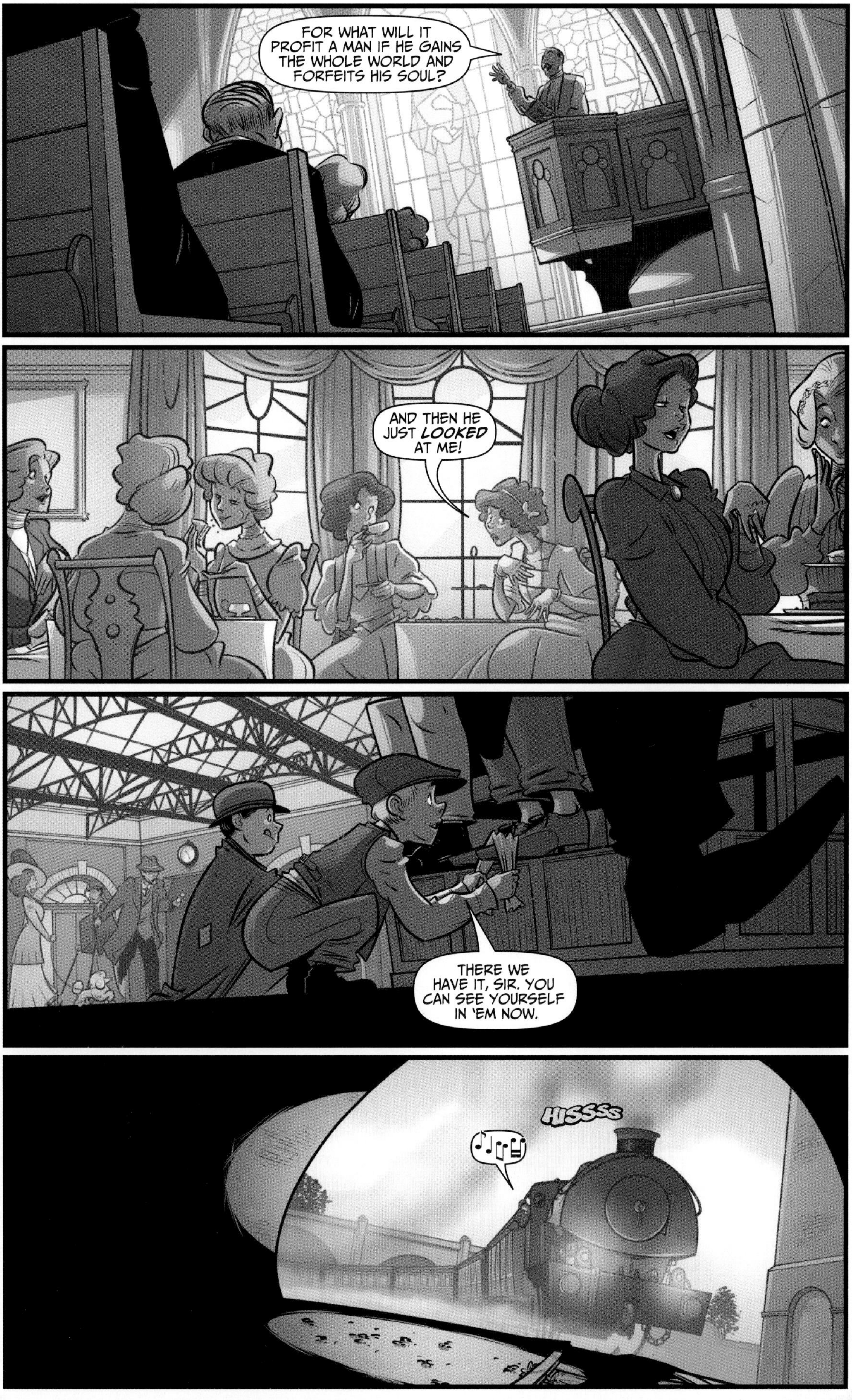
FOR WHAT WILL IT PROFIT A MAN IF HE GAINS THE WHOLE WORLD AND FORFEITS HIS SOUL?
AND THEN HE JUST LOOKED AT ME!
THERE WE HAVE IT, SIR. YOU CAN SEE YOURSELF IN 'EM NOW.
HISSSS

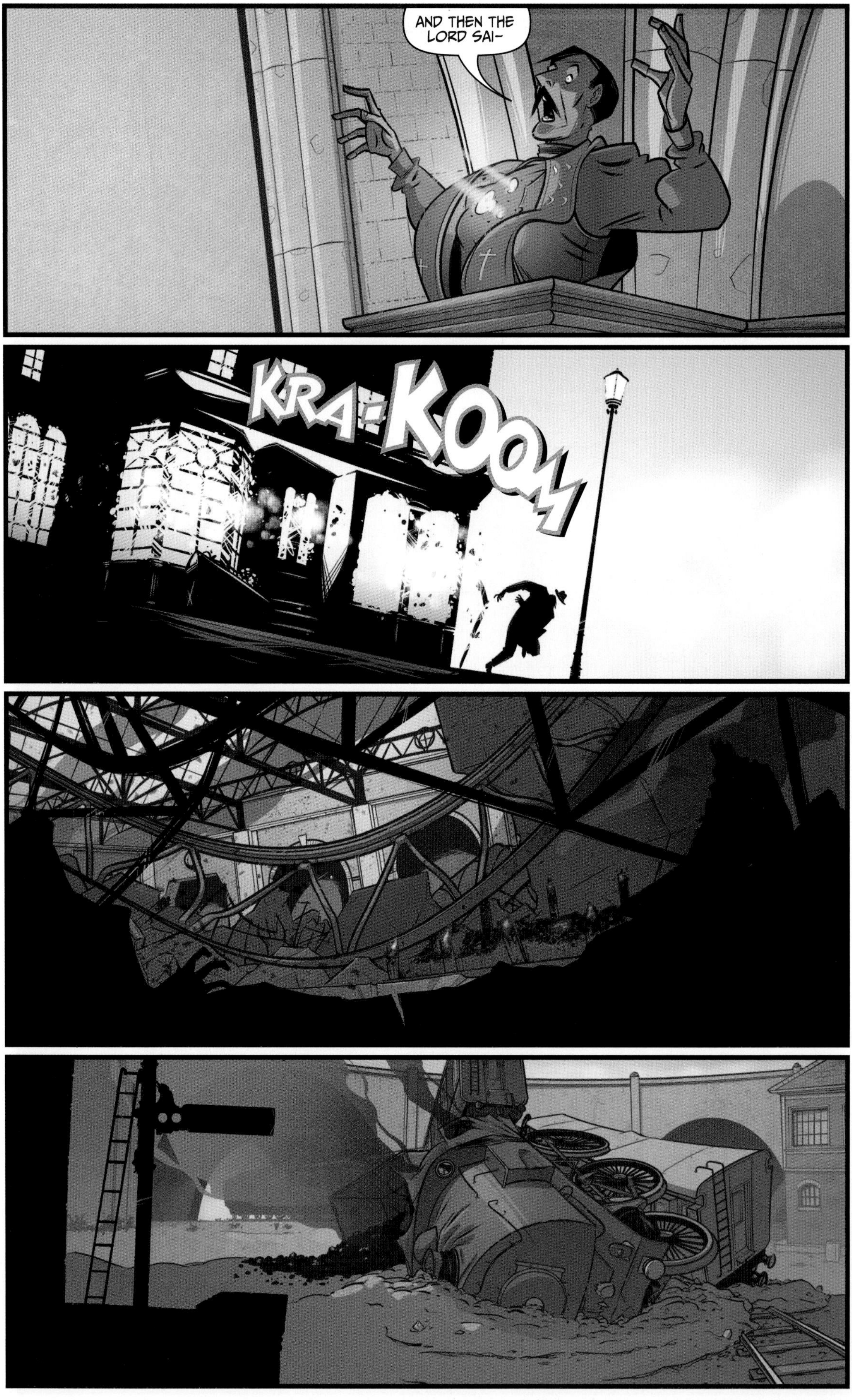
AND THEN THE LORD SAI-
KRA-KOOM

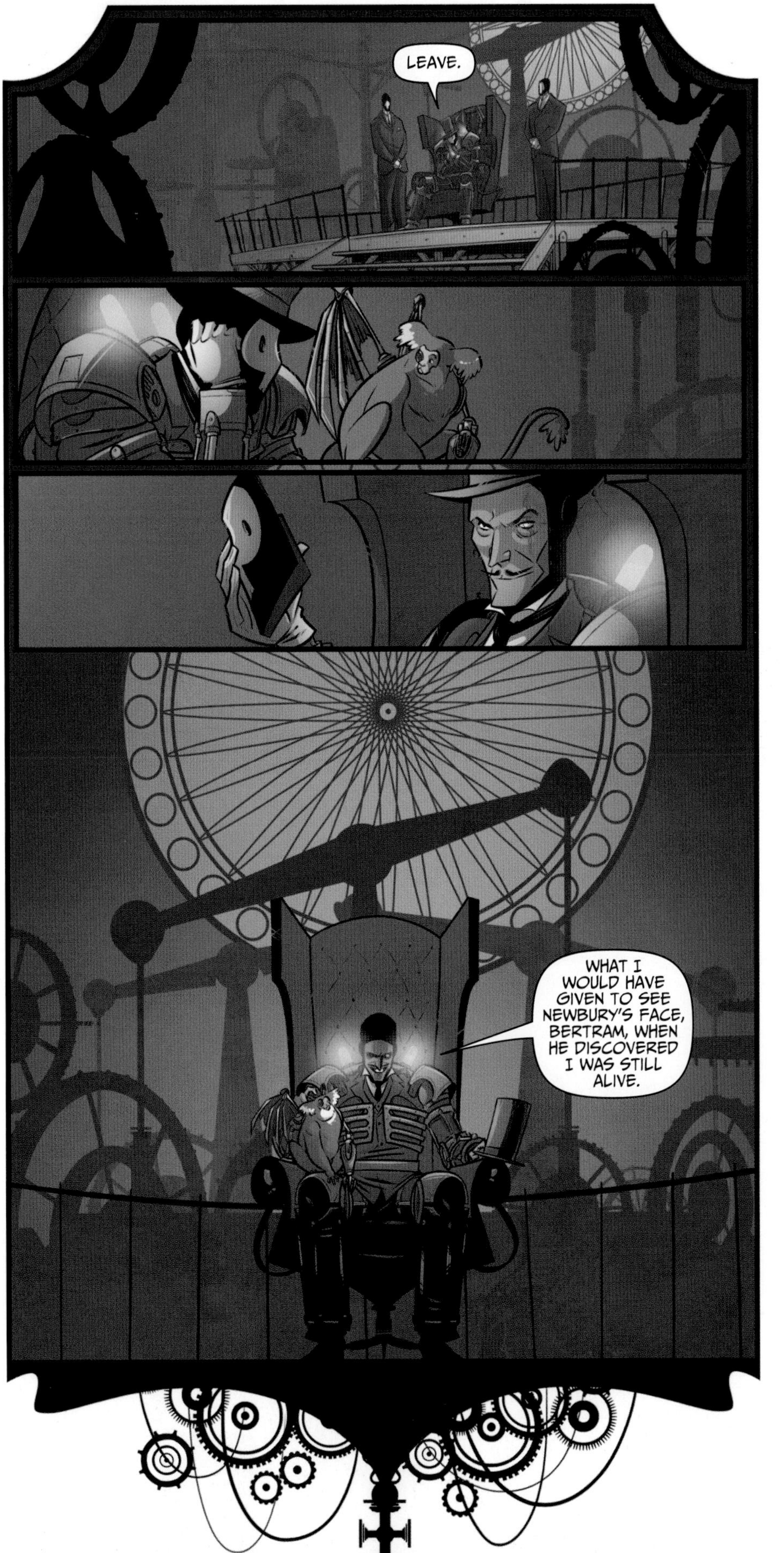
LEAVE.
WHAT I WOULD HAVE GIVEN TO SEE NEWBURY'S FACE, BERTRAM, WHEN HE DISCOVERED I WAS STILL ALIVE.

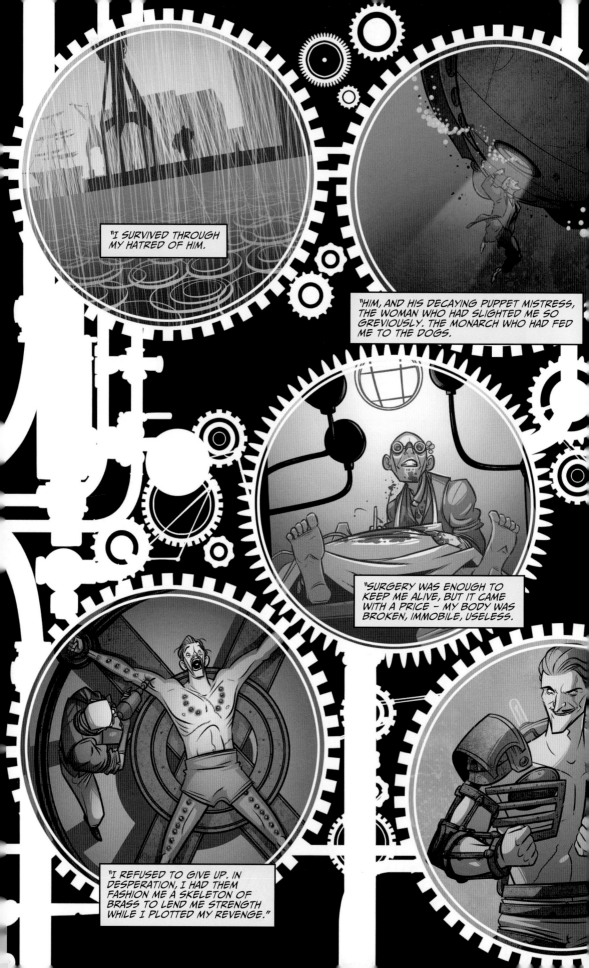

"I SURVIVED THROUGH MY HATRED OF HIM.

"HIM, AND HIS DECAYING PUPPET MISTRESS, THE WOMAN WHO HAD SLIGHTED ME SO GRIEVIOUSLY. THE MONARCH WHO HAD FED ME TO THE DOGS.

"SURGERY WAS ENOUGH TO KEEP ME ALIVE, BUT IT CAME WITH A PRICE – MY BODY WAS BROKEN, IMMOBILE, USELESS.

"I REFUSED TO GIVE UP. IN DESPERATION, I HAD THEM FASHION ME A SKELETON OF BRASS TO LEND ME STRENGTH WHILE I PLOTTED MY REVENGE."

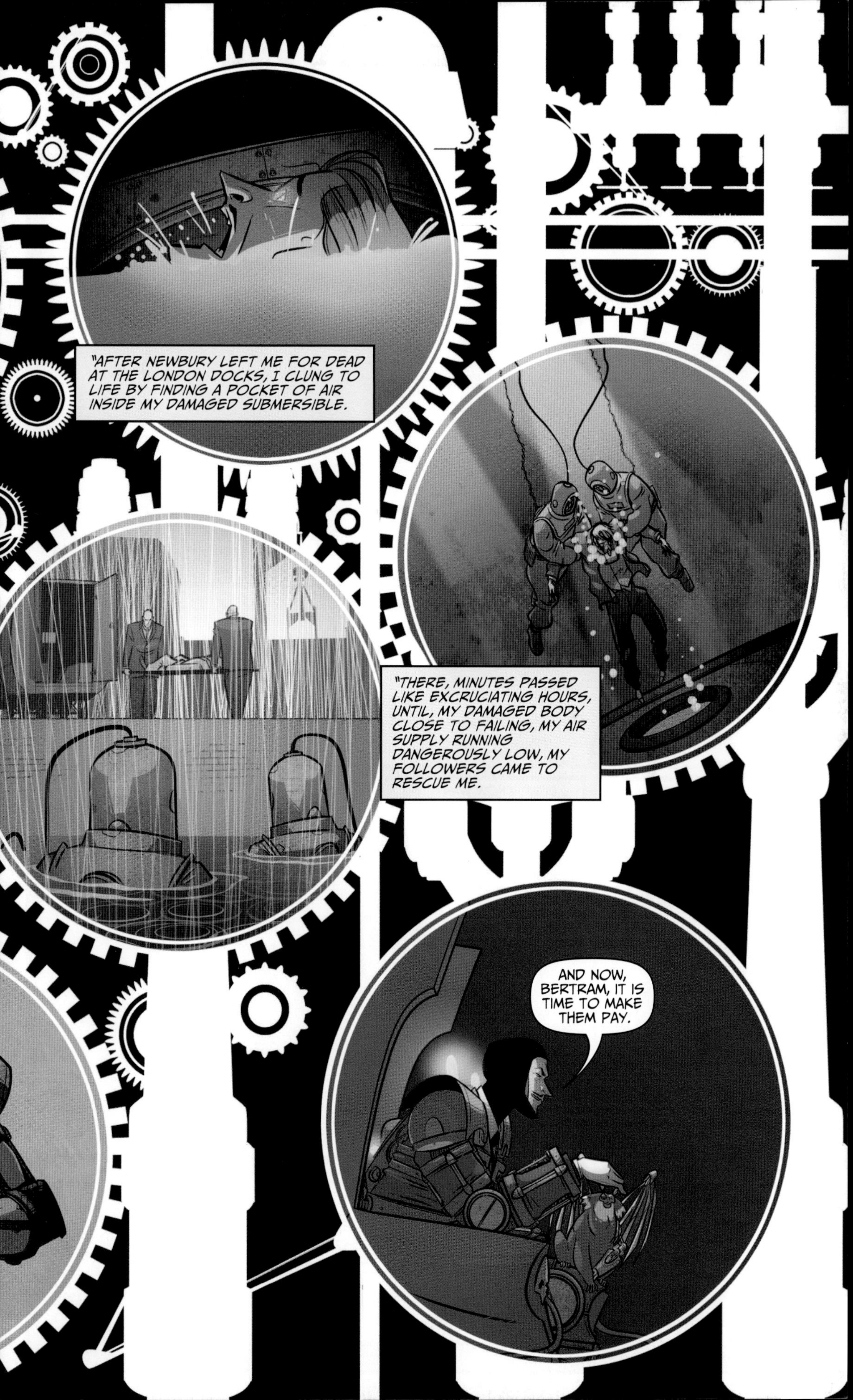
"AFTER NEWBURY LEFT ME FOR DEAD AT THE LONDON DOCKS, I CLUNG TO LIFE BY FINDING A POCKET OF AIR INSIDE MY DAMAGED SUBMERSIBLE.
"THERE, MINUTES PASSED LIKE EXCRUCIATING HOURS, UNTIL, MY DAMAGED BODY CLOSE TO FAILING, MY AIR SUPPLY RUNNING DANGEROUSLY LOW, MY FOLLOWERS CAME TO RESCUE ME.
AND NOW, BERTRAM, IT IS TIME TO MAKE THEM PAY.

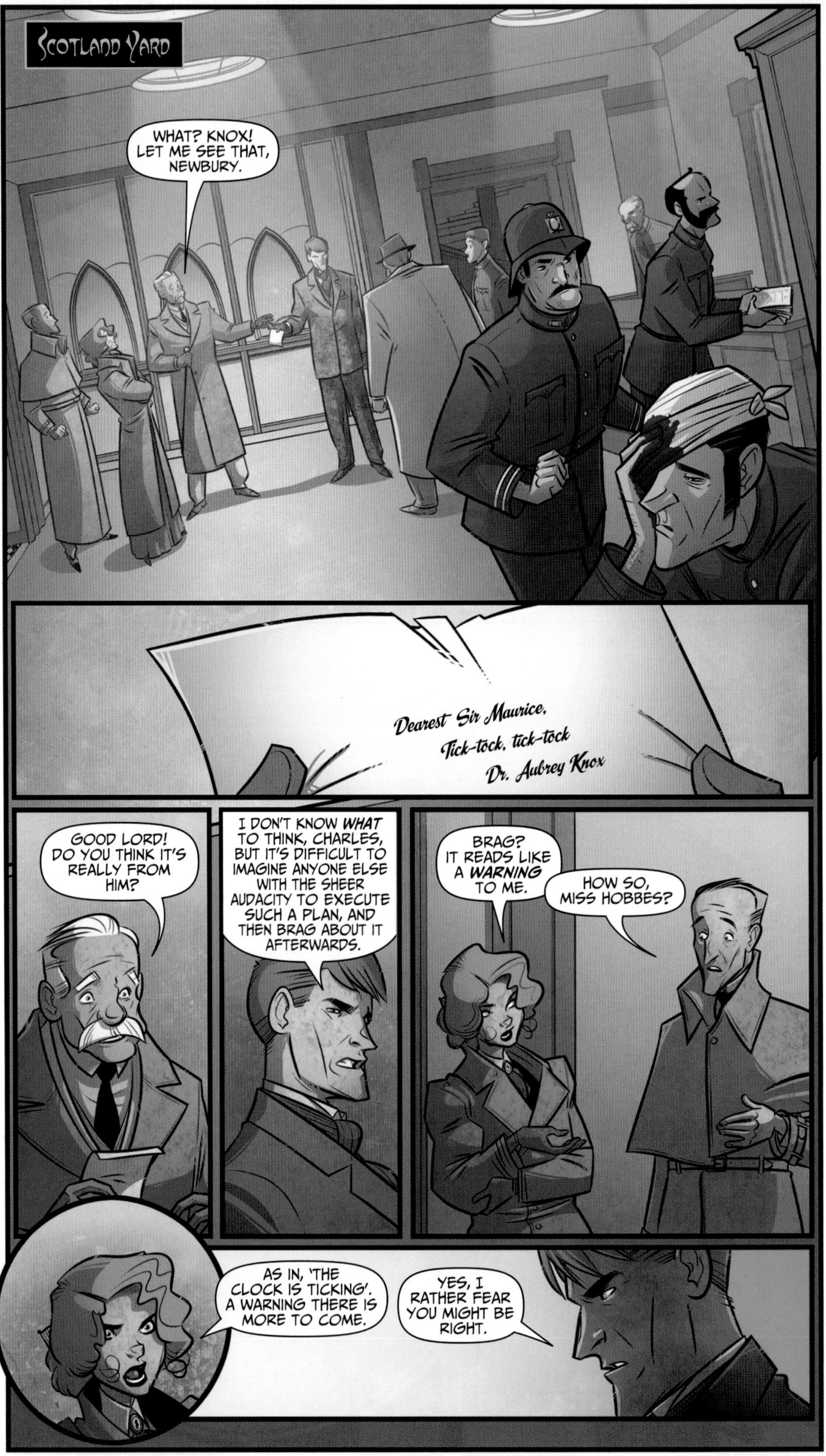
SCOTLAND YARD
WHAT? KNOX! LET ME SEE THAT, NEWBURY.
Dearest Sir Maurice,
Tick-tock, tick-tock
Dr. Aubrey Knox
GOOD LORD! DO YOU THINK IT'S REALLY FROM HIM?
I DON'T KNOW WHAT TO THINK, CHARLES, BUT IT'S DIFFICULT TO IMAGINE ANYONE ELSE WITH THE SHEER AUDACITY TO EXECUTE SUCH A PLAN, AND THEN BRAG ABOUT IT AFTERWARDS.
BRAG? IT READS LIKE A WARNING TO ME.
HOW SO, MISS HOBBES?
AS IN, 'THE CLOCK IS TICKING'. A WARNING THERE IS MORE TO COME.
YES, I RATHER FEAR YOU MIGHT BE RIGHT.

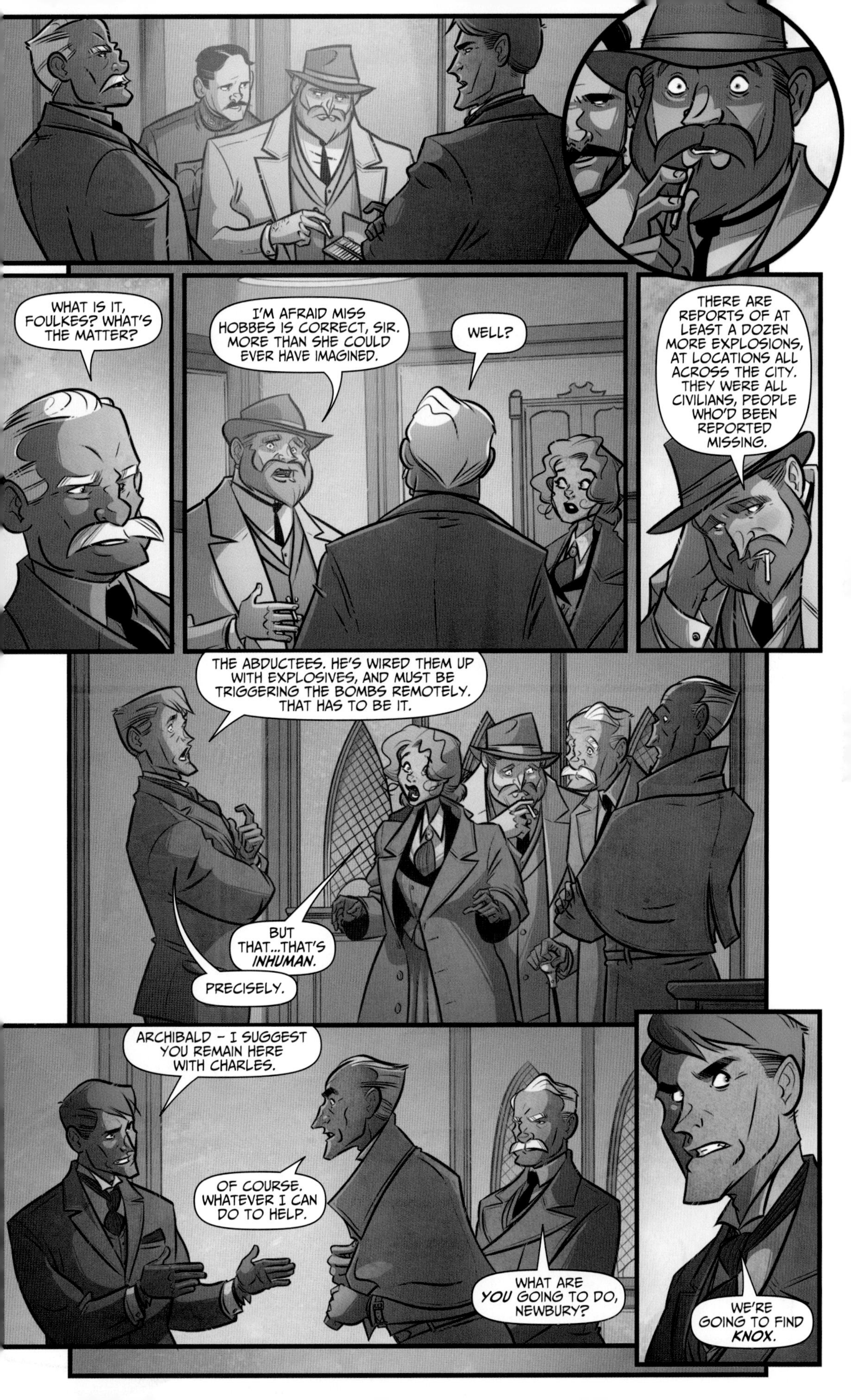
WHAT IS IT, FOULKES? WHAT'S THE MATTER?
I'M AFRAID MISS HOBBES IS CORRECT, SIR. MORE THAN SHE COULD EVER HAVE IMAGINED.
WELL?
THERE ARE REPORTS OF AT LEAST A DOZEN MORE EXPLOSIONS, AT LOCATIONS ALL ACROSS THE CITY. THEY WERE ALL CIVILIANS, PEOPLE WHO'D BEEN REPORTED MISSING.
THE ABDUCTEES. HE'S WIRED THEM UP WITH EXPLOSIVES, AND MUST BE TRIGGERING THE BOMBS REMOTELY. THAT HAS TO BE IT.
BUT THAT...THAT'S *INHUMAN.*
PRECISELY.
ARCHIBALD – I SUGGEST YOU REMAIN HERE WITH CHARLES.
OF COURSE. WHATEVER I CAN DO TO HELP.
WHAT ARE *YOU* GOING TO DO, NEWBURY?
WE'RE GOING TO FIND *KNOX.*

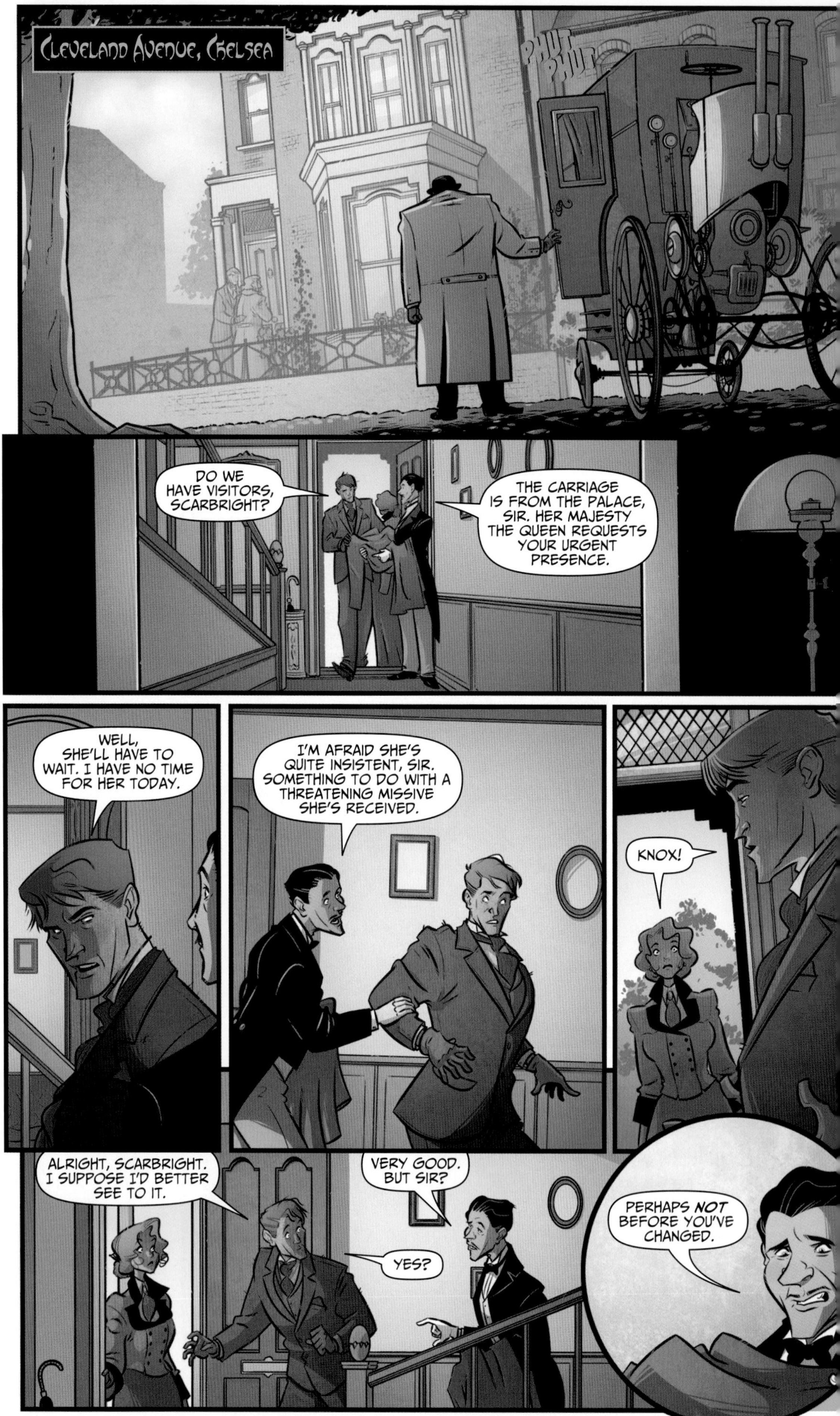
CLEVELAND AVENUE, CHELSEA
PHUT PHUT
DO WE HAVE VISITORS, SCARBRIGHT?
THE CARRIAGE IS FROM THE PALACE, SIR. HER MAJESTY THE QUEEN REQUESTS YOUR URGENT PRESENCE.
WELL, SHE'LL HAVE TO WAIT. I HAVE NO TIME FOR HER TODAY.
I'M AFRAID SHE'S QUITE INSISTENT, SIR. SOMETHING TO DO WITH A THREATENING MISSIVE SHE'S RECEIVED.
KNOX!
ALRIGHT, SCARBRIGHT. I SUPPOSE I'D BETTER SEE TO IT.
VERY GOOD. BUT SIR?
YES?
PERHAPS NOT BEFORE YOU'VE CHANGED.

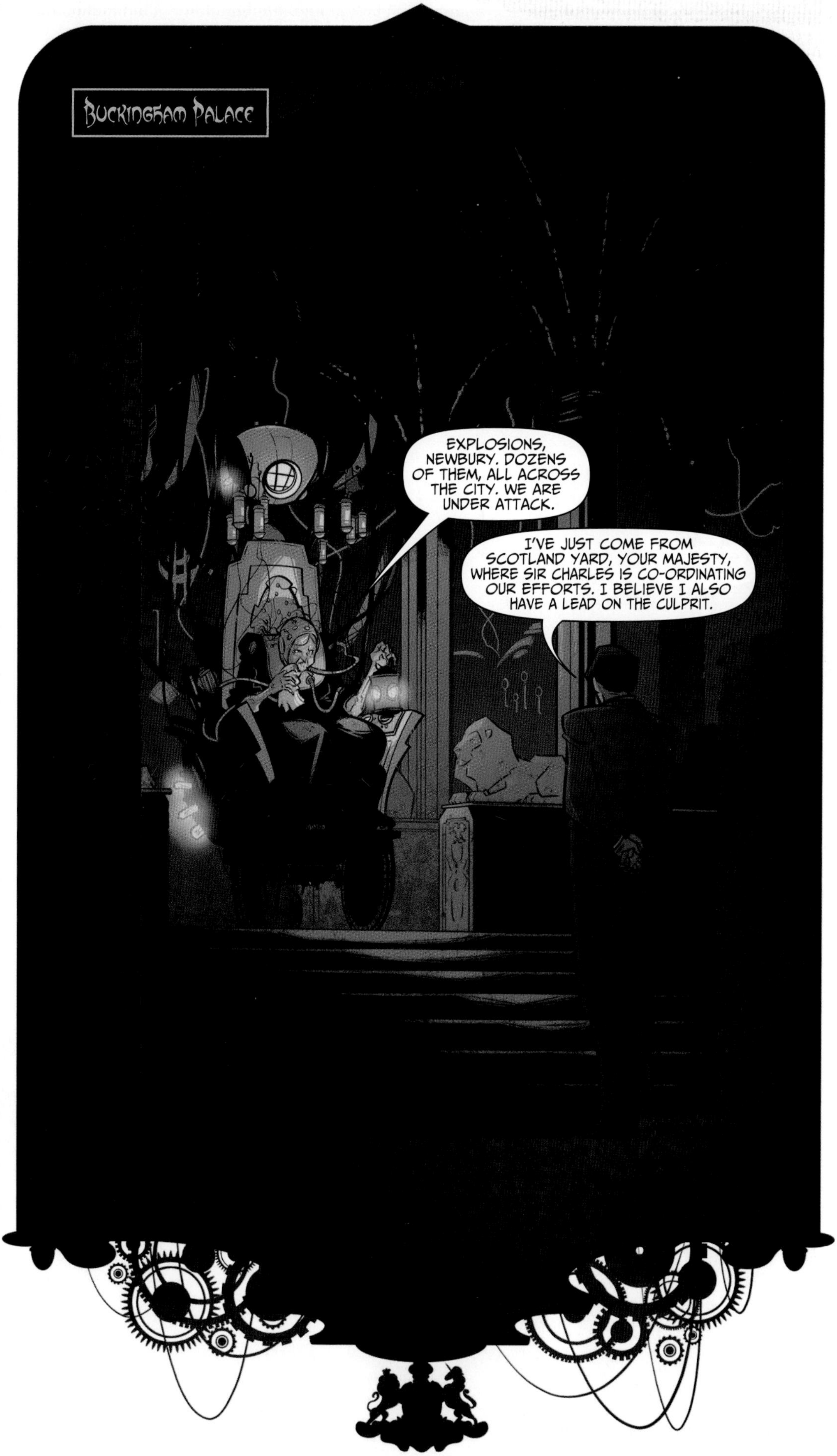
BUCKINGHAM PALACE
EXPLOSIONS, NEWBURY. DOZENS OF THEM, ALL ACROSS THE CITY. WE ARE UNDER ATTACK.
I'VE JUST COME FROM SCOTLAND YARD, YOUR MAJESTY, WHERE SIR CHARLES IS CO-ORDINATING OUR EFFORTS. I BELIEVE I ALSO HAVE A LEAD ON THE CULPRIT.

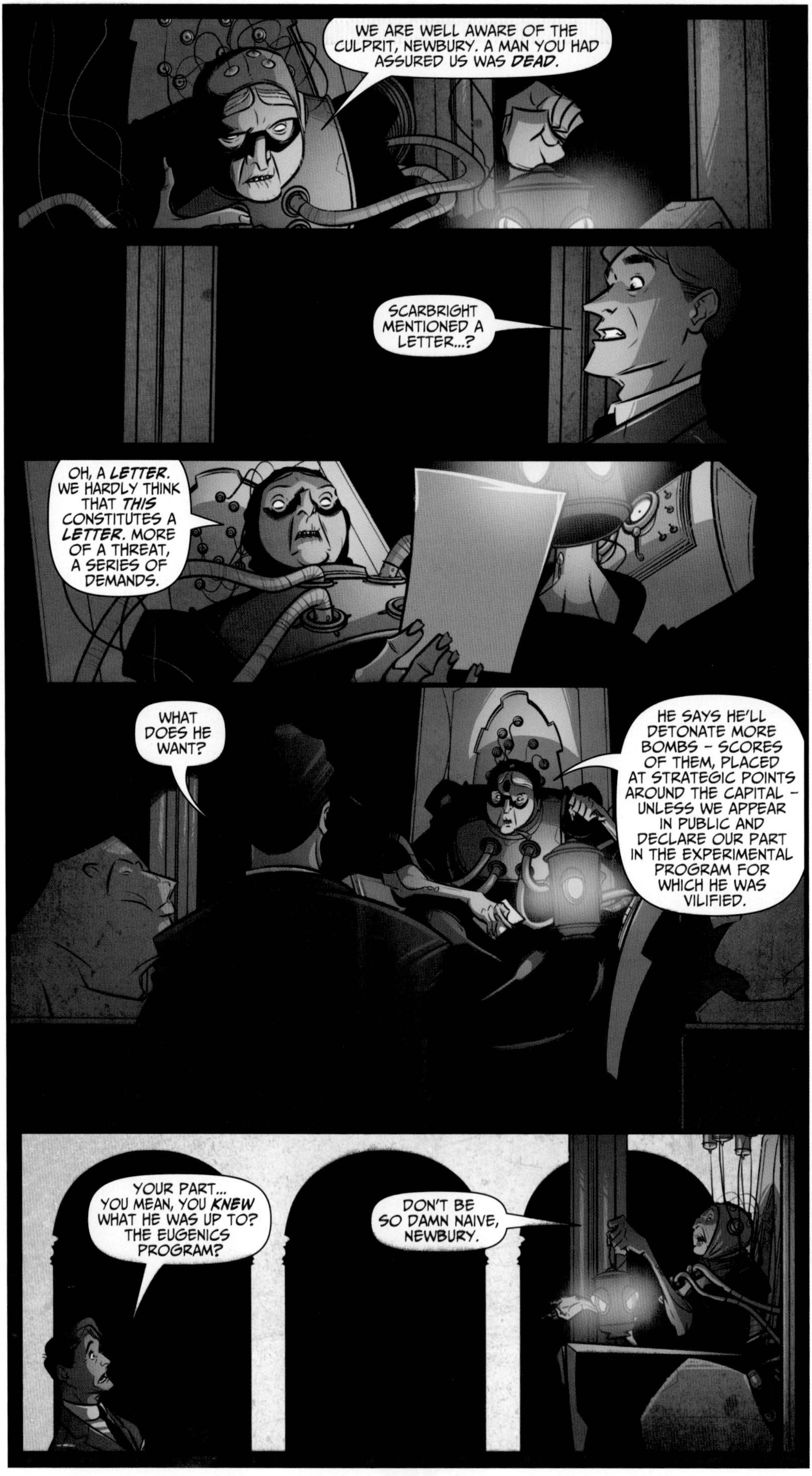
WE ARE WELL AWARE OF THE CULPRIT, NEWBURY. A MAN YOU HAD ASSURED US WAS *DEAD*.
SCARBRIGHT MENTIONED A LETTER...?
OH, A *LETTER*. WE HARDLY THINK THAT *THIS* CONSTITUTES A *LETTER*. MORE OF A THREAT, A SERIES OF DEMANDS.
WHAT DOES HE WANT?
HE SAYS HE'LL DETONATE MORE BOMBS – SCORES OF THEM, PLACED AT STRATEGIC POINTS AROUND THE CAPITAL – UNLESS WE APPEAR IN PUBLIC AND DECLARE OUR PART IN THE EXPERIMENTAL PROGRAM FOR WHICH HE WAS VILIFIED.
YOUR PART... YOU MEAN, YOU *KNEW* WHAT HE WAS UP TO? THE EUGENICS PROGRAM?
DON'T BE SO DAMN NAIVE, NEWBURY.

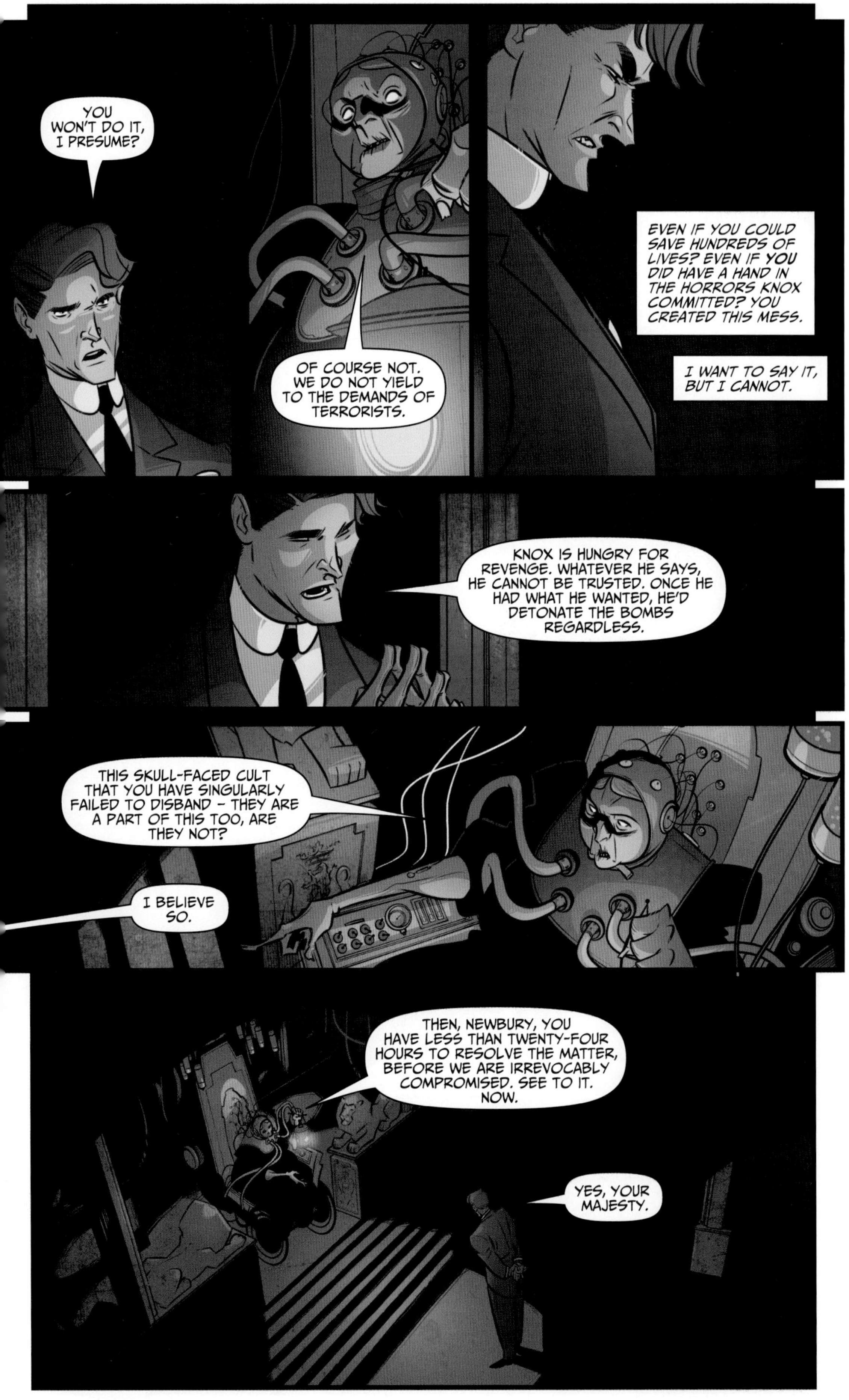
YOU WON'T DO IT, I PRESUME?
OF COURSE NOT. WE DO NOT YIELD TO THE DEMANDS OF TERRORISTS.
EVEN IF YOU COULD SAVE HUNDREDS OF LIVES? EVEN IF YOU DID HAVE A HAND IN THE HORRORS KNOX COMMITTED? YOU CREATED THIS MESS.
I WANT TO SAY IT, BUT I CANNOT.
KNOX IS HUNGRY FOR REVENGE. WHATEVER HE SAYS, HE CANNOT BE TRUSTED. ONCE HE HAD WHAT HE WANTED, HE'D DETONATE THE BOMBS REGARDLESS.
THIS SKULL-FACED CULT THAT YOU HAVE SINGULARLY FAILED TO DISBAND – THEY ARE A PART OF THIS TOO, ARE THEY NOT?
I BELIEVE SO.
THEN, NEWBURY, YOU HAVE LESS THAN TWENTY-FOUR HOURS TO RESOLVE THE MATTER, BEFORE WE ARE IRREVOCABLY COMPROMISED. SEE TO IT. NOW.
YES, YOUR MAJESTY.

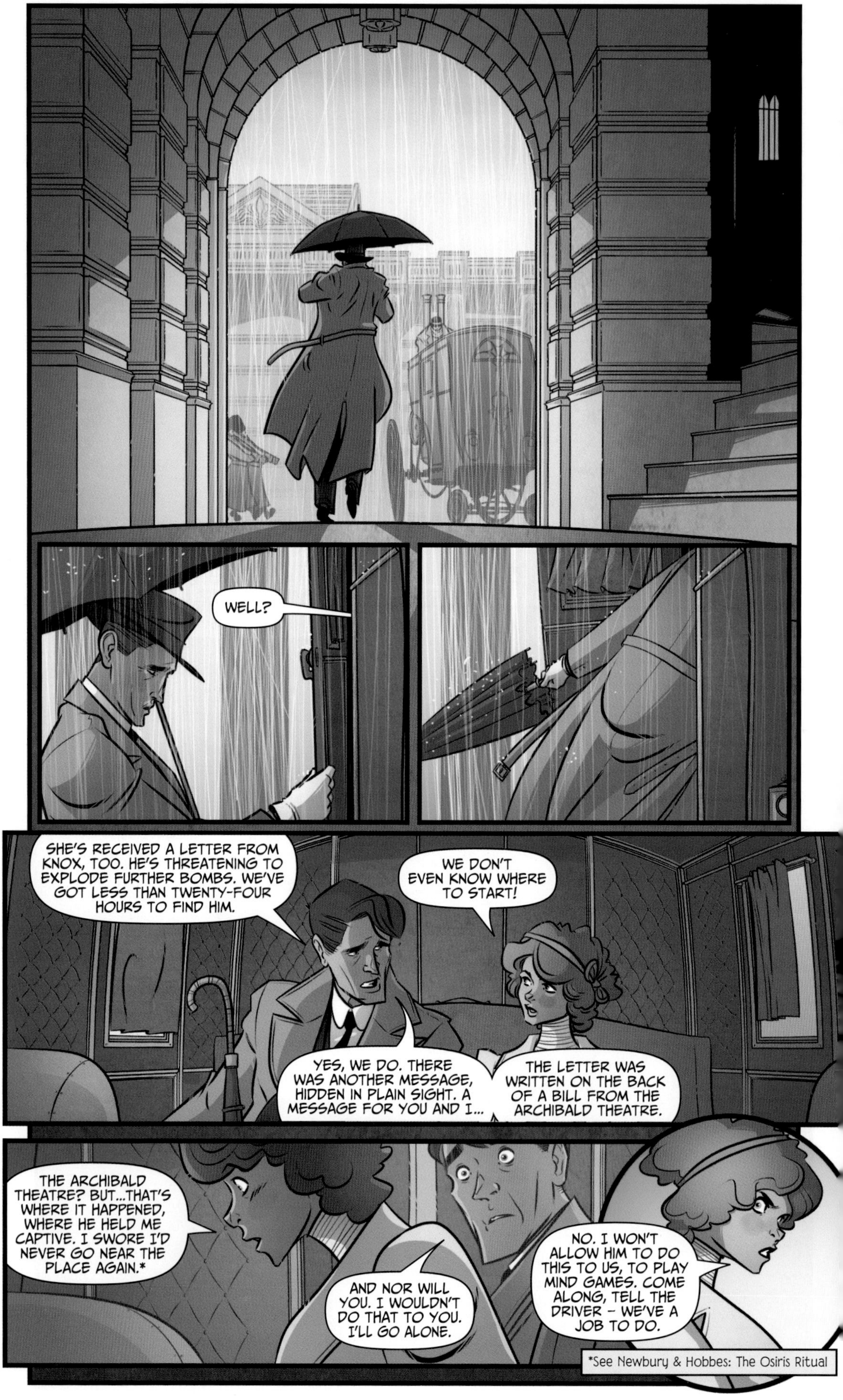
WELL?
SHE'S RECEIVED A LETTER FROM KNOX, TOO. HE'S THREATENING TO EXPLODE FURTHER BOMBS. WE'VE GOT LESS THAN TWENTY-FOUR HOURS TO FIND HIM.
WE DON'T EVEN KNOW WHERE TO START!
YES, WE DO. THERE WAS ANOTHER MESSAGE, HIDDEN IN PLAIN SIGHT. A MESSAGE FOR YOU AND I...
THE LETTER WAS WRITTEN ON THE BACK OF A BILL FROM THE ARCHIBALD THEATRE.
THE ARCHIBALD THEATRE? BUT...THAT'S WHERE IT HAPPENED, WHERE HE HELD ME CAPTIVE. I SWORE I'D NEVER GO NEAR THE PLACE AGAIN.*
AND NOR WILL YOU. I WOULDN'T DO THAT TO YOU. I'LL GO ALONE.
NO. I WON'T ALLOW HIM TO DO THIS TO US, TO PLAY MIND GAMES. COME ALONG, TELL THE DRIVER – WE'VE A JOB TO DO.
*See Newbury & Hobbes: The Osiris Ritual

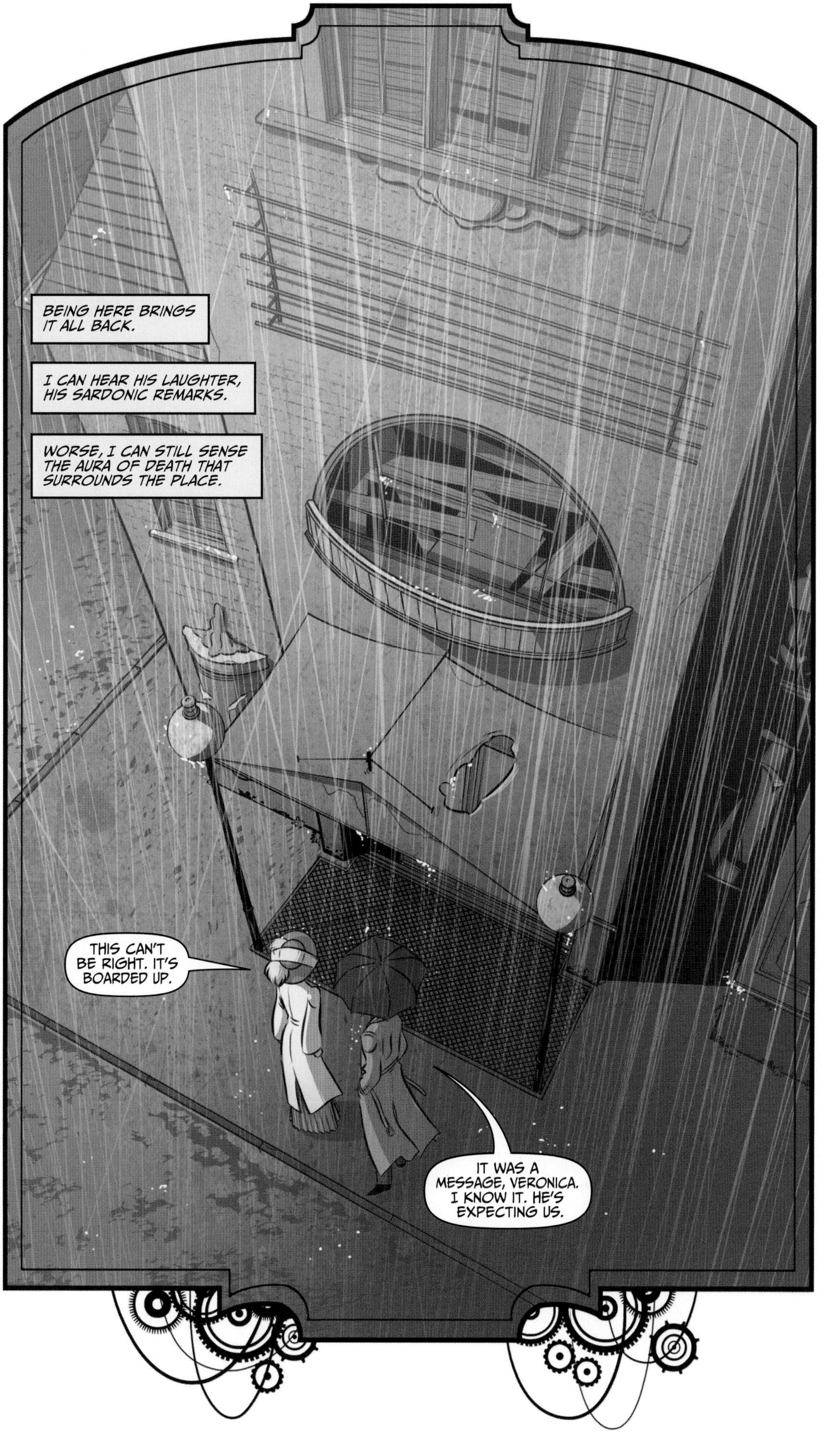
BEING HERE BRINGS IT ALL BACK.
I CAN HEAR HIS LAUGHTER, HIS SARDONIC REMARKS.
WORSE, I CAN STILL SENSE THE AURA OF DEATH THAT SURROUNDS THE PLACE.
THIS CAN'T BE RIGHT. IT'S BOARDED UP.
IT WAS A MESSAGE, VERONICA. I KNOW IT. HE'S EXPECTING US.

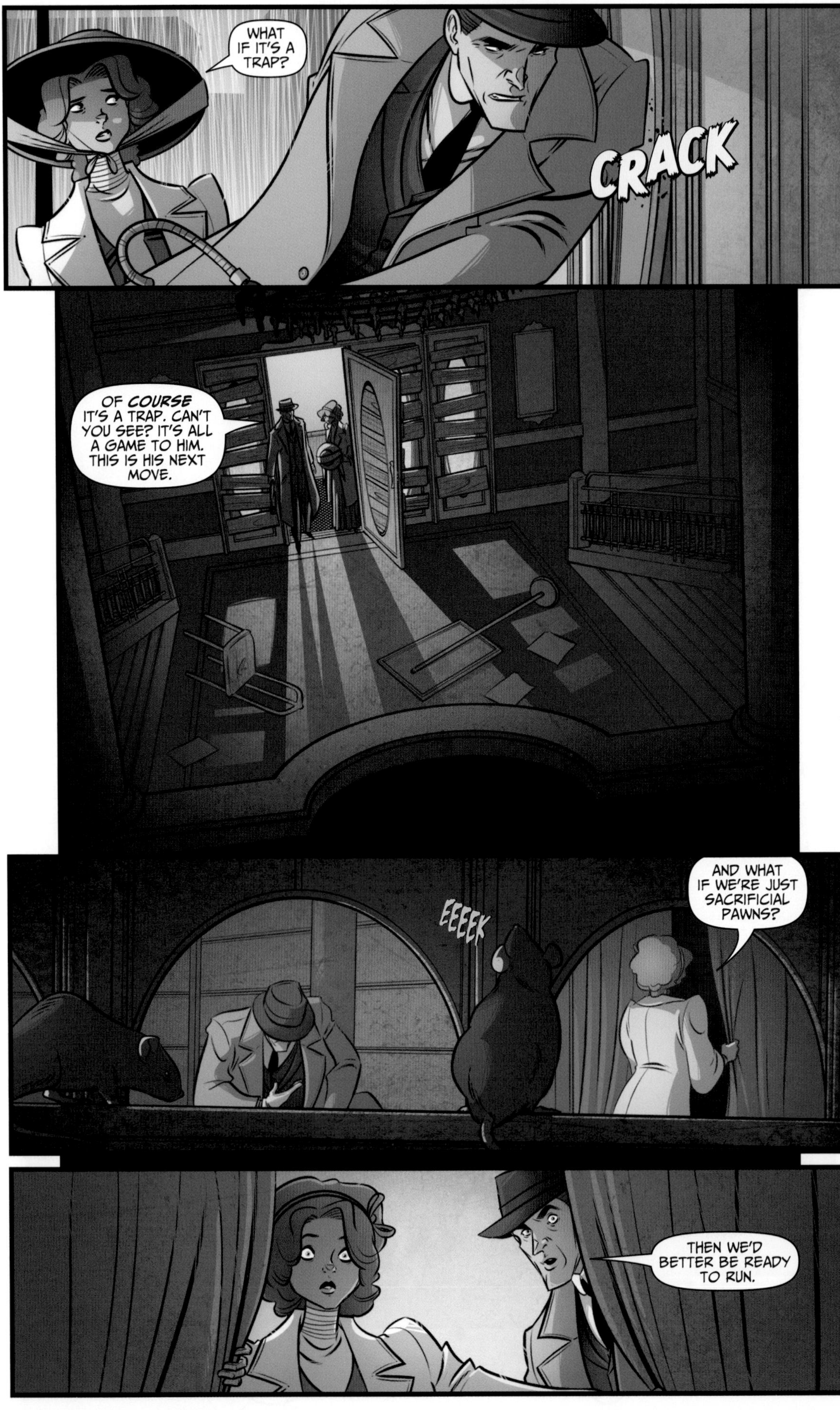
WHAT IF IT'S A TRAP?
CRACK
OF COURSE IT'S A TRAP. CAN'T YOU SEE? IT'S ALL A GAME TO HIM. THIS IS HIS NEXT MOVE.
AND WHAT IF WE'RE JUST SACRIFICIAL PAWNS?
EEEEK
THEN WE'D BETTER BE READY TO RUN.

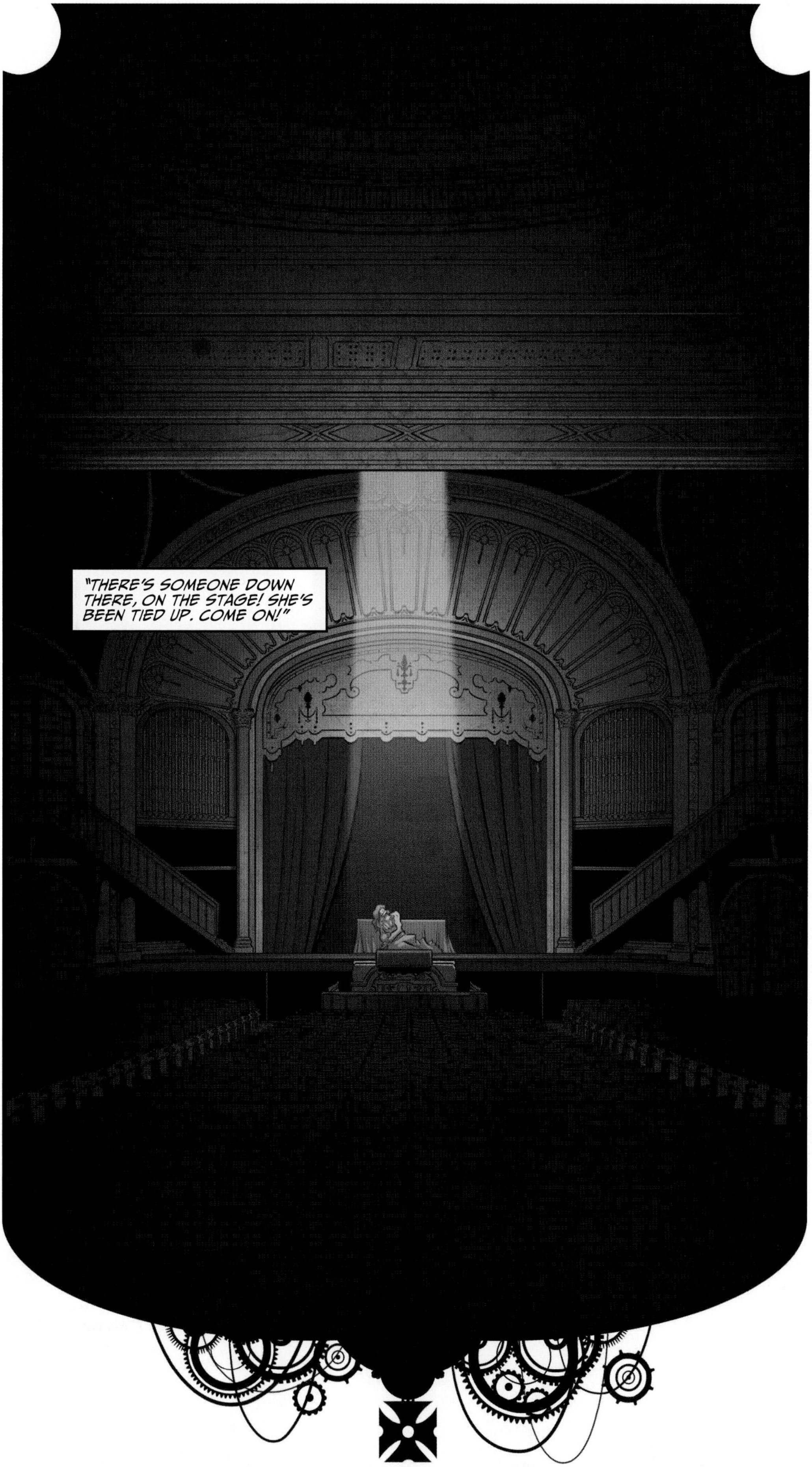
"THERE'S SOMEONE DOWN THERE, ON THE STAGE! SHE'S BEEN TIED UP. COME ON!"

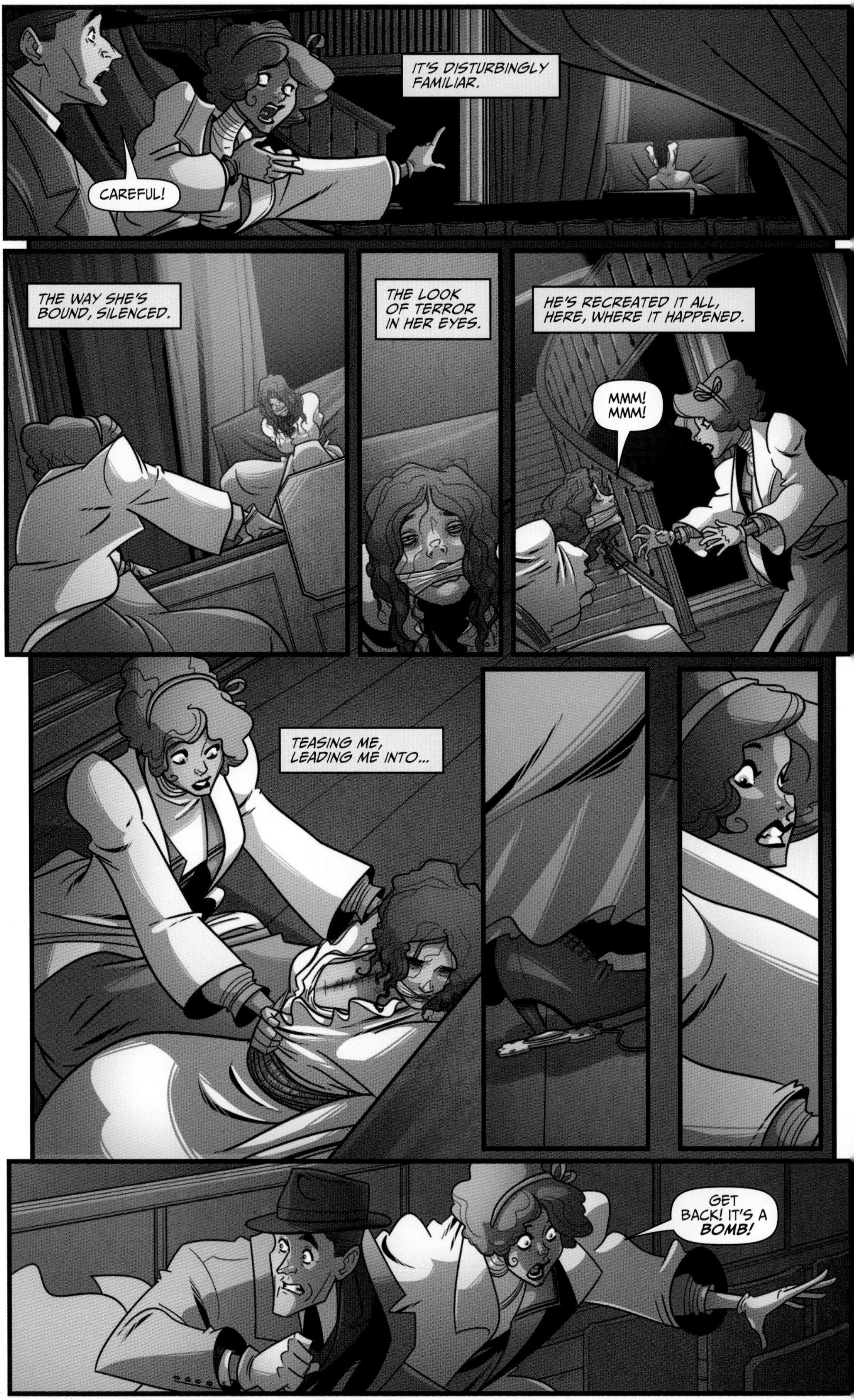
IT'S DISTURBINGLY FAMILIAR.
CAREFUL!
THE WAY SHE'S BOUND, SILENCED.
THE LOOK OF TERROR IN HER EYES.
HE'S RECREATED IT ALL, HERE, WHERE IT HAPPENED.
MMM! MMM!
TEASING ME, LEADING ME INTO...
GET BACK! IT'S A BOMB!

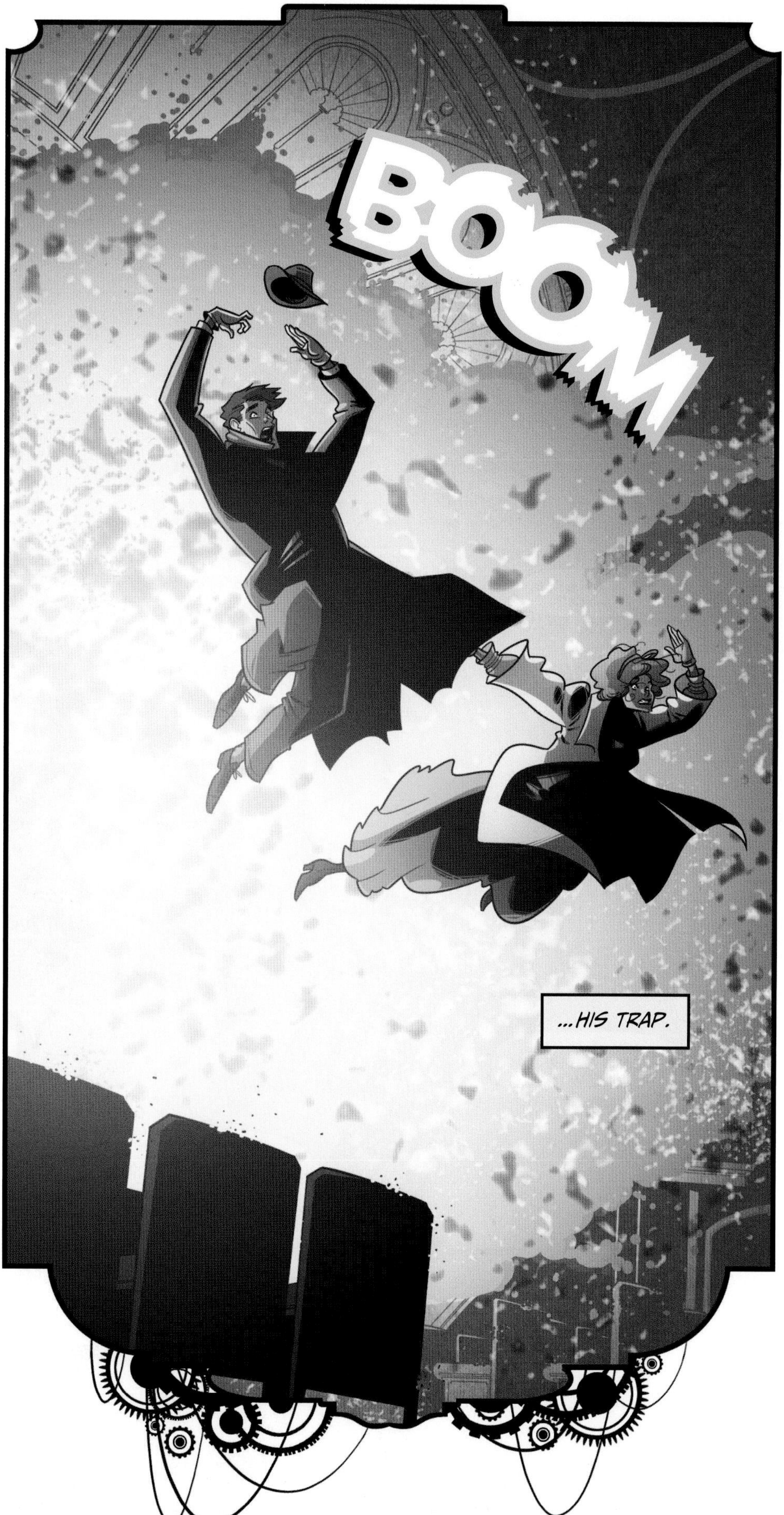
BOOM
...HIS TRAP.

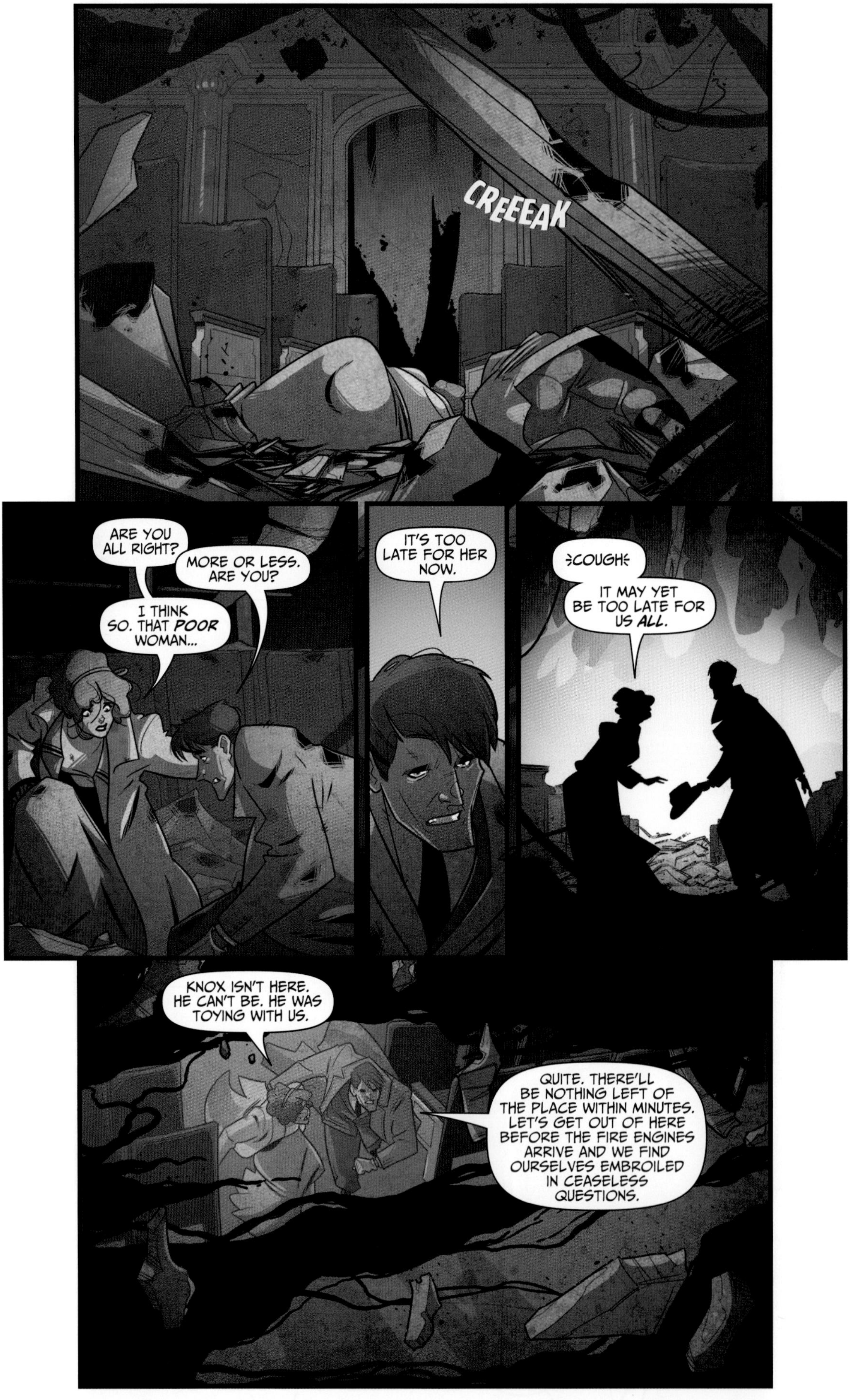
CREEEAK
ARE YOU ALL RIGHT?
MORE OR LESS. ARE YOU?
I THINK SO. THAT POOR WOMAN...
IT'S TOO LATE FOR HER NOW.
COUGH
IT MAY YET BE TOO LATE FOR US ALL.
KNOX ISN'T HERE. HE CAN'T BE. HE WAS TOYING WITH US.
QUITE. THERE'LL BE NOTHING LEFT OF THE PLACE WITHIN MINUTES. LET'S GET OUT OF HERE BEFORE THE FIRE ENGINES ARRIVE AND WE FIND OURSELVES EMBROILED IN CEASELESS QUESTIONS.

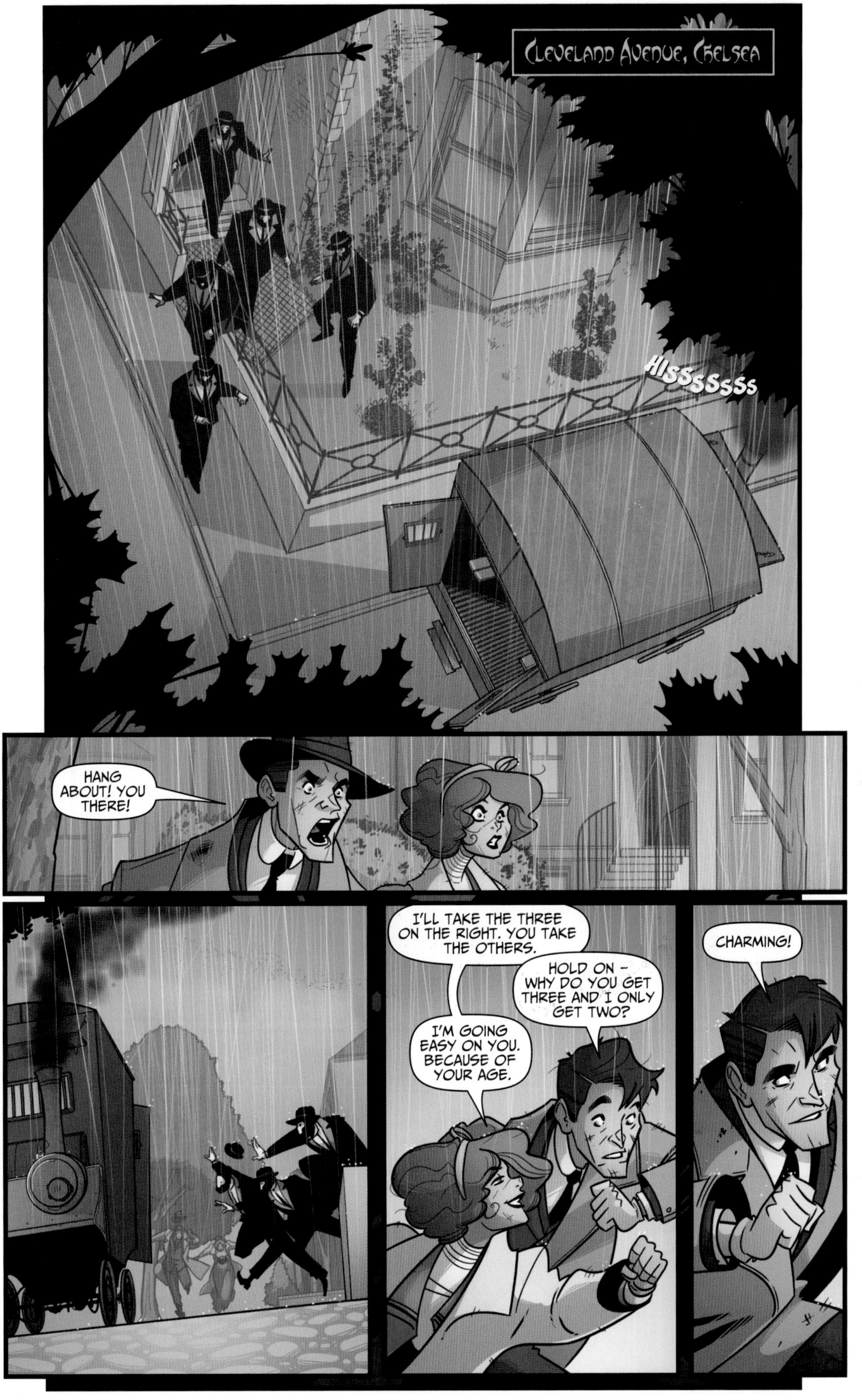
Cleveland Avenue, Chelsea
HISSSSSSS
HANG ABOUT! YOU THERE!
I'LL TAKE THE THREE ON THE RIGHT. YOU TAKE THE OTHERS.
HOLD ON – WHY DO YOU GET THREE AND I ONLY GET TWO?
I'M GOING EASY ON YOU. BECAUSE OF YOUR AGE.
CHARMING!

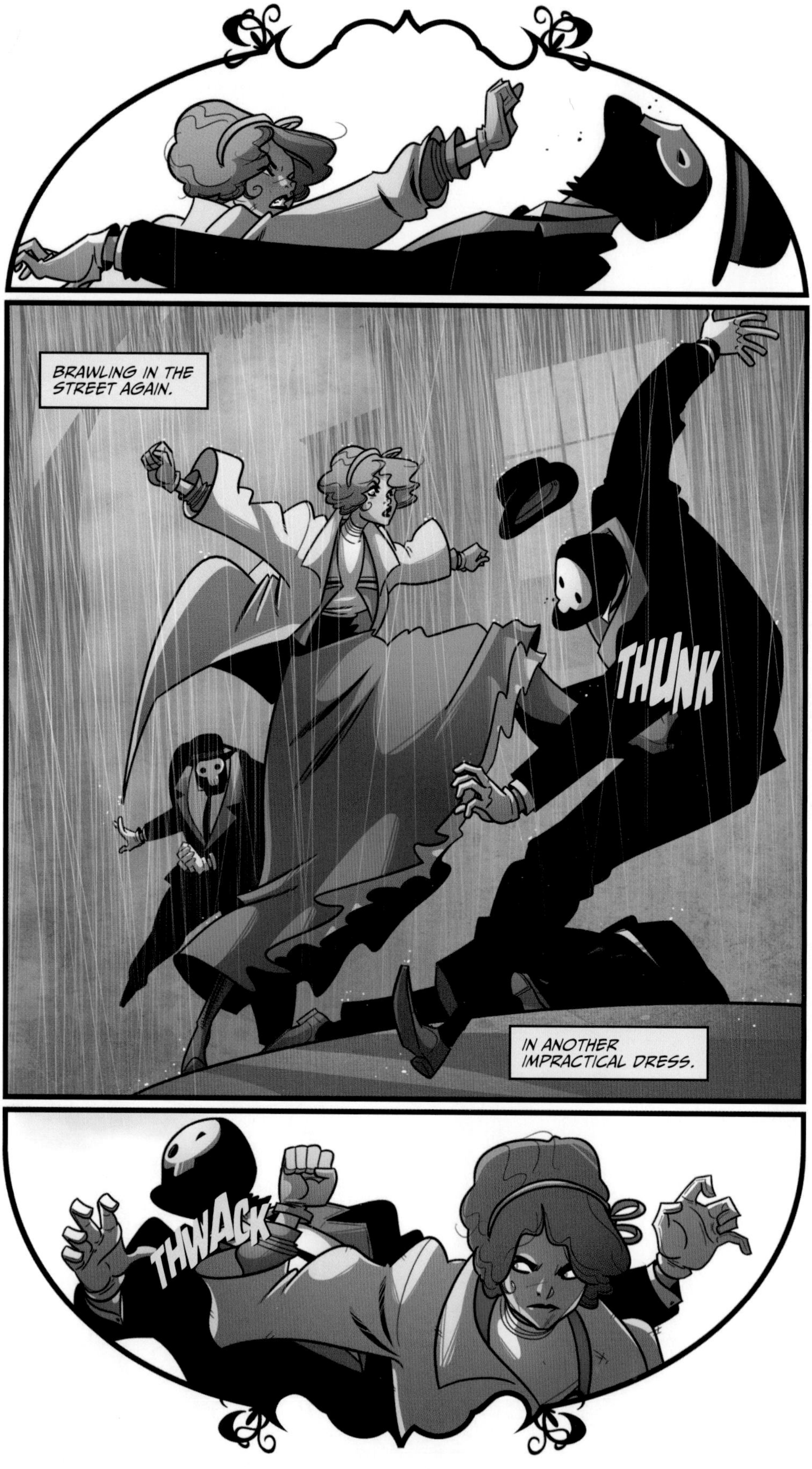
BRAWLING IN THE STREET AGAIN.
THUNK
IN ANOTHER IMPRACTICAL DRESS.
THWACK

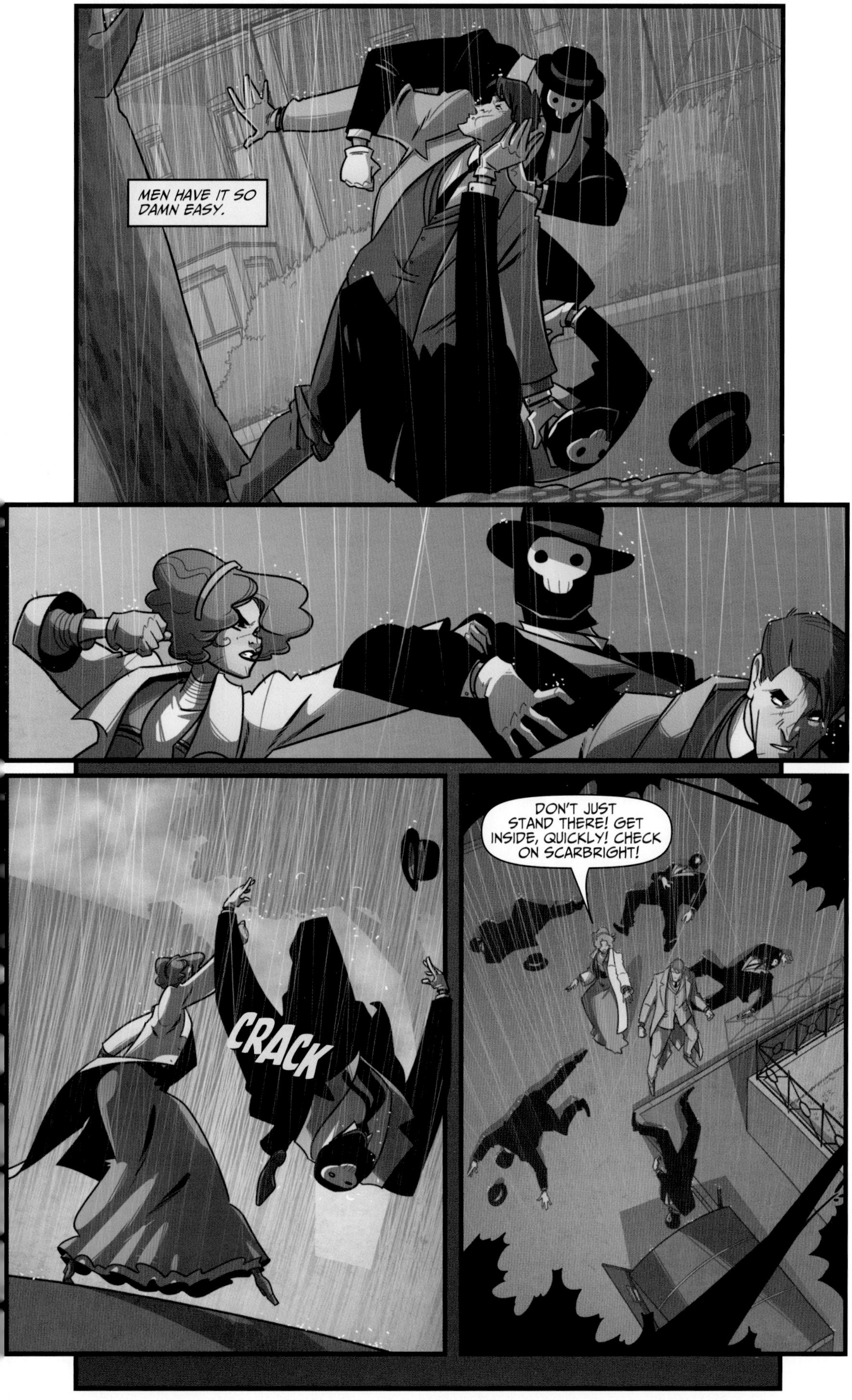
MEN HAVE IT SO DAMN EASY.
CRACK
DON'T JUST STAND THERE! GET INSIDE, QUICKLY! CHECK ON SCARBRIGHT!

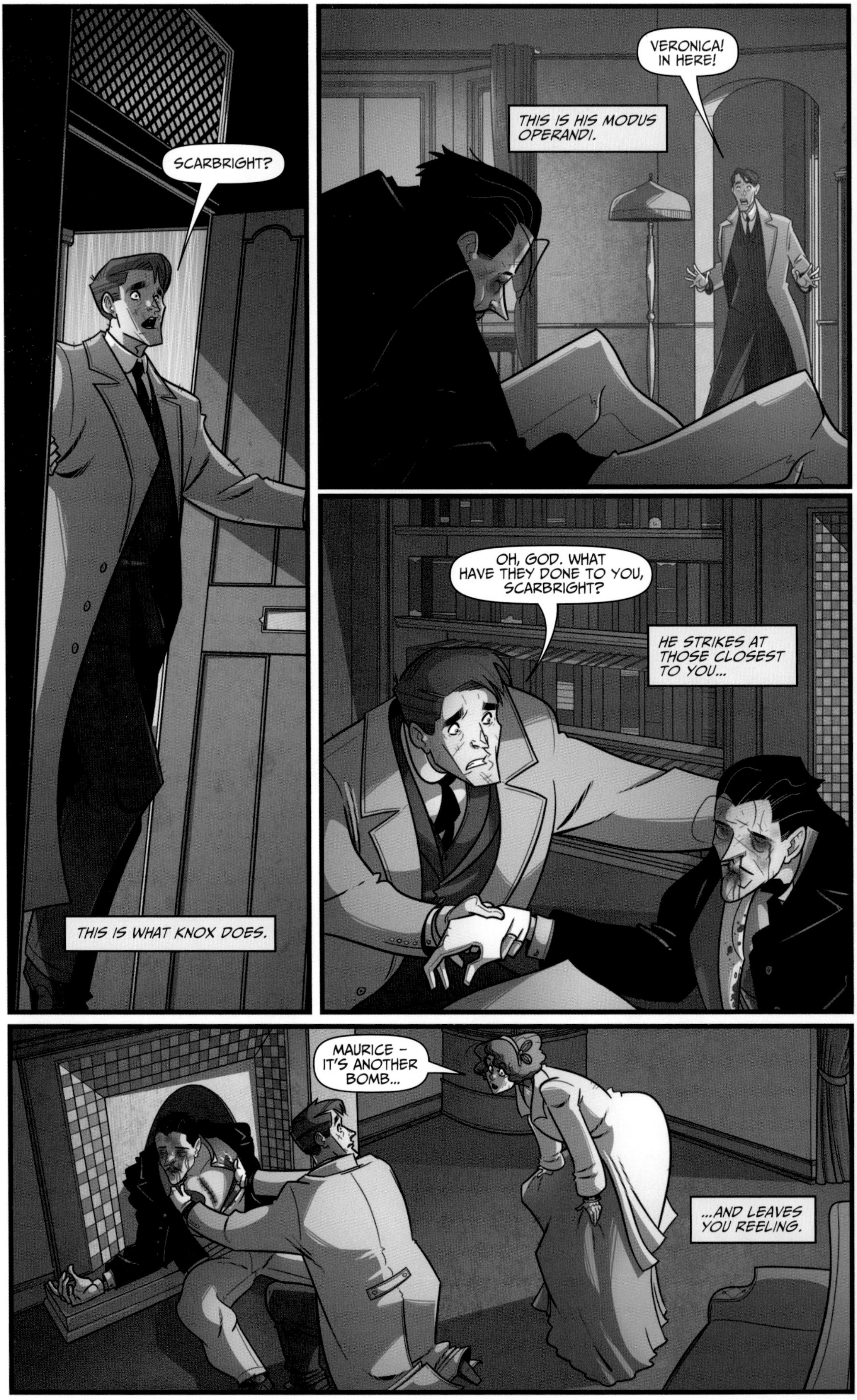
SCARBRIGHT?
THIS IS WHAT KNOX DOES.
THIS IS HIS MODUS OPERANDI.
VERONICA! IN HERE!
OH, GOD. WHAT HAVE THEY DONE TO YOU, SCARBRIGHT?
HE STRIKES AT THOSE CLOSEST TO YOU...
MAURICE – IT'S ANOTHER BOMB...
...AND LEAVES YOU REELING.

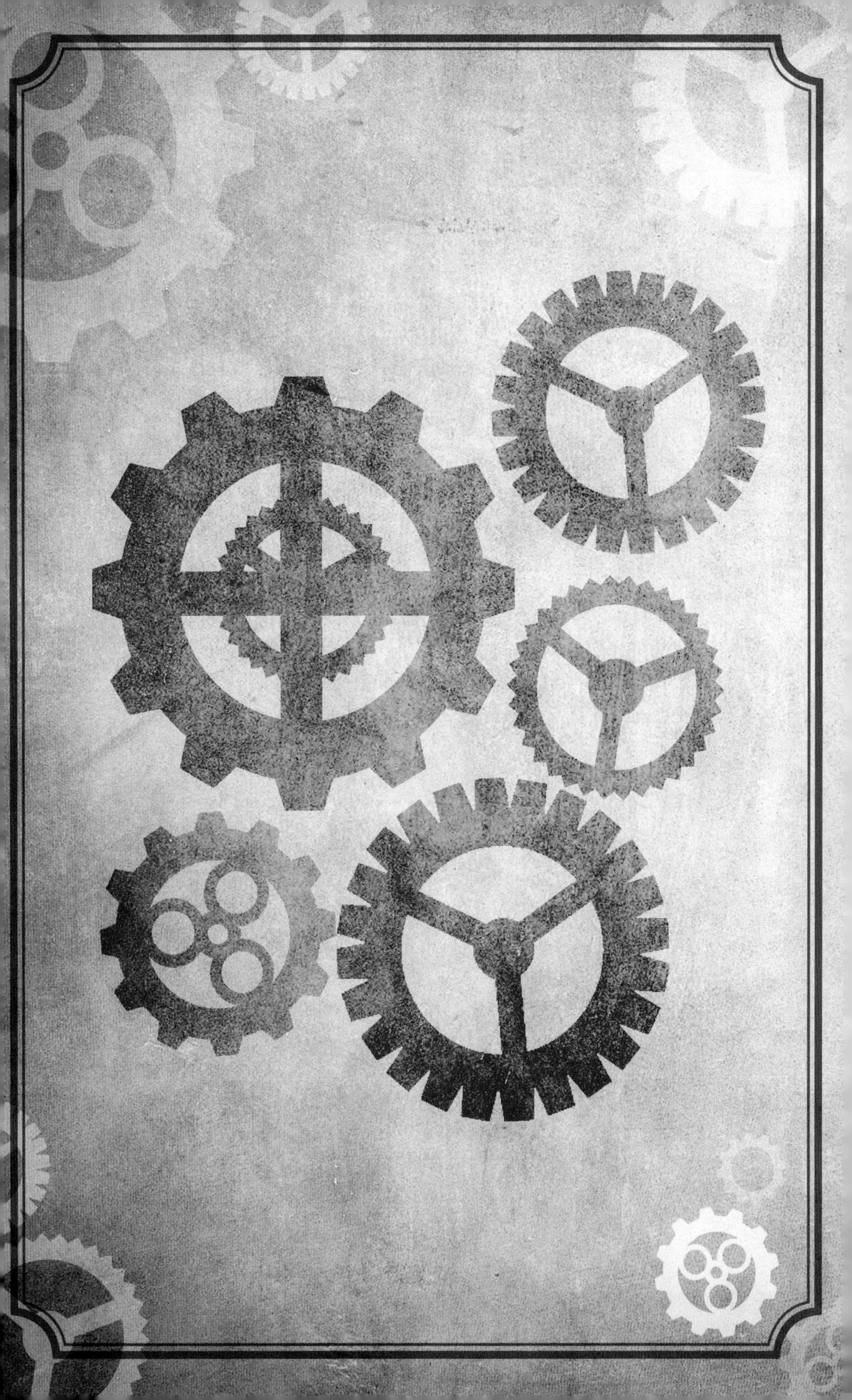

ILLUSTRATION BY **DAN BOULTWOOD**

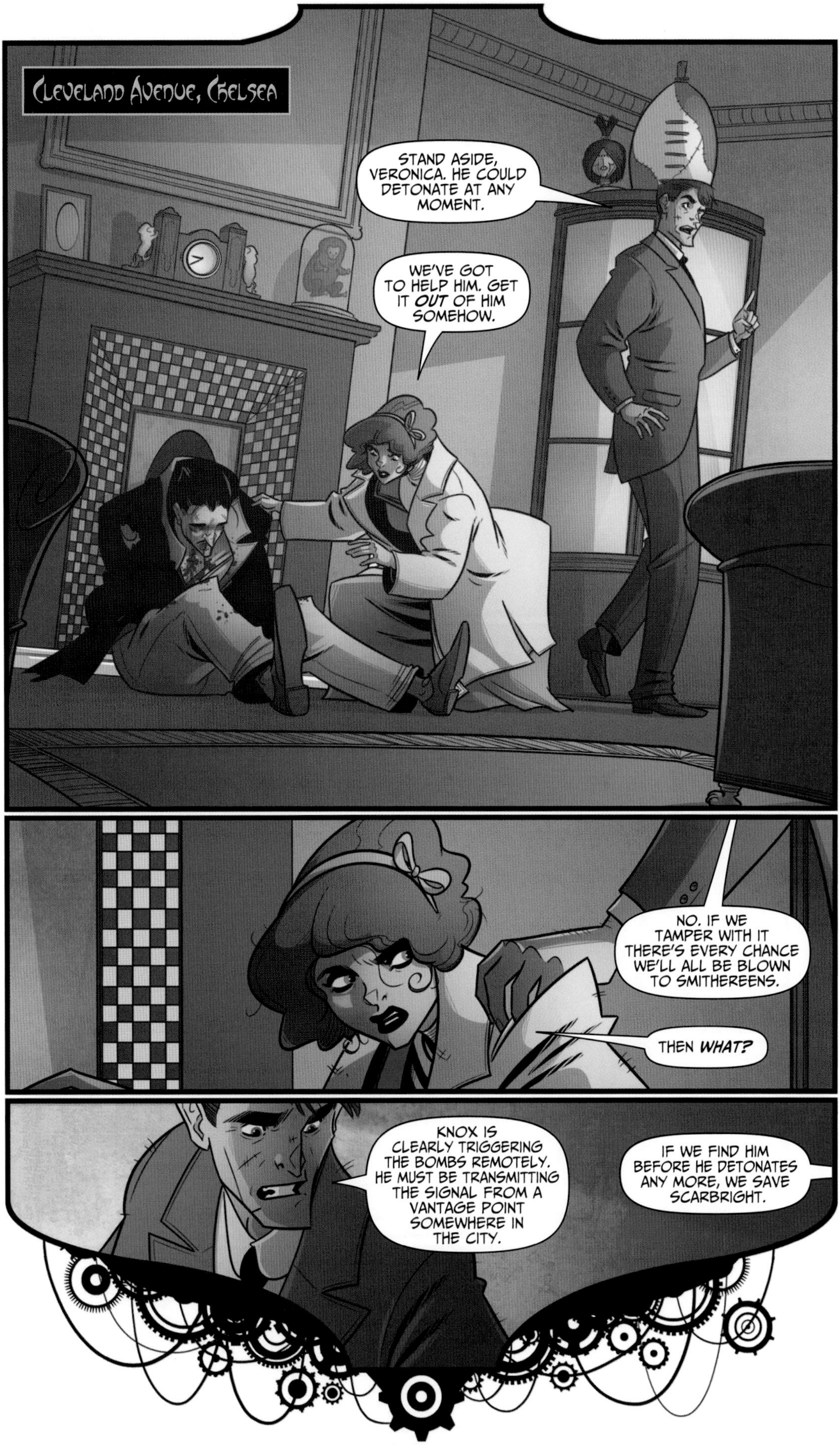
Cleveland Avenue, Chelsea
STAND ASIDE, VERONICA. HE COULD DETONATE AT ANY MOMENT.
WE'VE GOT TO HELP HIM. GET IT *OUT* OF HIM SOMEHOW.
NO. IF WE TAMPER WITH IT THERE'S EVERY CHANCE WE'LL ALL BE BLOWN TO SMITHEREENS.
THEN ***WHAT?***
KNOX IS CLEARLY TRIGGERING THE BOMBS REMOTELY. HE MUST BE TRANSMITTING THE SIGNAL FROM A VANTAGE POINT SOMEWHERE IN THE CITY.
IF WE FIND HIM BEFORE HE DETONATES ANY MORE, WE SAVE SCARBRIGHT.

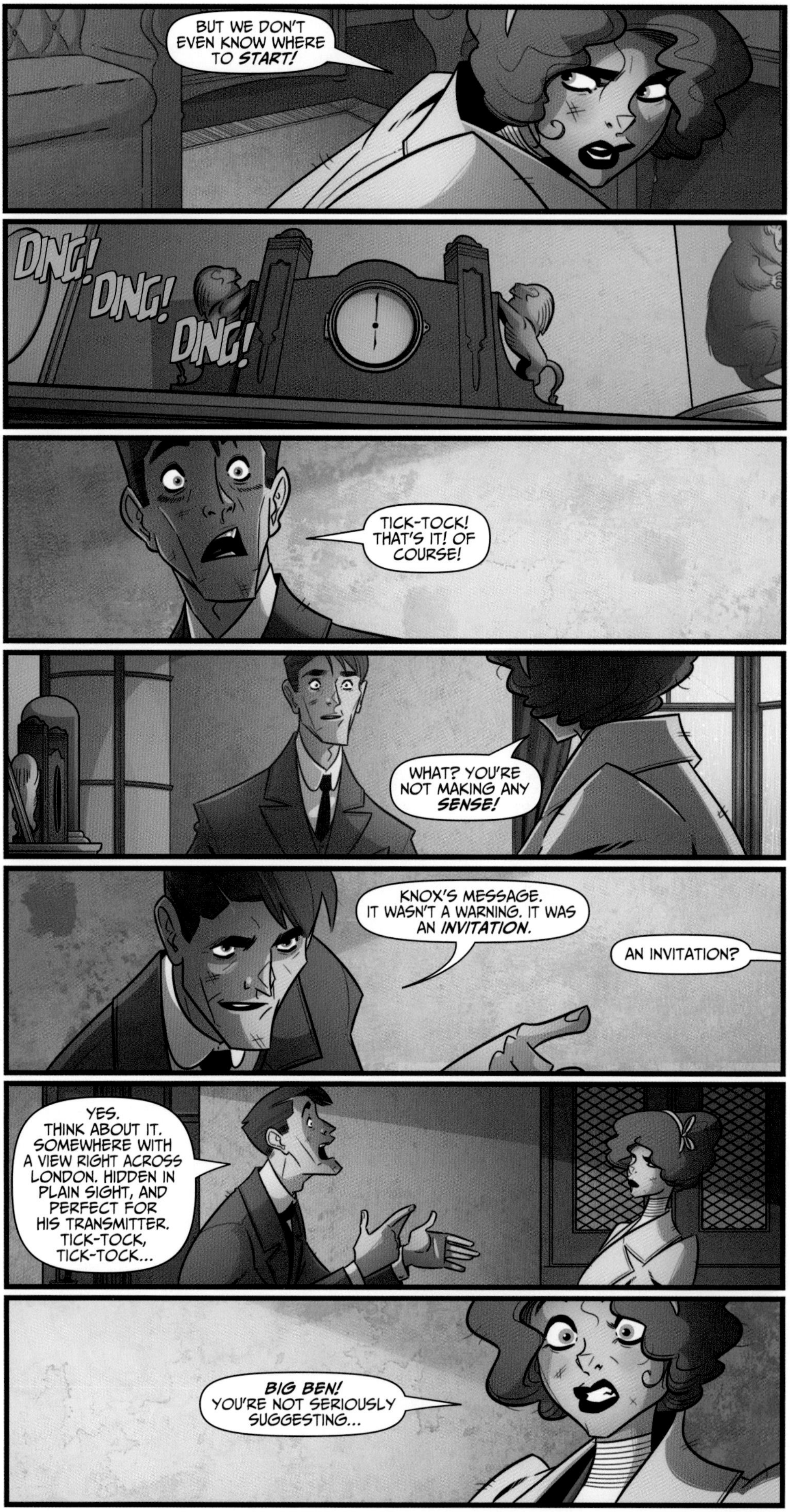

BUT WE DON'T EVEN KNOW WHERE TO *START!*
DING! DING! DING!
TICK-TOCK! THAT'S IT! OF COURSE!
WHAT? YOU'RE NOT MAKING ANY *SENSE!*
KNOX'S MESSAGE. IT WASN'T A WARNING. IT WAS AN *INVITATION.*
AN INVITATION?
YES. THINK ABOUT IT. SOMEWHERE WITH A VIEW RIGHT ACROSS LONDON. HIDDEN IN PLAIN SIGHT, AND PERFECT FOR HIS TRANSMITTER. TICK-TOCK, TICK-TOCK...
BIG BEN! YOU'RE NOT SERIOUSLY SUGGESTING...

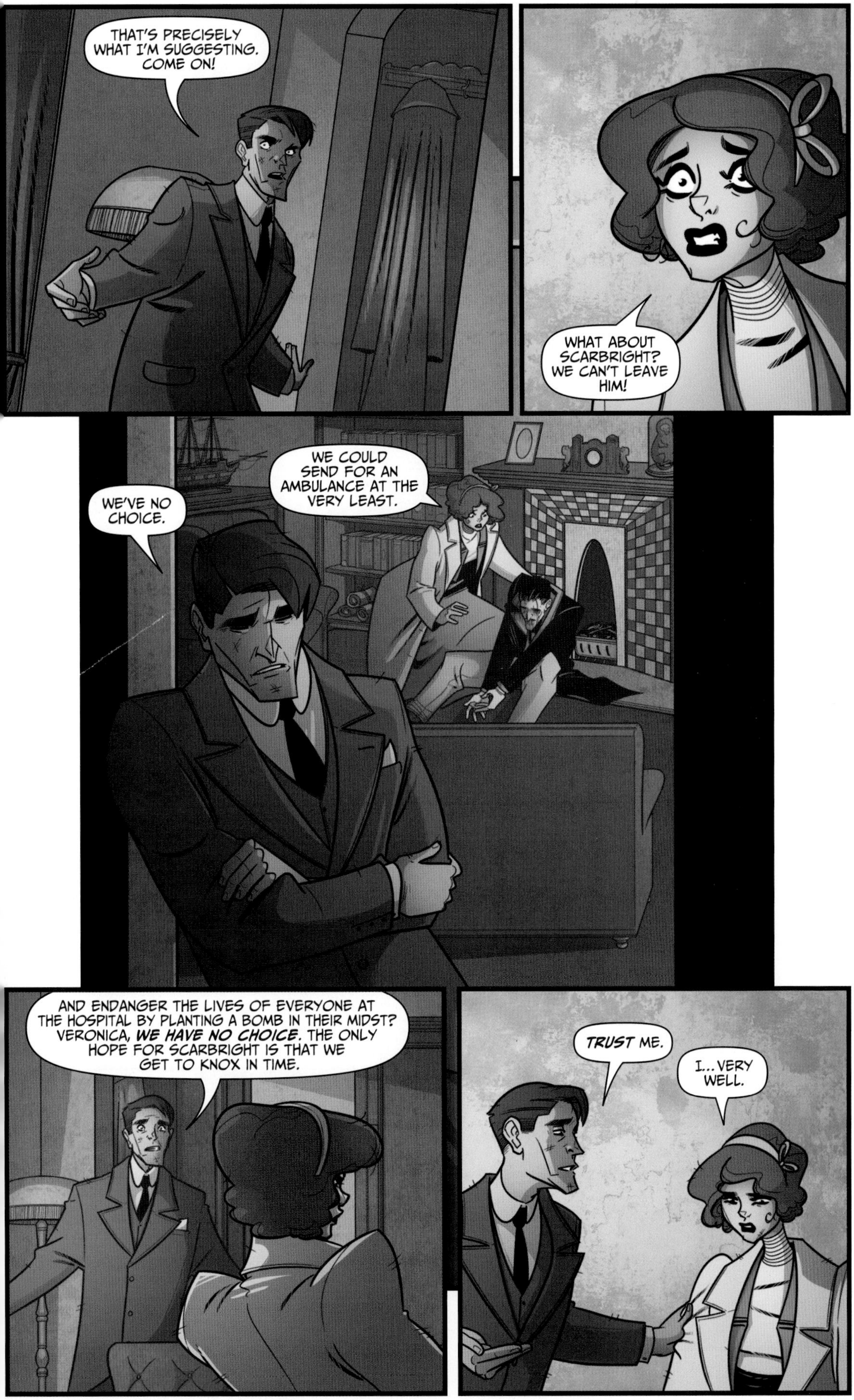
THAT'S PRECISELY WHAT I'M SUGGESTING. COME ON!
WHAT ABOUT SCARBRIGHT? WE CAN'T LEAVE HIM!
WE'VE NO CHOICE.
WE COULD SEND FOR AN AMBULANCE AT THE VERY LEAST.
AND ENDANGER THE LIVES OF EVERYONE AT THE HOSPITAL BY PLANTING A BOMB IN THEIR MIDST? VERONICA, *WE HAVE NO CHOICE*. THE ONLY HOPE FOR SCARBRIGHT IS THAT WE GET TO KNOX IN TIME.
TRUST ME.
I... VERY WELL.

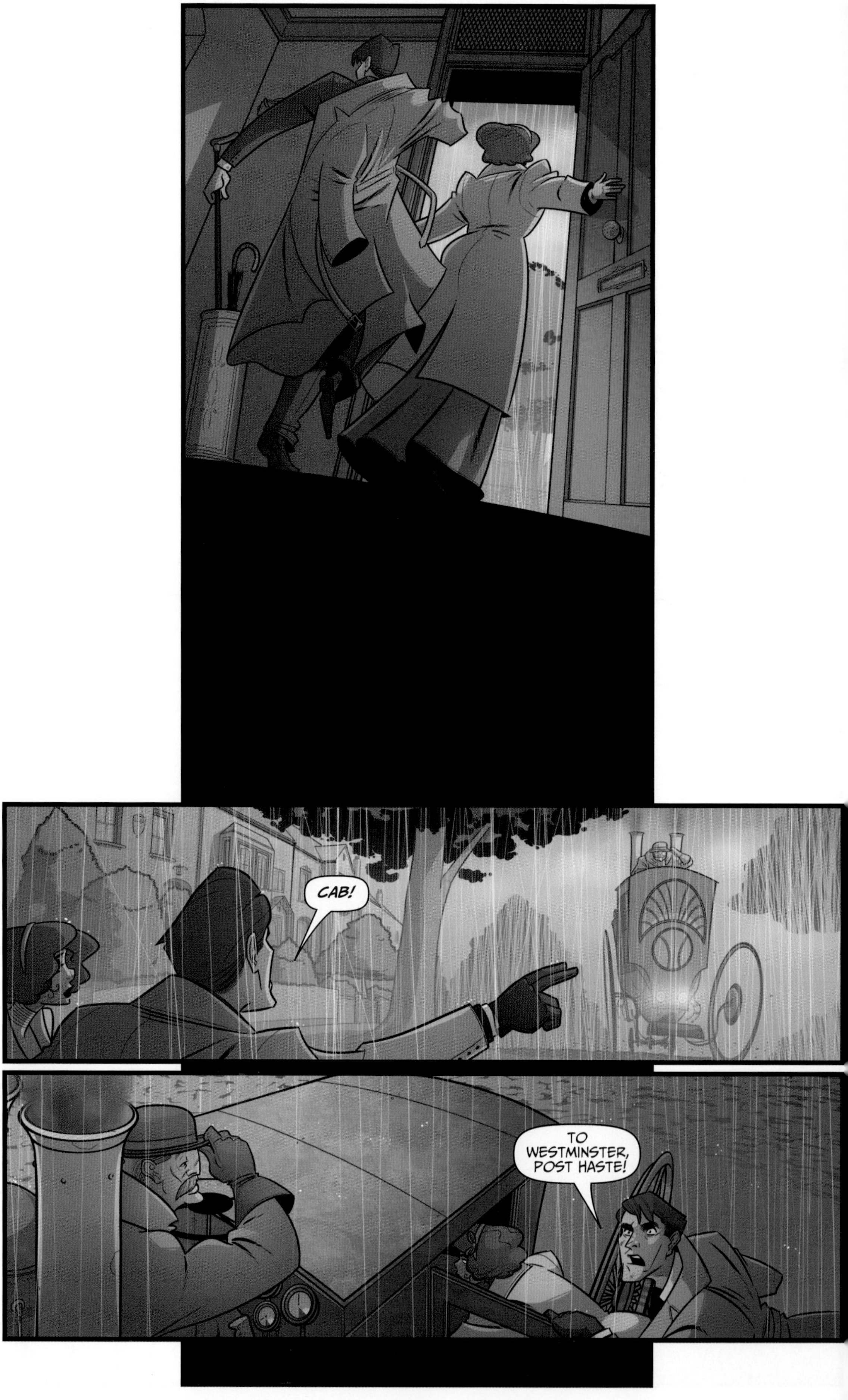
CAB!
TO WESTMINSTER, POST HASTE!

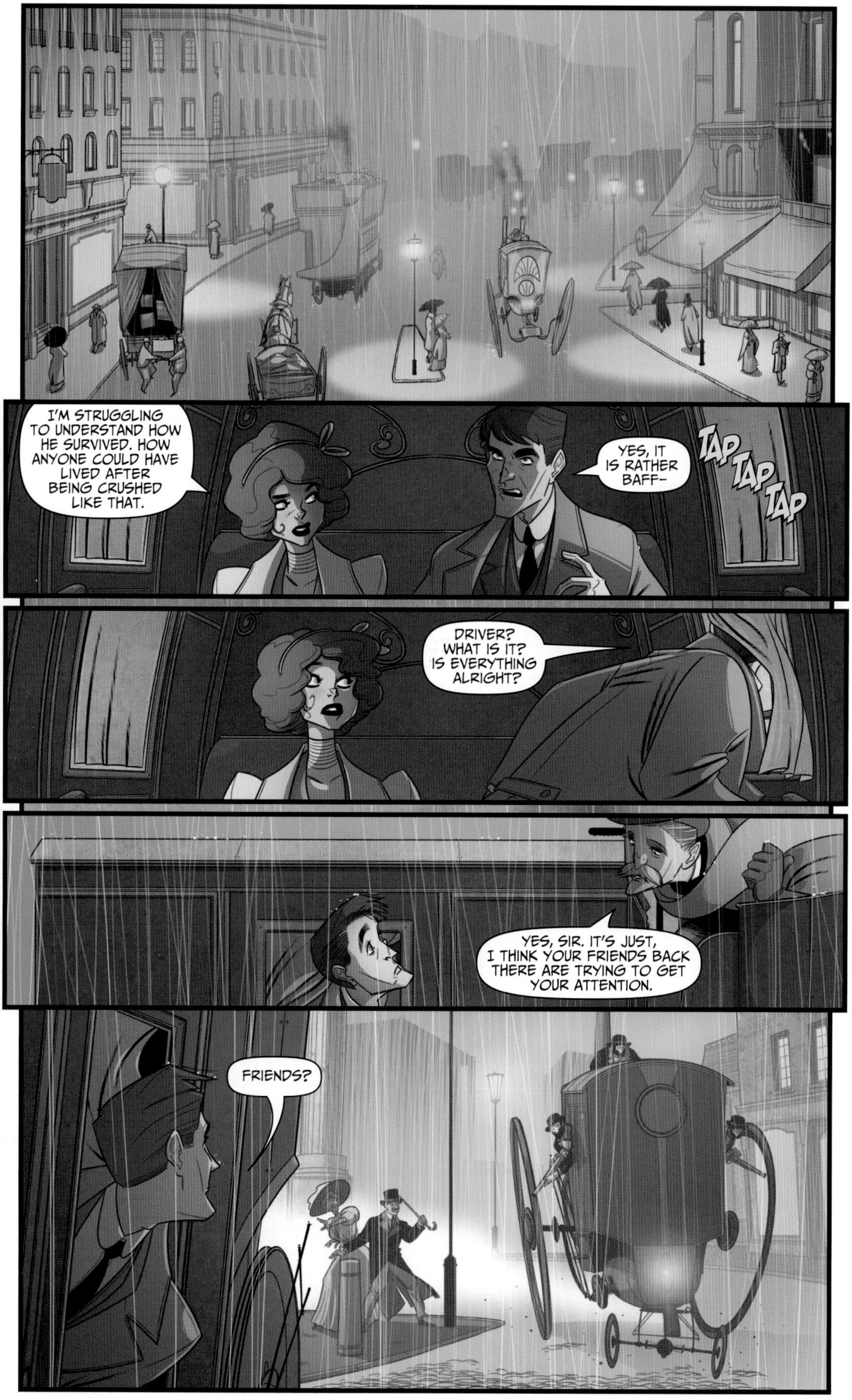
I'M STRUGGLING TO UNDERSTAND HOW HE SURVIVED. HOW ANYONE COULD HAVE LIVED AFTER BEING CRUSHED LIKE THAT.
YES, IT IS RATHER BAFF-
TAP TAP TAP
DRIVER? WHAT IS IT? IS EVERYTHING ALRIGHT?
YES, SIR. IT'S JUST, I THINK YOUR FRIENDS BACK THERE ARE TRYING TO GET YOUR ATTENTION.
FRIENDS?

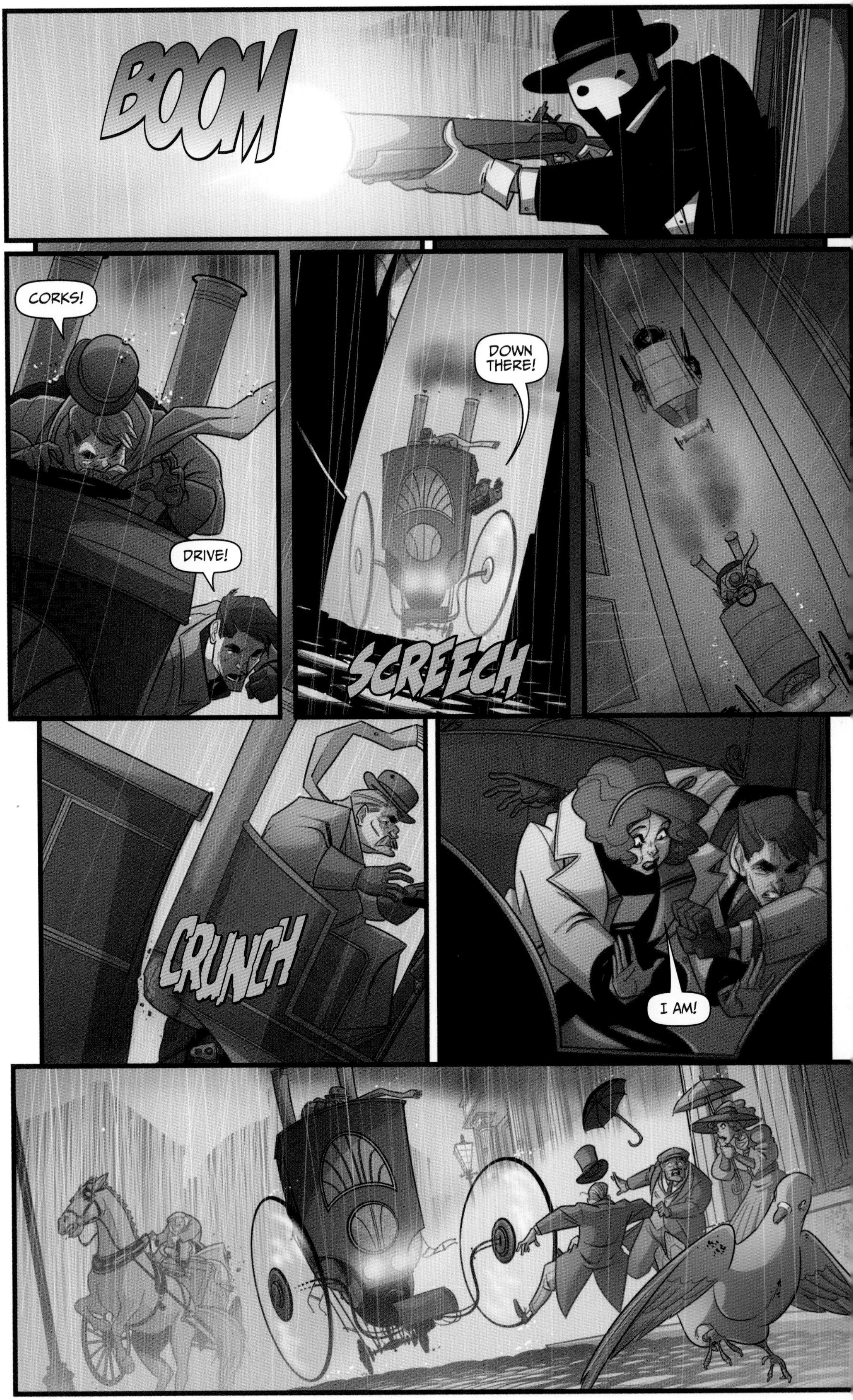
BOOM
CORKS!
DRIVE!
DOWN THERE!
SCREECH
CRUNCH
I AM!

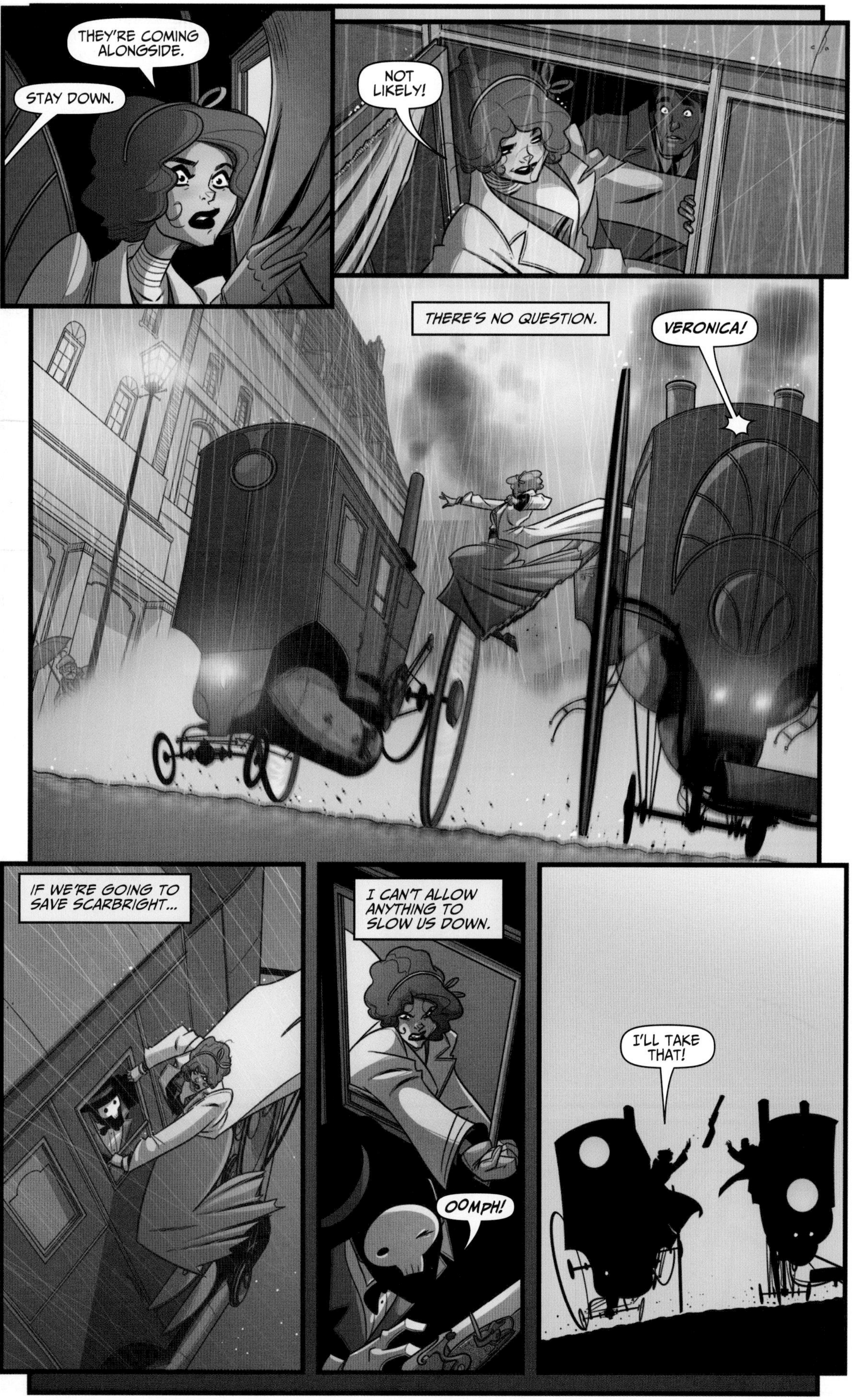
THEY'RE COMING ALONGSIDE.
STAY DOWN.
NOT LIKELY!
THERE'S NO QUESTION.
VERONICA!
IF WE'RE GOING TO SAVE SCARBRIGHT...
I CAN'T ALLOW ANYTHING TO SLOW US DOWN.
OOMPH!
I'LL TAKE THAT!

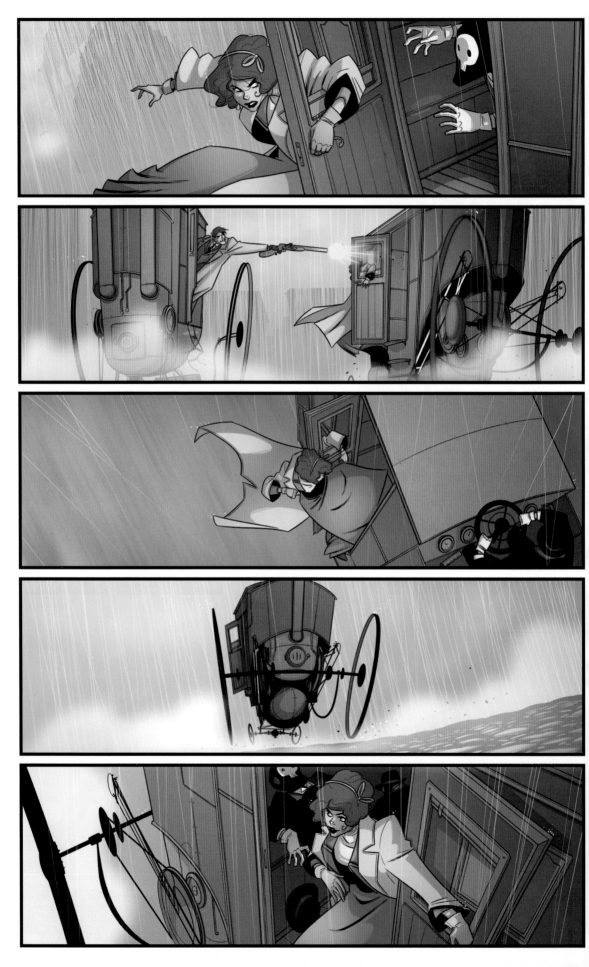

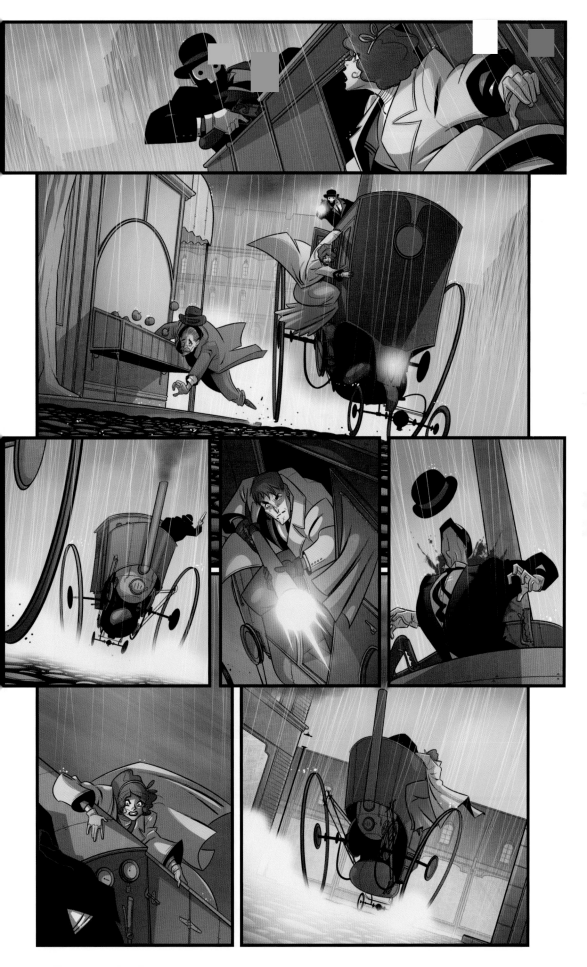

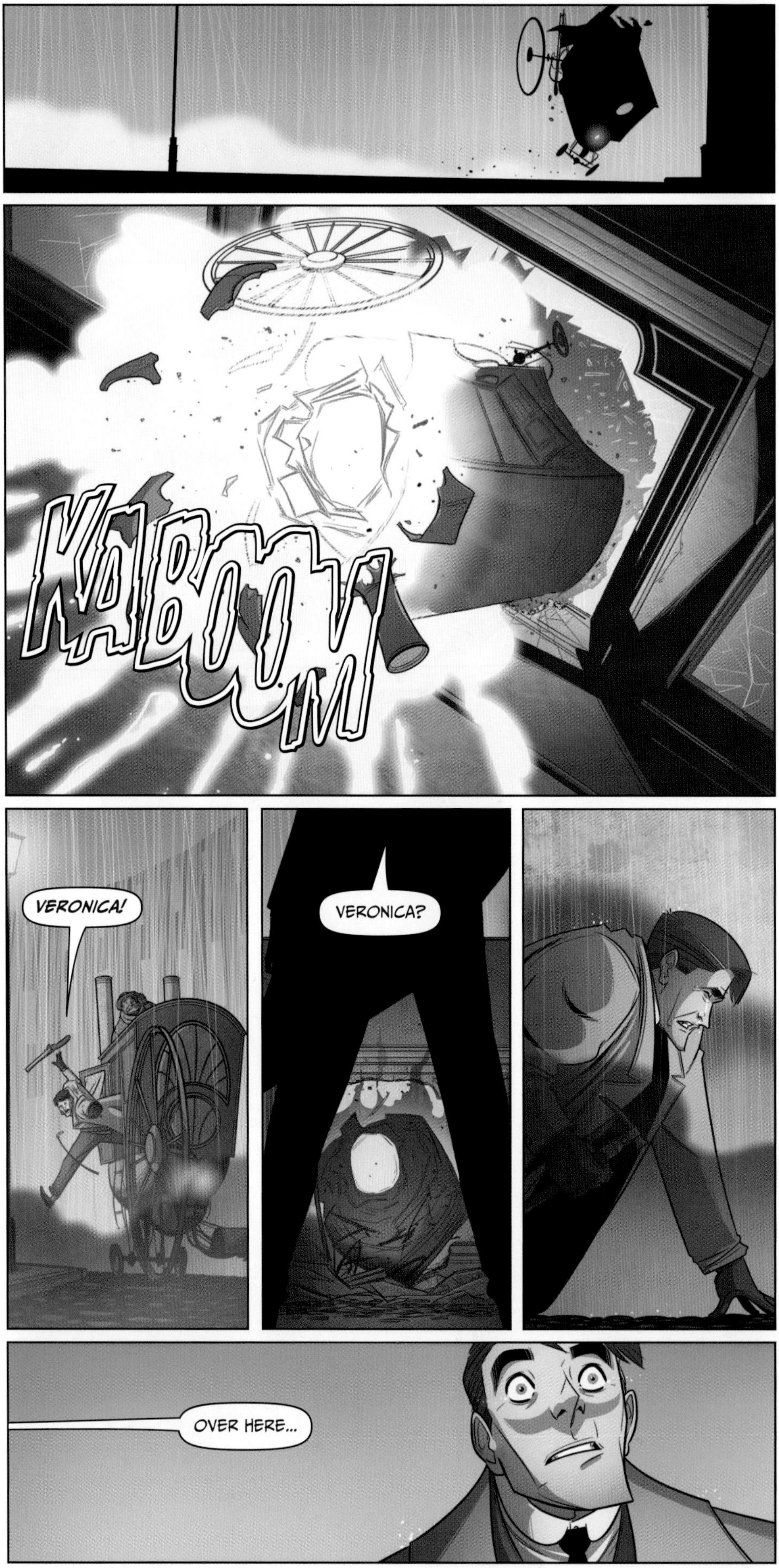
KABOOM
VERONICA!
VERONICA?
OVER HERE...

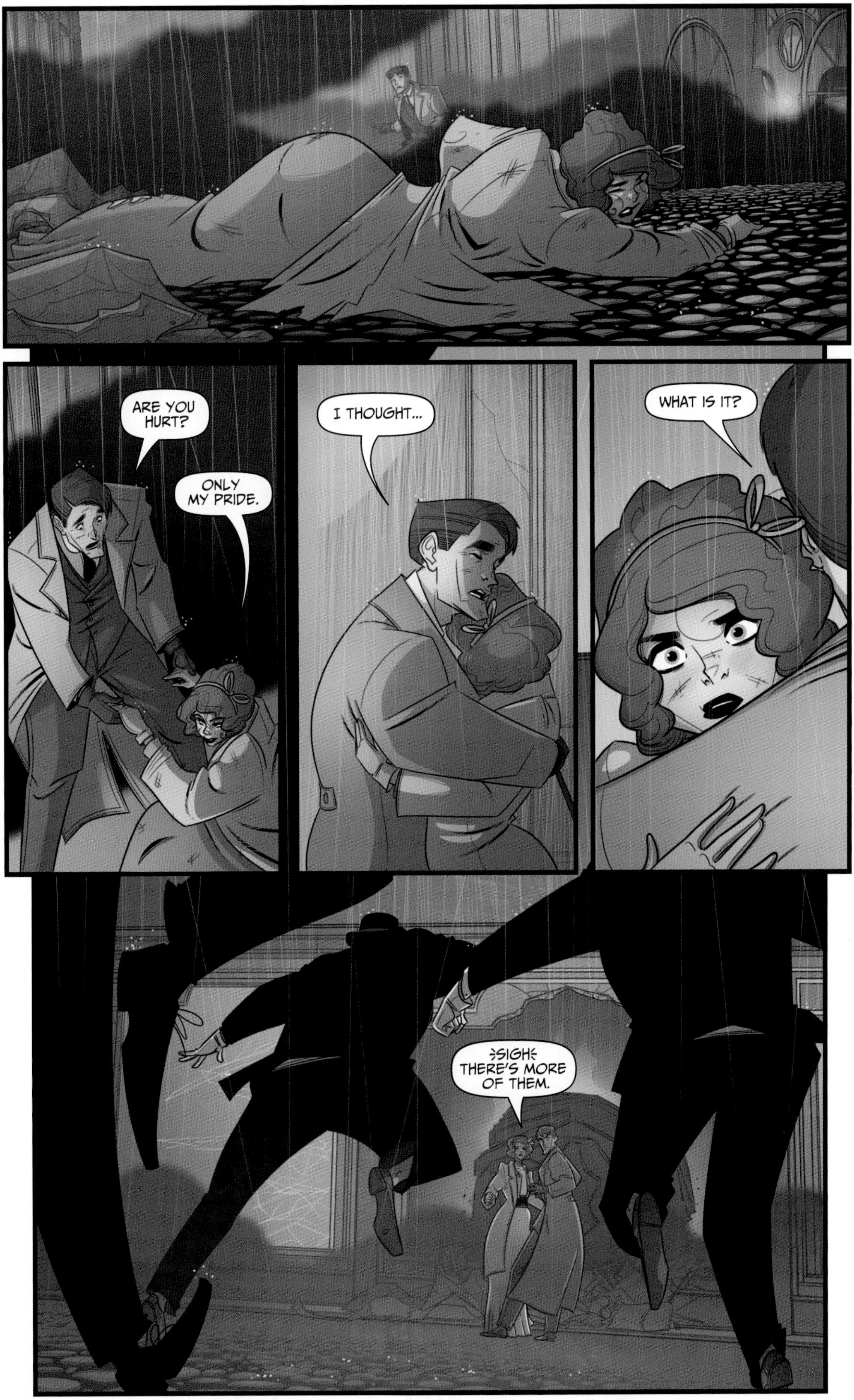
ARE YOU HURT?
ONLY MY PRIDE.
I THOUGHT...
WHAT IS IT?
SIGH
THERE'S MORE OF THEM.

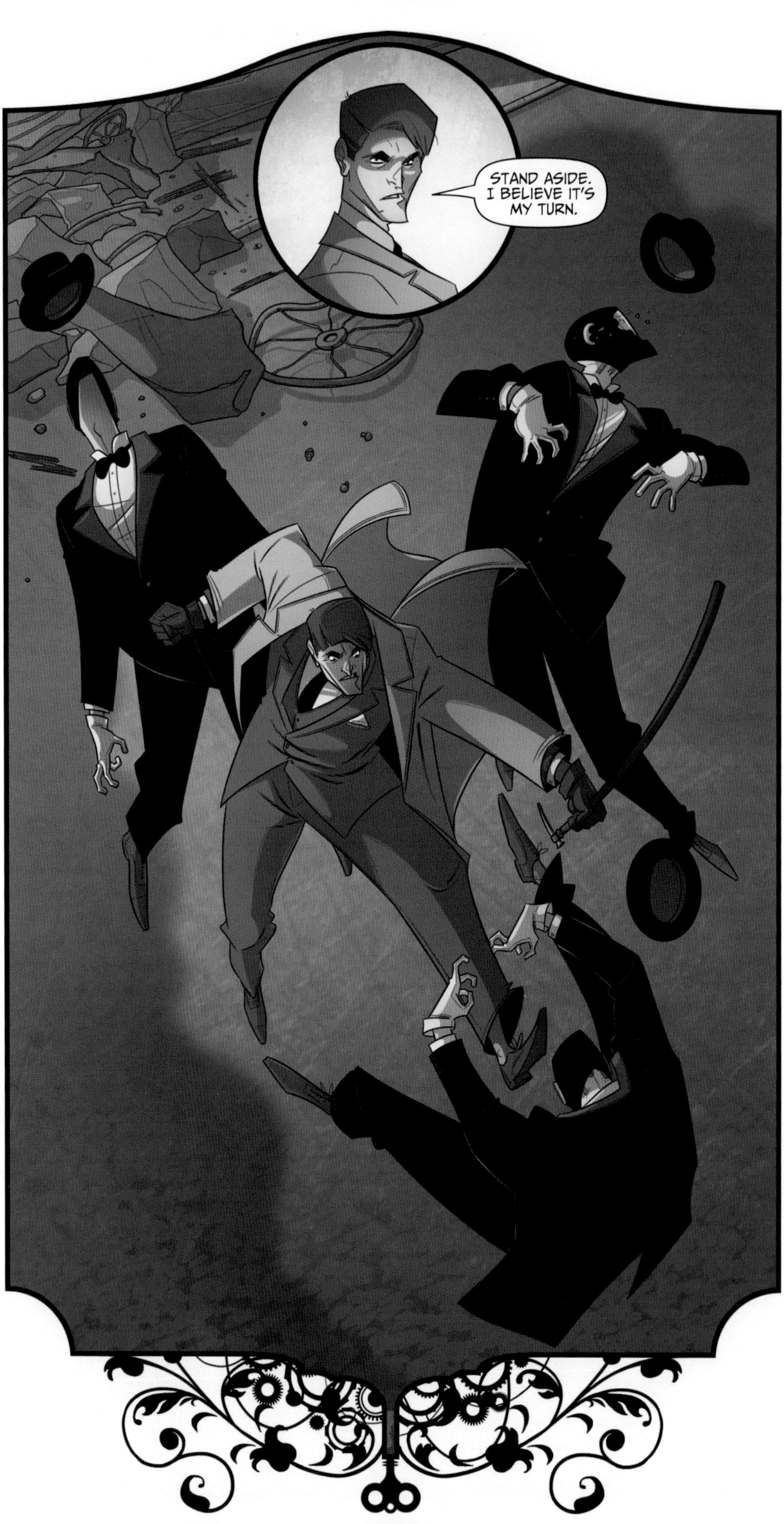
STAND ASIDE. I BELIEVE IT'S MY TURN.

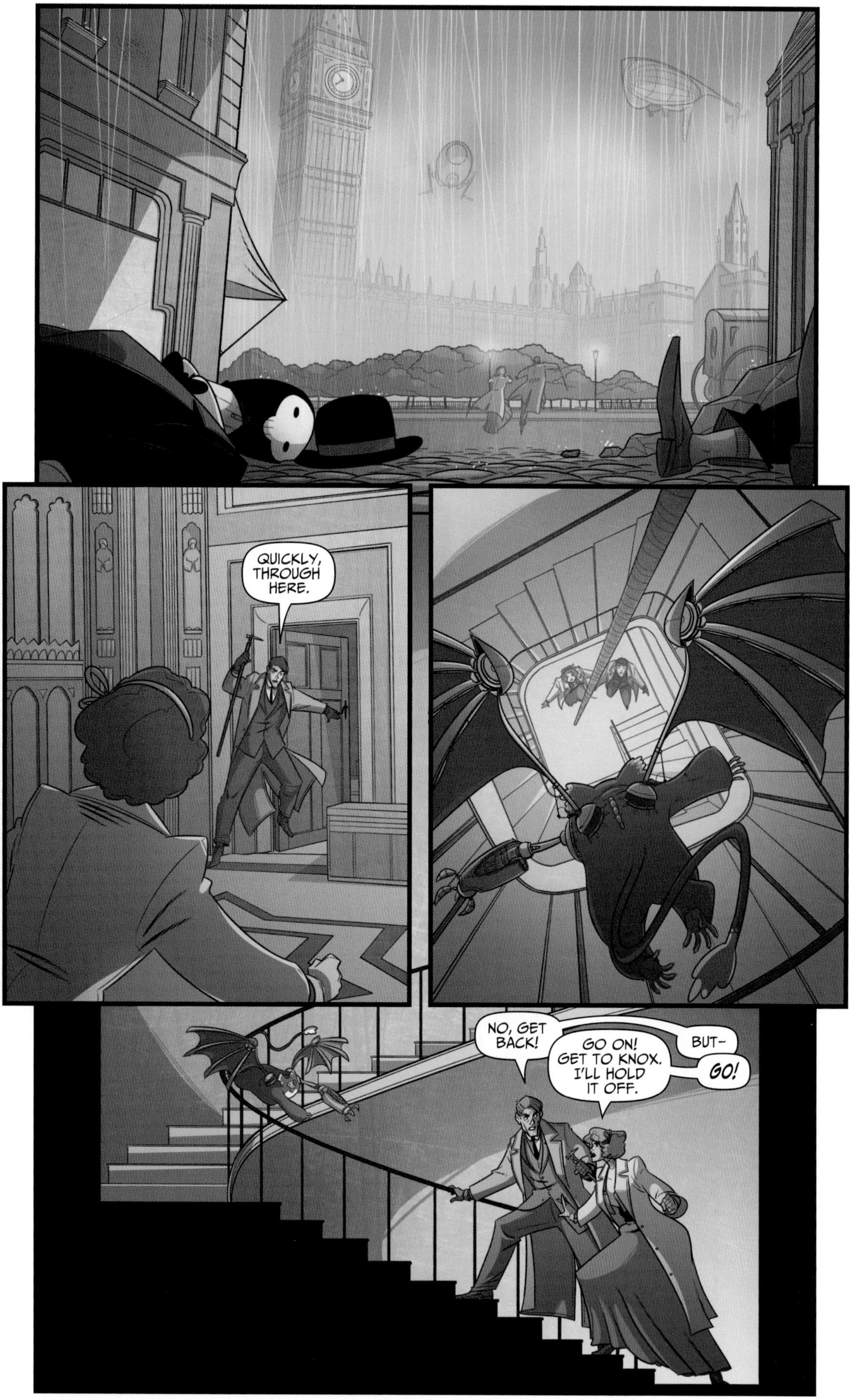
QUICKLY, THROUGH HERE.
NO, GET BACK!
GO ON! GET TO KNOX. I'LL HOLD IT OFF.
BUT-
GO!

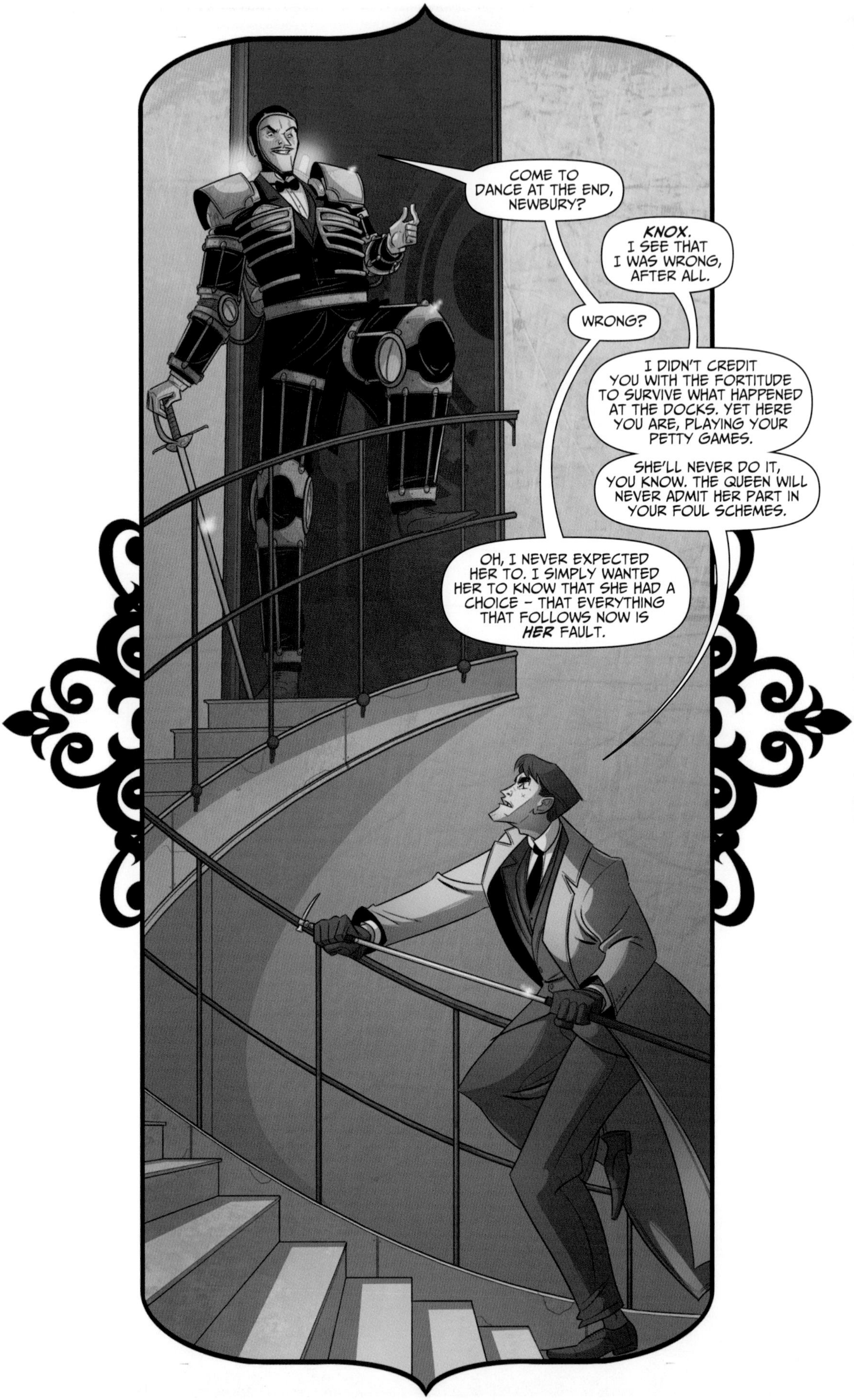
COME TO DANCE AT THE END, NEWBURY?
KNOX. I SEE THAT I WAS WRONG, AFTER ALL.
WRONG?
I DIDN'T CREDIT YOU WITH THE FORTITUDE TO SURVIVE WHAT HAPPENED AT THE DOCKS. YET HERE YOU ARE, PLAYING YOUR PETTY GAMES.
SHE'LL NEVER DO IT, YOU KNOW. THE QUEEN WILL NEVER ADMIT HER PART IN YOUR FOUL SCHEMES.
OH, I NEVER EXPECTED HER TO. I SIMPLY WANTED HER TO KNOW THAT SHE HAD A CHOICE - THAT EVERYTHING THAT FOLLOWS NOW IS HER FAULT.

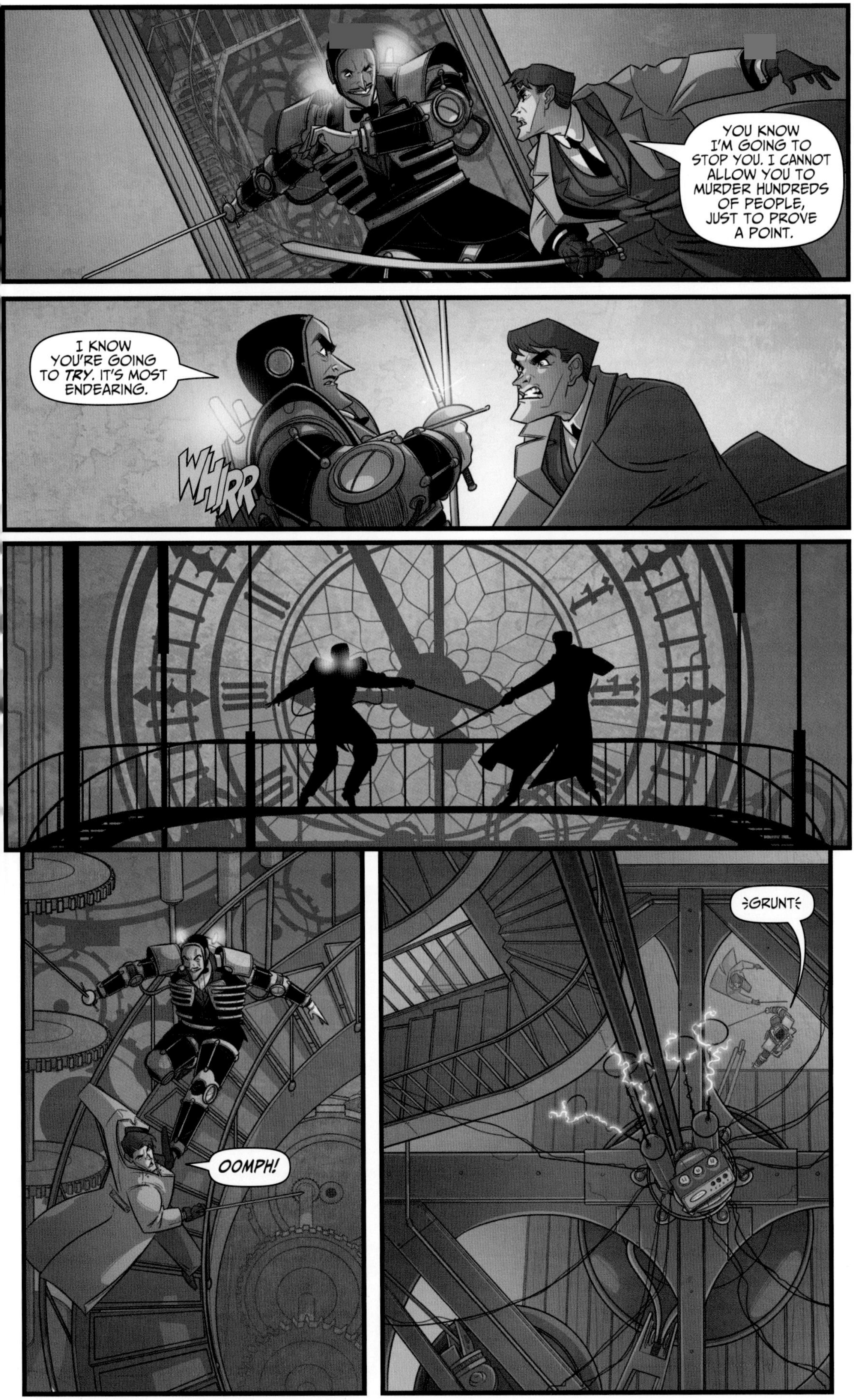
YOU KNOW I'M GOING TO STOP YOU. I CANNOT ALLOW YOU TO MURDER HUNDREDS OF PEOPLE, JUST TO PROVE A POINT.
I KNOW YOU'RE GOING TO TRY. IT'S MOST ENDEARING.
WHIRR
OOMPH!
GRUNT

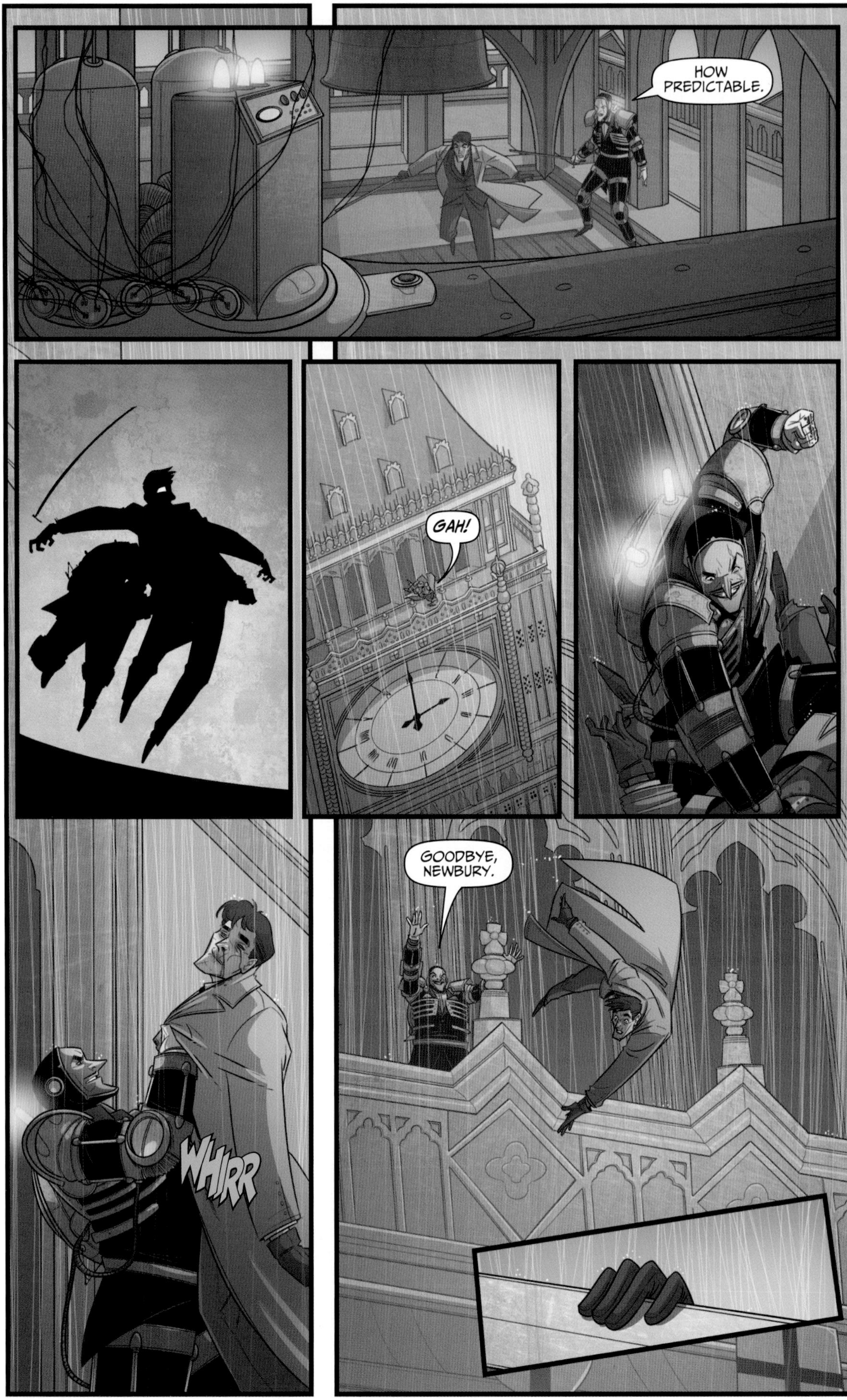
HOW PREDICTABLE.
GAH!
WHIRR
GOODBYE, NEWBURY.

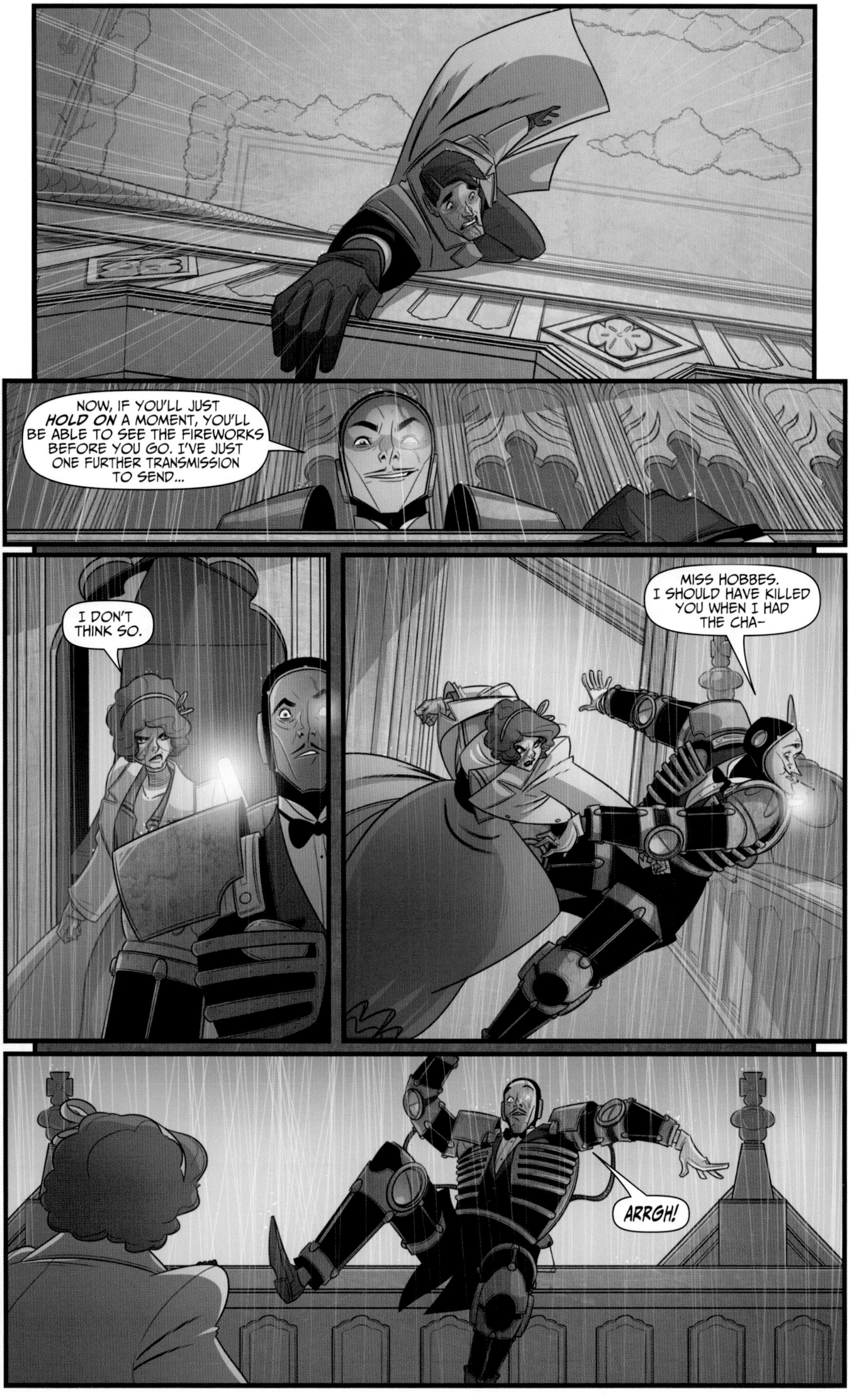
NOW, IF YOU'LL JUST HOLD ON A MOMENT, YOU'LL BE ABLE TO SEE THE FIREWORKS BEFORE YOU GO. I'VE JUST ONE FURTHER TRANSMISSION TO SEND...
I DON'T THINK SO.
MISS HOBBES. I SHOULD HAVE KILLED YOU WHEN I HAD THE CHA-
ARRGH!

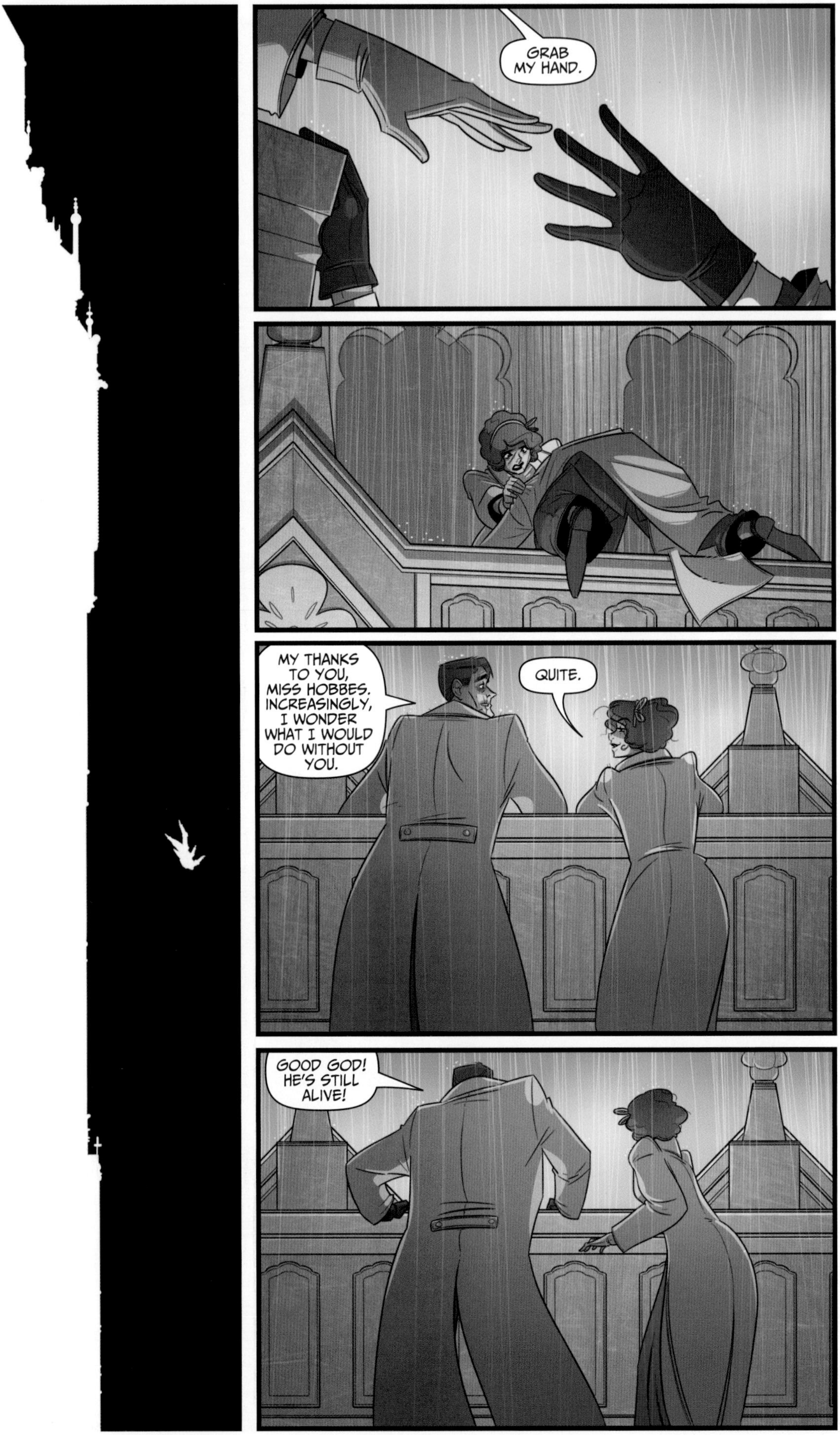
GRAB MY HAND.
MY THANKS TO YOU, MISS HOBBES. INCREASINGLY, I WONDER WHAT I WOULD DO WITHOUT YOU.
QUITE.
GOOD GOD! HE'S STILL ALIVE!

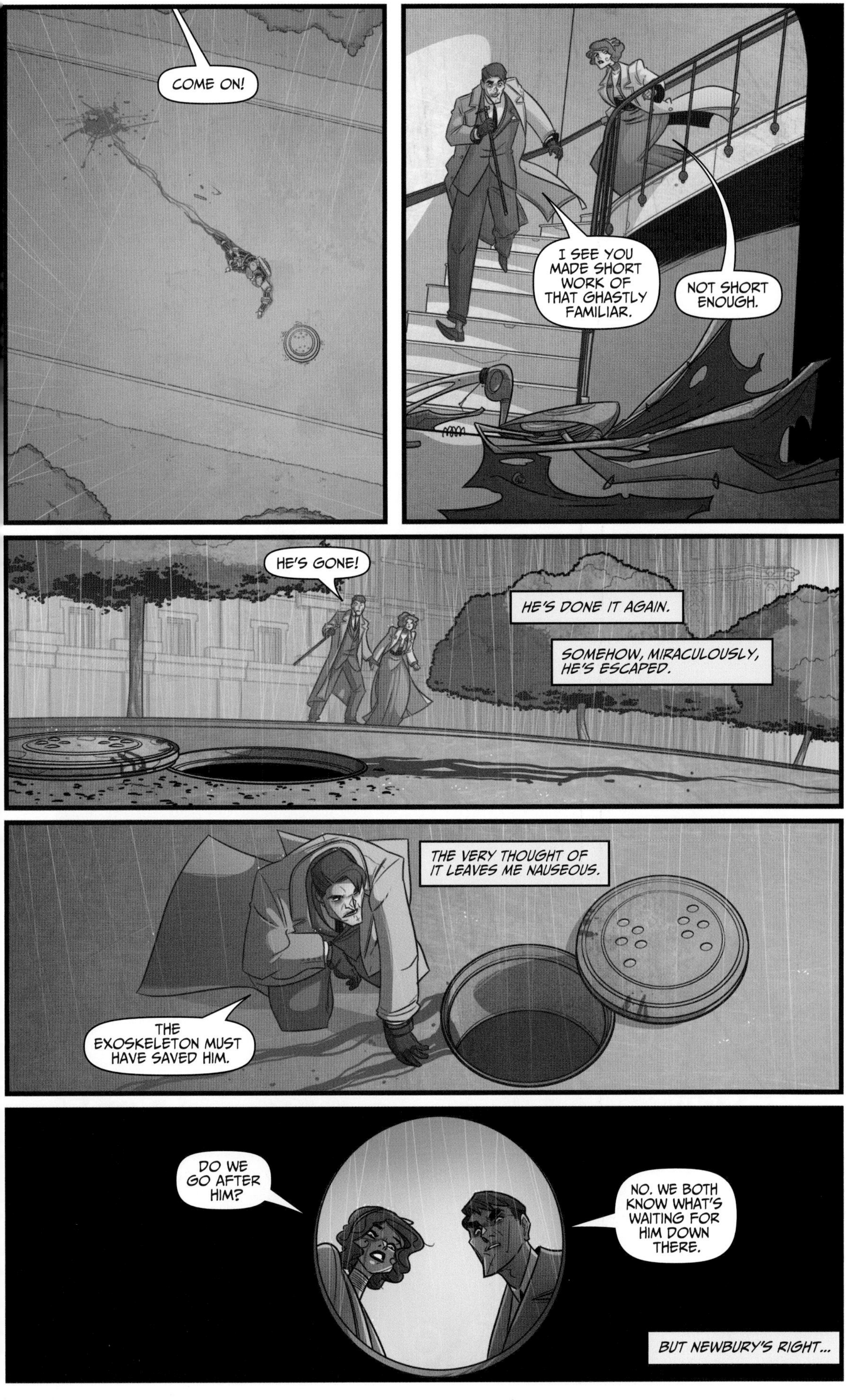
COME ON!
I SEE YOU MADE SHORT WORK OF THAT GHASTLY FAMILIAR.
NOT SHORT ENOUGH.
HE'S GONE!
HE'S DONE IT AGAIN.
SOMEHOW, MIRACULOUSLY, HE'S ESCAPED.
THE VERY THOUGHT OF IT LEAVES ME NAUSEOUS.
THE EXOSKELETON MUST HAVE SAVED HIM.
DO WE GO AFTER HIM?
NO. WE BOTH KNOW WHAT'S WAITING FOR HIM DOWN THERE.
BUT NEWBURY'S RIGHT...

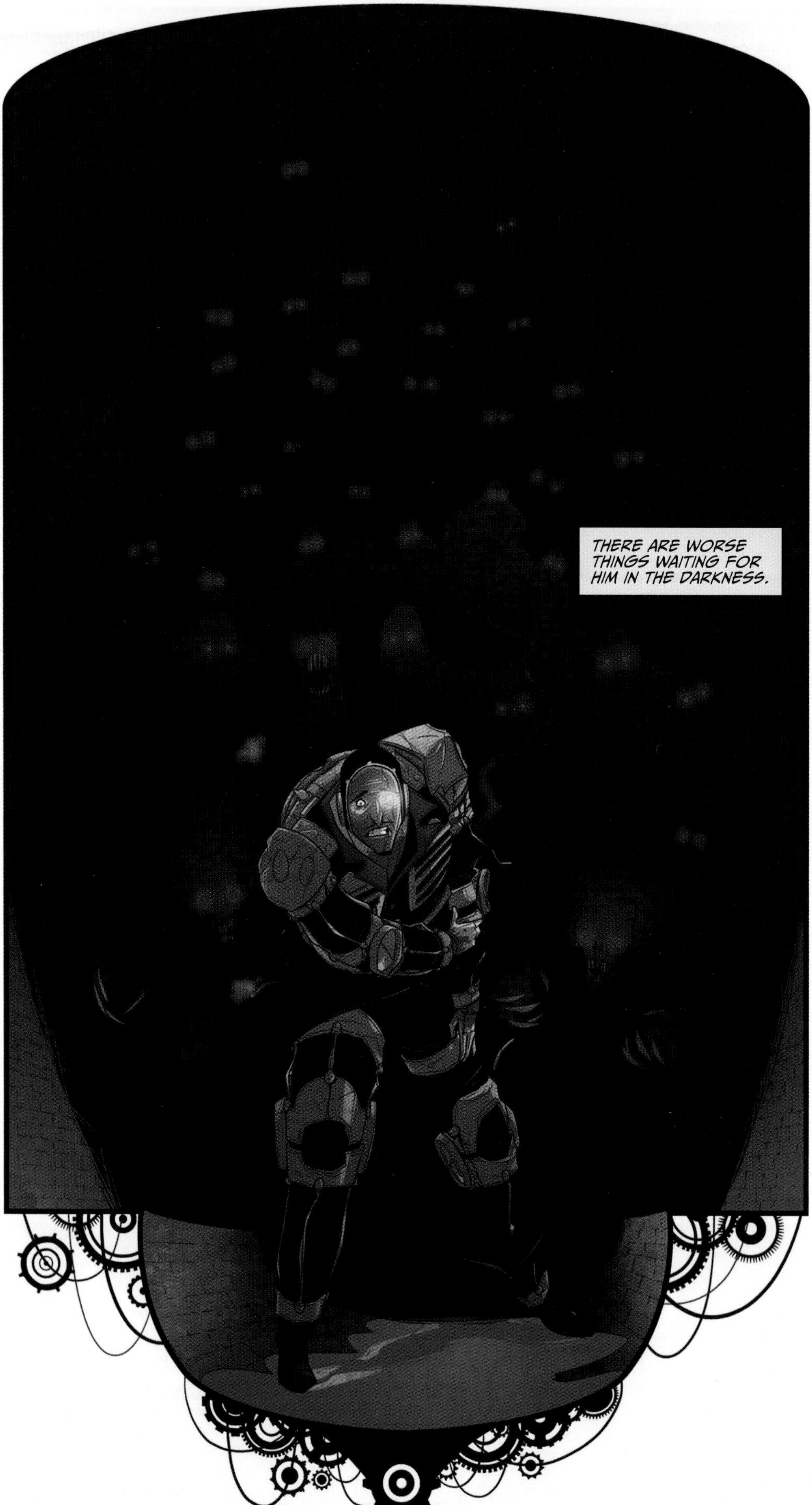
THERE ARE WORSE THINGS WAITING FOR HIM IN THE DARKNESS.

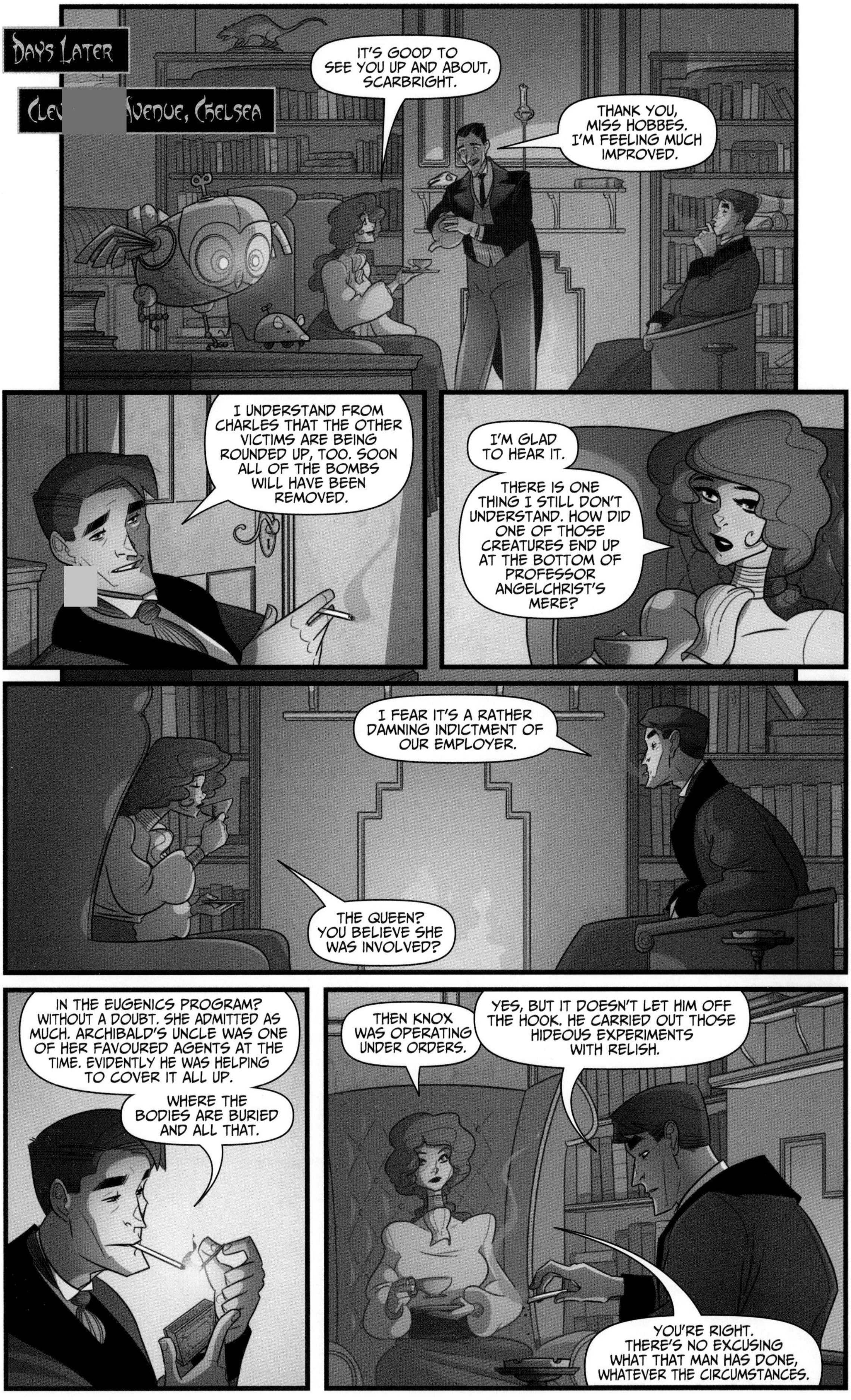

Days Later
Clev Avenue, Chelsea
IT'S GOOD TO SEE YOU UP AND ABOUT, SCARBRIGHT.
THANK YOU, MISS HOBBES. I'M FEELING MUCH IMPROVED.
I UNDERSTAND FROM CHARLES THAT THE OTHER VICTIMS ARE BEING ROUNDED UP, TOO. SOON ALL OF THE BOMBS WILL HAVE BEEN REMOVED.
I'M GLAD TO HEAR IT.
THERE IS ONE THING I STILL DON'T UNDERSTAND. HOW DID ONE OF THOSE CREATURES END UP AT THE BOTTOM OF PROFESSOR ANGELCHRIST'S MERE?
I FEAR IT'S A RATHER DAMNING INDICTMENT OF OUR EMPLOYER.
THE QUEEN? YOU BELIEVE SHE WAS INVOLVED?
IN THE EUGENICS PROGRAM? WITHOUT A DOUBT. SHE ADMITTED AS MUCH. ARCHIBALD'S UNCLE WAS ONE OF HER FAVOURED AGENTS AT THE TIME. EVIDENTLY HE WAS HELPING TO COVER IT ALL UP.
WHERE THE BODIES ARE BURIED AND ALL THAT.
THEN KNOX WAS OPERATING UNDER ORDERS.
YES, BUT IT DOESN'T LET HIM OFF THE HOOK. HE CARRIED OUT THOSE HIDEOUS EXPERIMENTS WITH RELISH.
YOU'RE RIGHT. THERE'S NO EXCUSING WHAT THAT MAN HAS DONE, WHATEVER THE CIRCUMSTANCES.

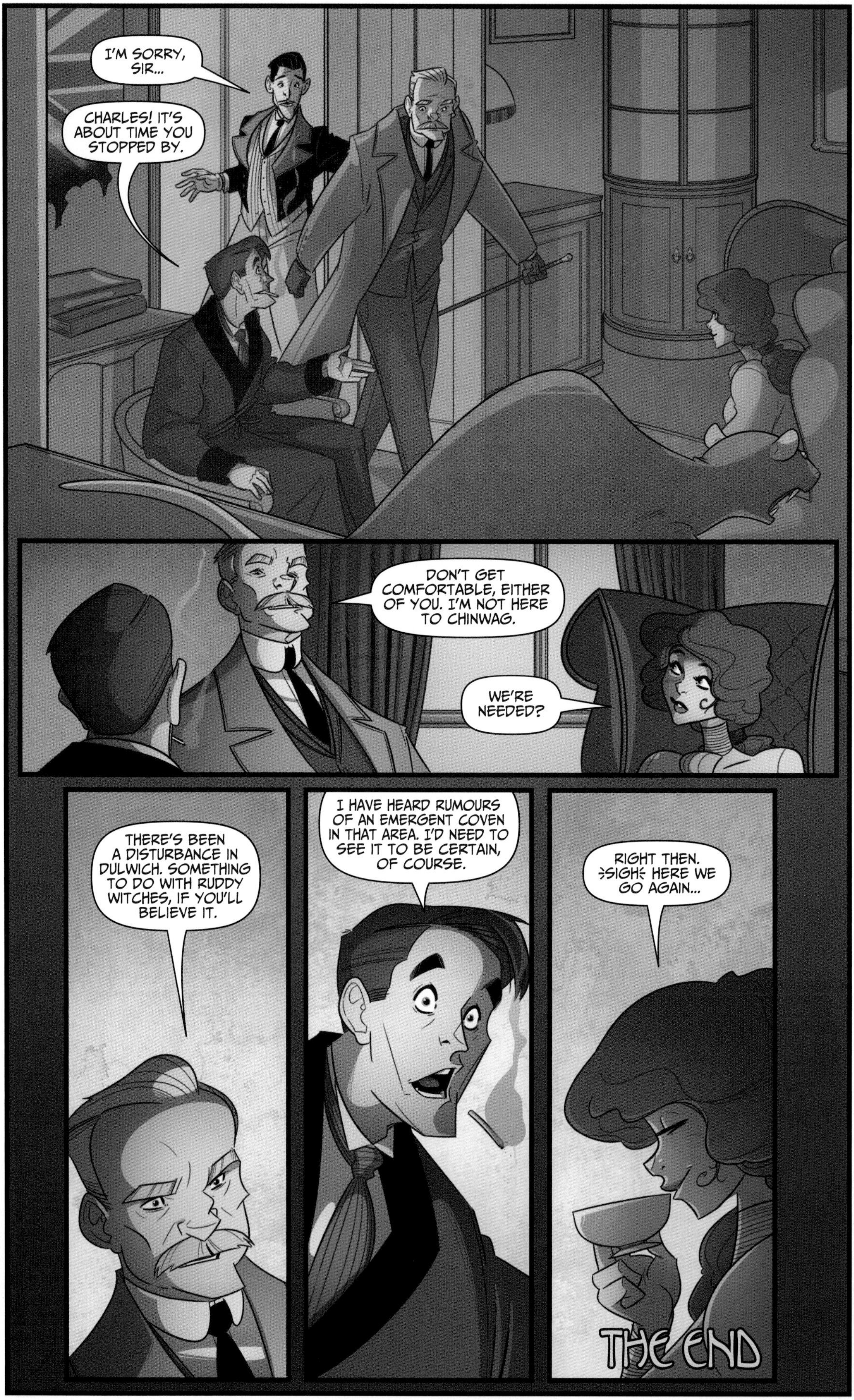
I'M SORRY, SIR...
CHARLES! IT'S ABOUT TIME YOU STOPPED BY.
DON'T GET COMFORTABLE, EITHER OF YOU. I'M NOT HERE TO CHINWAG.
WE'RE NEEDED?
THERE'S BEEN A DISTURBANCE IN DULWICH. SOMETHING TO DO WITH RUDDY WITCHES, IF YOU'LL BELIEVE IT.
I HAVE HEARD RUMOURS OF AN EMERGENT COVEN IN THAT AREA. I'D NEED TO SEE IT TO BE CERTAIN, OF COURSE.
RIGHT THEN. *SIGH* HERE WE GO AGAIN...
THE END

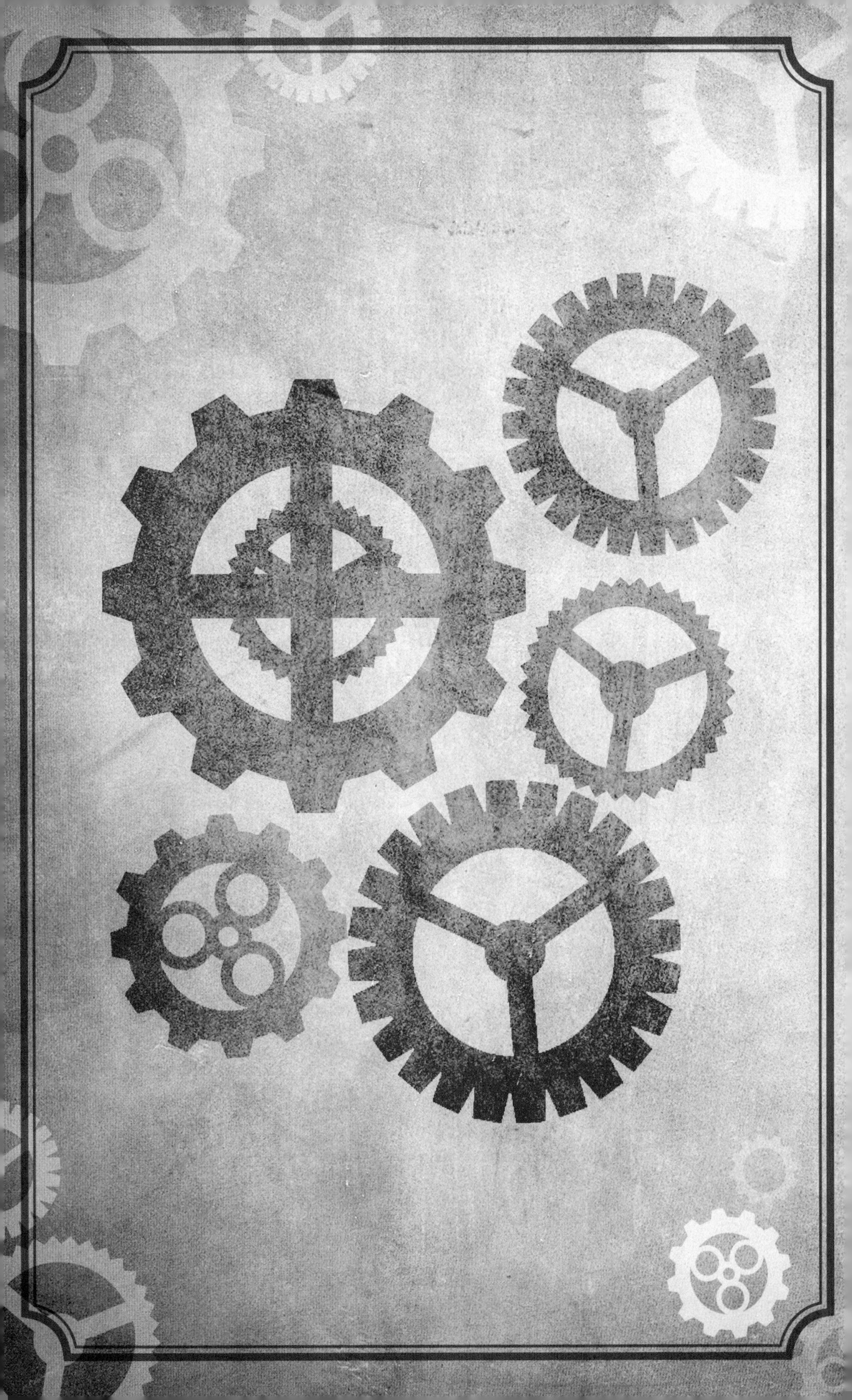

COVERS GALLERY

#1 COVER C BY **ARIANNA FLOREAN**

#3 COVER B BY **V.V. GLASS**

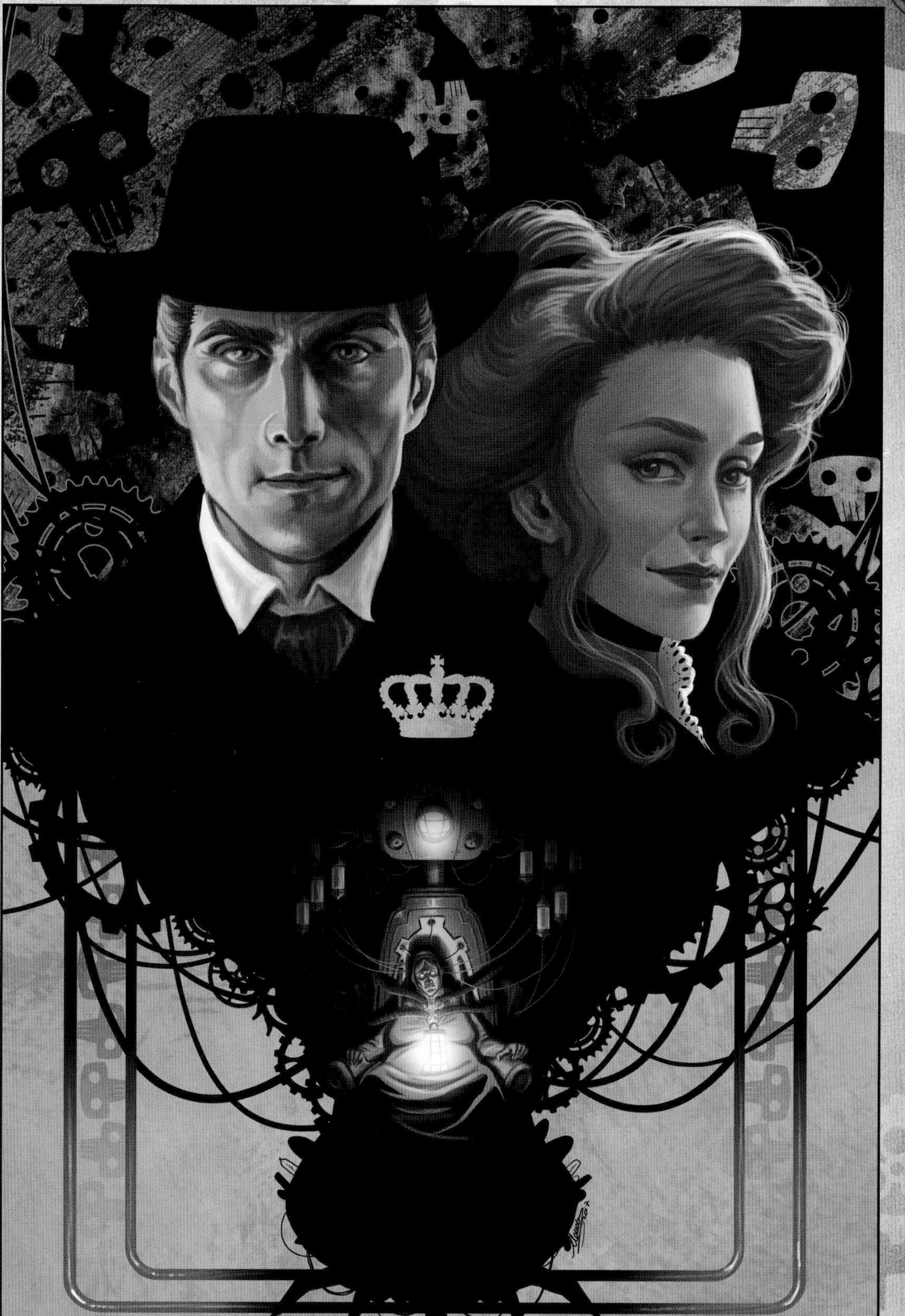

#2 COVER B BY **CLAUDIA IANNICIELLO**

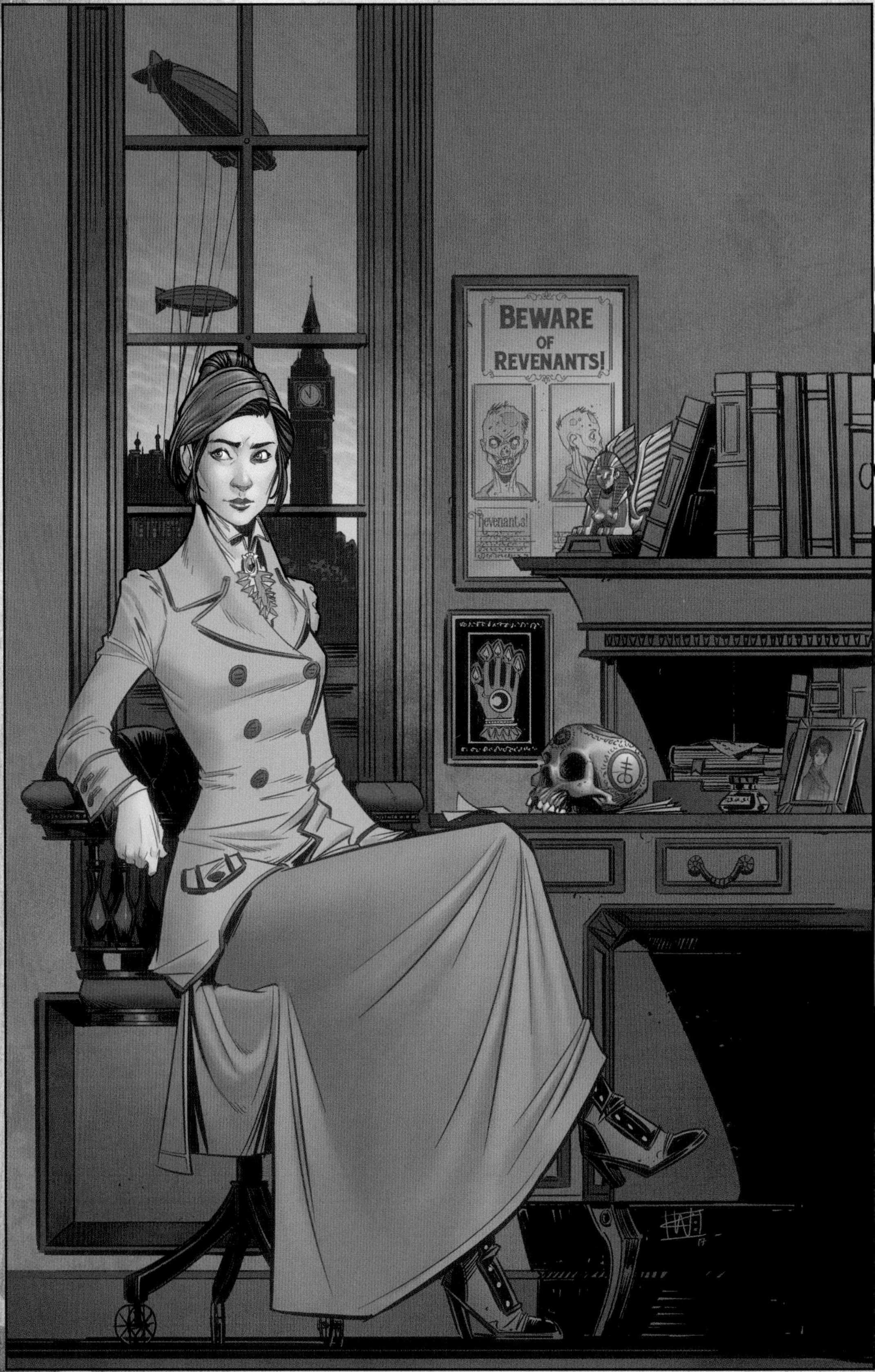
BEWARE
OF
REVENANTS!
Revenants!

#1 COVER B BY **CHRIS WILDGOOSE & ANDRE MAY**

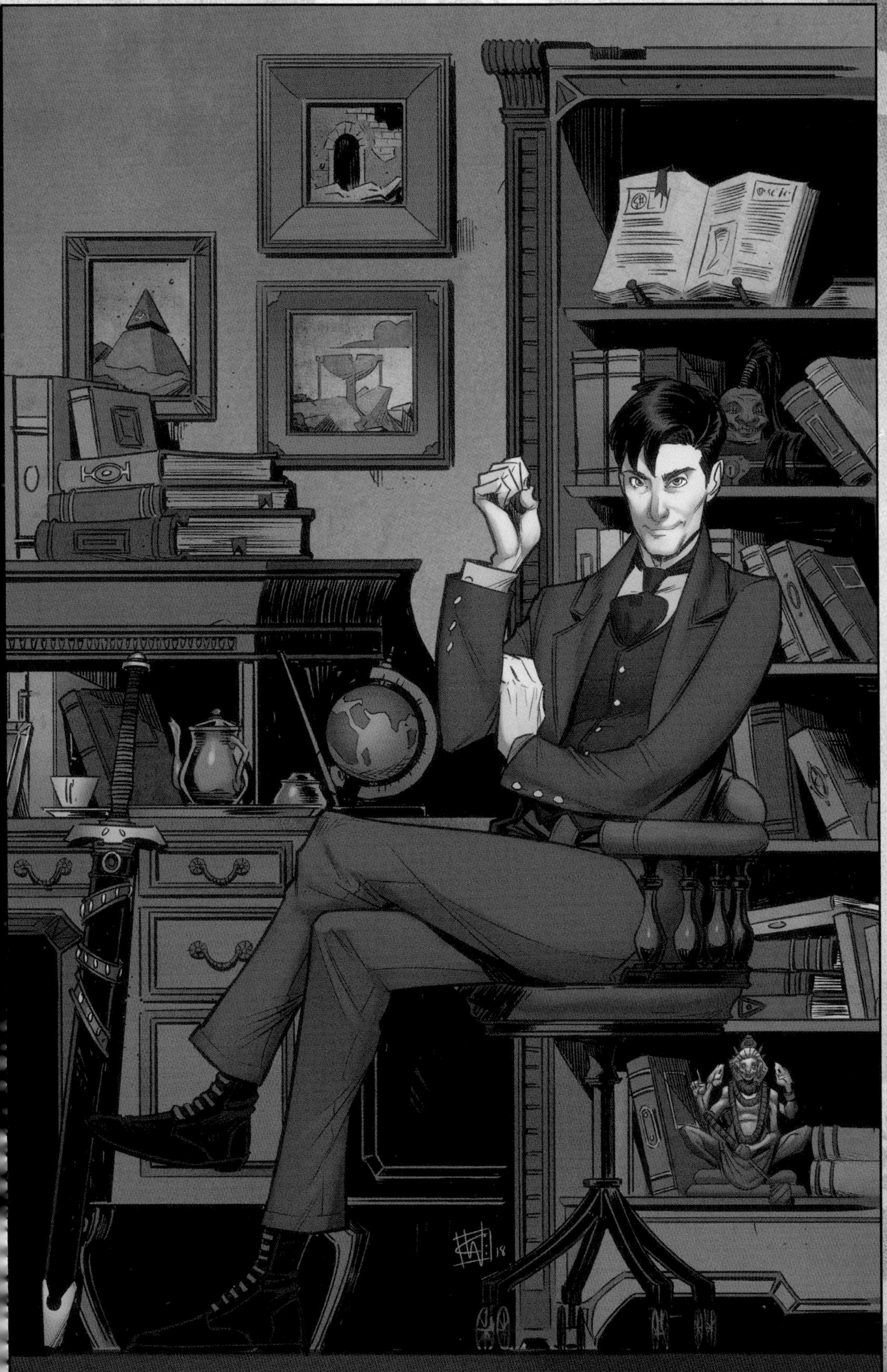

#4 COVER B BY **CHRIS WILDGOOSE & ANDRE MAY**

A FRIEND TO THE DEAD

A Newbury & Hobbes Story

By George Mann

"Corpses? Did you say *corpses*?"

"I did, Charles."

"Rising from the *dead*?"

"So the woman claims."

"Well, it's clearly some ill-conceived joke. Either that or she's lost complete control of her faculties. I mean, the dead don't simply wake up of an evening and decide to take a constitutional."

Newbury leaned back in his chair, taking a long draw on his cigarette. He considered Bainbridge's statement as he allowed smoke to ripple from his nostrils. "Well, you *say* that…"

"What do you mean, 'I *say* that'? You can't seriously believe these claims, Newbury. Miss Hobbes, a little help here…" Bainbridge turned in his seat, peering around to where

Veronica was standing before the bookcase a few feet away, leafing through the pages of one of Newbury's clippings folders.

They had gathered in Newbury's drawing room to hear the details of the new case with which he'd been presented that morning – a private matter, brought to his attention by a distraught young woman who'd sought him out in desperation after the police had failed to take the matter seriously. Judging by Bainbridge's incredulous expression, Newbury could quite well imagine the reception she'd received at the Yard.

"Oh, I think the two of you can manage perfectly well on your own," said Veronica, offering Newbury a playful smile before returning to her reading.

"Once again," sighed Bainbridge, "I find myself the sole voice of reason." He reached for his pipe. "She claims to have *seen* one of these wandering corpses?"

Newbury smiled. "She did. The 'shambling form of a man', dressed in filthy rags and stumbling between the headstones."

"Describes every drunk I've ever encountered," said Bainbridge.

Newbury laughed. "Quite. In and of itself, such a sighting would barely be worthy of our attention."

"But?" said Veronica, without lifting her eyes from the page.

"But when you consider that her husband's grave was found to have been recently disturbed – along with several others – I'm inclined to at least carry out some preliminary investigations."

Bainbridge shook his head. "This is madness, even for you. Disturbed graves, walking corpses... I can't believe you're even entertaining the idea of wasting your time with this."

"The woman seemed sincere, Charles. She's terrified that something untoward has become of her husband. And frankly, we need to be certain we're not dealing with some new strain of the revenant plague that's incubating inside the recently deceased."

"What a thought," said Bainbridge. He chewed thoughtfully on the end of his pipe, and then seemed to come to a decision. "All right, then. Where do we start?"

Newbury grinned. "With the husband's grave, of course."

The Church of St Barnabas in Southwark had seen better days. Where once it had stood as a stoic beacon against the bitter English weather, now it was losing its long battle with the elements, covered in a heavy patina of moss and ivy, as if the earth itself were reaching up to slowly claim it.

Two of the stained-glass windows had been boarded over, and the tower had developed an alarming lean, subsidence threatening to cause the whole building to topple. The roof was missing tiles and had been badly patched with tattered sheets of waxed canvas.

Newbury wondered how big the congregation must be. It was still an operating church – that much was clear from the fact the vicar was still carrying out funeral services, and presumably others, too – but Newbury couldn't believe the place attracted a healthy flock. It seemed so desolate, abandoned. Even now, in the mid-afternoon, mist wreathed the field of listing headstones around them, and the grass – unkempt and damp – was punctuated by patches of nettles and strangling weeds. Someone had long since stopped caring about the place.

A thud from the bottom of the nearby grave suggested the gravedigger, Samson, had finally earned his coin. "That's the bugger," came the voice from the muddy pit, loud and rude in the otherwise silent graveyard.

Newbury looked to the vicar, the Reverend James Baker, who was standing beside Bainbridge, arms folded across his chest. He looked flustered. He was in his fifties, Newbury guessed, with bushy grey eyebrows and the deep worry lines around his eyes. He was otherwise lean and muscular, and surprisingly tall, giving him a willowy appearance that belied his true frame. "Well, open it then," he snapped, and

Newbury couldn't tell whether his temper spoke of concern or impatience.

The gravedigger issued a grunt of acknowledgement. A few moments later, they heard the nails pop as he prised open the lid.

"Empty. Just like the last one."

Beside Newbury, Veronica sighed. She approached the edge of the grave, peering down. "No sign that the lid has been tampered with?"

"Hard to tell, miss," said Samson. "If someone has messed with it, they put it back all right."

Reverend Baker cleared his throat. "Well, I think we've all seen enough, don't you?" He glanced at Bainbridge. "I suggest we retreat to the vicarage for tea and leave poor Samson here to finish backfilling the grave."

"Very well," said Bainbridge. "I've got some questions to put to you regarding the funeral arrangements of the...umm...*victims* in question."

Baker nodded. "Of course." He beckoned for the others to follow. "Come along, this way."

The vicarage was a significantly more welcoming prospect than the church, and in a much more satisfactory state of repair. Newbury sat at the kitchen table beside Veronica, who was picking idly at a slice of sponge cake. It looked rather stale.

"No, I can assure you, Sir Charles – the bodies were very much in situ when the coffins were committed to the ground. There are numerous witnesses – family members who attended the services and such like."

"And you've seen nothing? No sign of grave robbers operating during the night? It's clear the graves have been disturbed. No voices or sounds of digging?"

"Nothing, I'm afraid. It's usually deathly quiet around here after dark, if you'll forgive my turn of phrase. Although I'm forced to admit – it

seems likely that I've missed something."

Bainbridge made a sound akin to a dissatisfied *humph*.

"Well, it's clear the bodies haven't climbed from the graves themselves," ventured Newbury. "Revenants would hardly stop to re-affix the coffin lids and backfill the graves behind them."

"So we can rule out an outbreak of post-mortem Revenants," said Bainbridge. "Thank God for that." He looked to Reverend Baker apologetically.

"I wouldn't be so sure of that," said Veronica. She'd stopped prodding the remains of her sponge cake. Slowly, she rose to her feet. She circled the table to stand before the sink, peering out of the window into the misty graveyard beyond. "*Look*, out there." She jabbed a finger towards the looming silhouette of the church. The others gathered around her, squinting to see. "There's someone out there. They way they're walking – it's shambolic, as if they have little control over their limbs...it reminds me of–"

"A Revenant!" finished Newbury. He ran to the kitchen door, heart racing. "Come on. This could be the answer we're looking for. We must get a better look at it. There's no time to lose!"

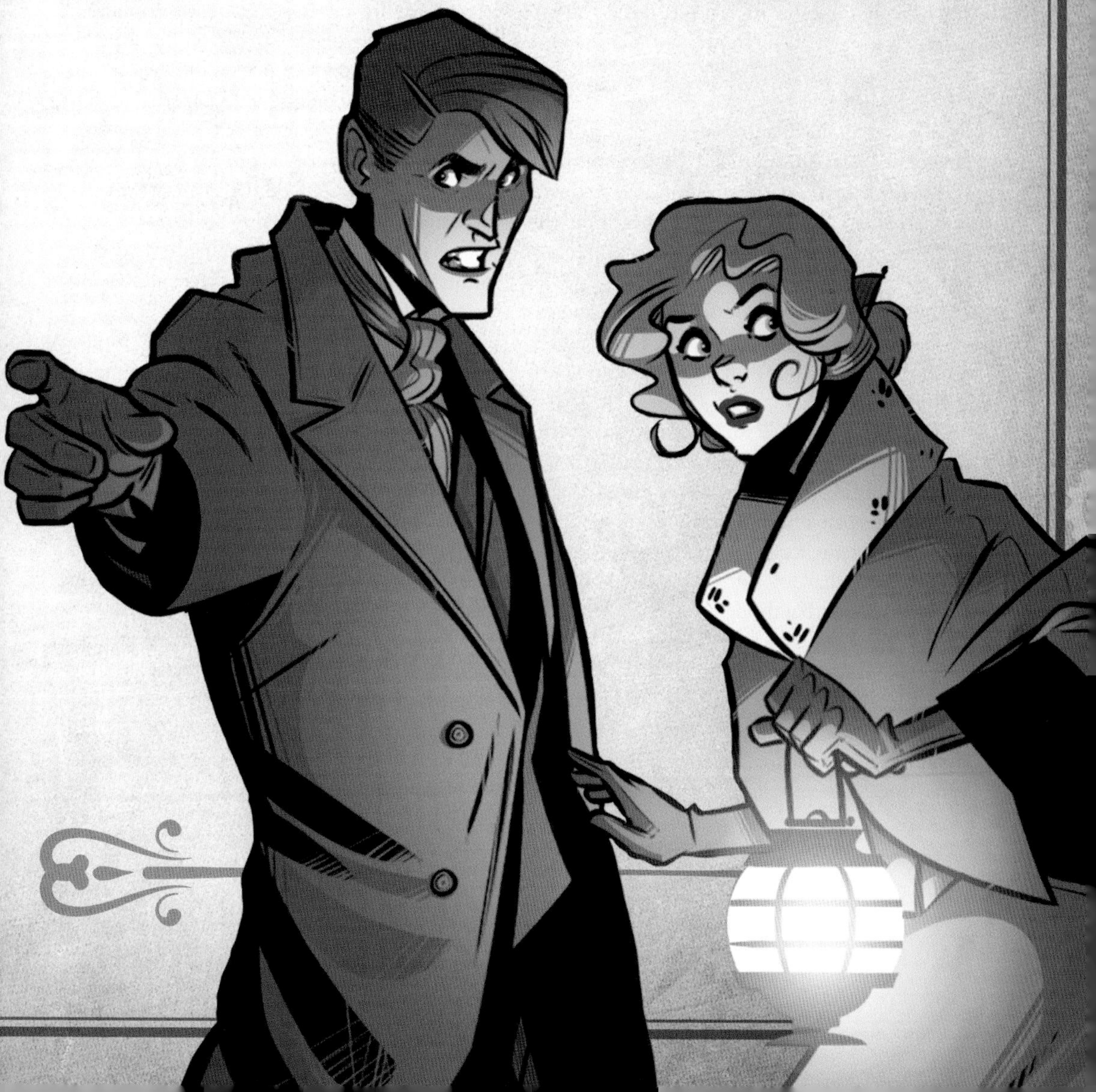

"Sir Maurice?"

Newbury peered into the swirling mist. Veronica's voice seemed distant, muffled by the syrupy fog that clung to the headstones, wrapping everything in its chill embrace. He couldn't see more than a few feet ahead of him, and in his haste to pursue the creature, he'd lost all sense of direction.

He ran a hand through his hair, listening – but there was nothing but the shrill cawing of a distant crow. Somewhere out there, amongst the forest of listing stones, lurked the creature they'd seen from the vicarage window. The thought of it made his skin crawl. It could be just yards away, and he wouldn't know until it was already on top of him, tearing at his throat...

"Sir Maurice?"

"Over here," he called. "Stay where you are. I'm coming." He set out in the direction of the vicarage, where the lamplight from the window glowed soft and diffuse, a welcome beacon in the fog. Veronica and Bainbridge were waiting for him by the door.

"You could have got yourself killed, running off like that," muttered Bainbridge. He cleared his throat. "Still… don't suppose you found anything useful?"

Newbury laughed. "No. Whatever it was, it didn't hang around."

"Probably for the best," said Veronica. "We're ill prepared for an encounter tonight. I suggest we retire for the evening and return tomorrow afresh."

"Agreed," said Bainbridge.

"All right," said Newbury. "Tomorrow, then, we catch ourselves a Revenant."

"If only there was something we could do about this damnable fog," muttered Bainbridge, as the three of them stalked through the maze of headstones, searching for any sign of the creature they'd glimpsed the previous evening. "It's diabolical."

"It's London," said Newbury.

"Aye, but I don't have to like it."

Newbury laughed, but it was mirthless.

Veronica touched Bainbridge's arm. She passed him a small silver hipflask. "Here. Take a nip from that."

"Much obliged." Bainbridge took a long draw, coughing as the alcohol hit his palate.

"We've been out here for hours. What say we retreat to the vica–" Veronica stopped short at the sound of an eerie growl, coming from somewhere close by in the fog. It was animalistic, inhuman.

Newbury tightened his grip on his pistol. "Come on. Follow me." He set off at a run, the others falling in behind him. His feet sunk into the damp loam as he raced across the graveyard in the direction of the sound. He could see nothing save for the looming shapes of the headstones, which seemed to swim out of the miasma towards him, threatening to send him tumbling with every step. And yet still there was no sign of the damnable creature.

He heard Bainbridge cry out behind him, and lurched to a halt, swinging his pistol up and around, expecting to see a Revenant bursting out of the fog… but there was only Bainbridge, mired in the soil of a freshly filled grave, his left leg buried up to the knee. Veronica was already by his side, hauling him out of the pit of loose earth.

Newbury walked over to join them, catching his breath. "Are you hurt?"

"No, no. I'm fine," said Bainbridge, trying, in vain, to wipe the mud from his trouser leg. He stopped suddenly. "Hold on. What's this?" He stooped to retrieve something from the ground, and then flinched, dropping it in abject disgust.

Newbury peered at the object in trepidation.

It was a severed human hand, pale and peeling. The stump was ragged where it had been torn off at the wrist, and there were impressions that looked disturbingly like teeth marks just above the thumb.

"We must have unearthed it as I pulled you free from the grave," said Veronica, her lips curling in disgust. "Someone's tried to bury it here, in another recent grave."

"It looks as if the entire grave has been disturbed," said Newbury. "We'll have to watch our step. Are you good to walk?"

"Aye," said Bainbridge. "I'll be fine."

"Very well." Newbury set out again, brandishing his gun, slower now. Ahead, the church tower emerged from the tubercular haze, a stark, angular silhouette. He edged closer until the building fully resolved from the murk. The wooden door was ajar. He paused on the threshold. Inside, someone, or something, was drawing heavy breath.

Cautiously, he beckoned the others forward, nudging the door open with the nose of his gun. He peered into the gloomy interior of the church hall.

There in the aisle, hunched over the glossy mess of a fresh corpse, was a thing that had once been a man, but was now little more than a shambling corpse, riddled with the Revenant plague, its clothes reduced to threads, its hair hanging long and limp, its skin yellowed and peeling. Tatters of bloody flesh hung from its open mouth.

It looked up at Newbury and issued a low, threatening growl.

Newbury backed away, levelling his pistol as the revenant slowly rose to its full height.

It was taller and broader than him; around six foot, with ropey muscles and a wiry frame, despite its half-rotted appearance. Its fingertips ended in gnarled talons that dripped with gore. Flecks of torn flesh still clung to its jagged, blackened teeth. The stench was horrendous, ripe with decay and the iron tang of congealed blood. The half-eaten corpse at the creature's feet had belonged to a woman and couldn't have been more than a few days old – although it was difficult to be certain, now that her belly had been opened and her pale face was smeared with blood.

The revenant's eyes remain fixed on Newbury as it edged forward, sniffing the air, enamoured by the prospect of a fresh kill. He could see its body coiling as it moved, muscles tensing as it prepared to pounce. He knew from experience how fast the things could move.

Behind Newbury, Veronica and Bainbridge filed into the church. Neither of them uttered a word. Bainbridge made a series of short, sharp movements, and the ensuing mechanical *whirr* told Newbury that he had activated the electrical mechanism inside his cane.

The creature emitted a low growl, and then launched itself at Newbury, talons flashing.

Newbury squeezed the trigger of his pistol, and it barked loudly in the cavernous interior of the church. Two shots punched holes in the creature's chest but did little to slow it. It struck Newbury hard in the shoulder, causing him to topple backwards, colliding with Veronica and sending them both sprawling to the floor. Veronica rolled as she struck the slabs, breaking clear of the tangle, but Newbury was pinned beneath the weight of the monstrous creature, his pistol lost in the

fall. Pain flared in his shoulder as the creature's talons raked his flesh.

He grabbed for its throat, scrabbling until his fingers found purchase. He pushed its head back in an effort to hold its gnashing jaws from his face.

Newbury could sense Bainbridge to his left, his cane crackling with electrical discharge, but knew that his own proximity to the creature made it impossible for Bainbridge to deploy the weapon without risk of electrifying him, too. He was going to have to try to throw the thing clear. No easy feat, given its inhuman strength, its primal determination.

The muscles in his forearm burned with the exertion of holding the creature at bay. Gore spattered his face as the revenant hissed through broken teeth.

"That's enough now, Matthew. Let the man be."

The voice had come from somewhere off to Newbury's right, originating in the shadowy aisle that flanked the main hall. He heard footsteps drawing closer. The revenant seemed to hesitate, but its yellow eyes remained trained on Newbury's throat.

"What the devil?" This from Bainbridge, who clearly had a better view of proceedings than Newbury.

"Reverend Baker?" said Veronica. "You *know* this creature?"

Baker ignored the question. "Matthew. *Listen* to me, now. Focus on my voice. You don't need to do this. You know this is wrong. Fight your instincts. Remember what I taught you."

The revenant emitted another low growl.

"Matthew?"

And resumed its attack. Newbury felt his arm buckling, the creature's jaws pushing closer to his face. Its breath was hot and foul against his cheek. "Charles…"

Suddenly the world was ringing. The crack of an explosion echoed through the cavernous hall. The creature astride him went limp. Something wet pattered against his face, ran down his arms. He shoved the creature hard and it rolled off of him, collapsing to the slabs beside him with a wet, sickening thud.

Veronica was immediately by his side, helping him back to his feet. He wiped at his eyes, trying to make sense of what was going on. His hands were covered in blood.

Reverend Baker was on his knees beside the now headless corpse of the revenant, cradling the body up into his arms, tears streaming from his eyes. Beside him, on the ground, rested a still-smoking shotgun.

"Oh, Matthew. I'm so sorry, son. I'm so sorry."

"*Son?*" Bainbridge deactivated his cane with a twist of the headstock. "You mean to say this...*this*..." he paused for a moment, his expression softening, "...this was your son."

Baker looked up at him with pleading eyes. "He was once, yes. Not so very long ago. Until he contracted the plague from some fallen woman in Whitechapel."

Newbury stepped forward, placed a gentle hand on the vicar's shoulder. "And you meant to prevent him from killing. From feeding on the living."

Baker nodded. "It was me, all along. I disinterred the recently deceased, brought them here for him to feed. I thought...I thought...well, I thought it was the lesser sin. If it prevented him from taking the life of another..."

"You saved him from that," said Veronica. "You stopped him from becoming a killer."

"And now I have become one myself," said Baker. He issued a wracking sob, his entire body shaking.

"No," said Newbury. "He was no longer your son. He was beyond that. I owe you my life."

Baker shook his head. "All of those people, denied their proper rest. Their poor families. What have I done?"

"What any of us would have done," said Bainbridge. He looked to Newbury. "Come along. Fetch a spade. It's time to put an end to this whole sorry mess."

Baker scrambled to his feet. "A spade? You mean to bury him? Matthew?"

Bainbridge nodded. "And return that poor woman's body to whichever grave it came from."

Baker seemed barely able to comprehend what Bainbridge was saying. "I'll come quietly after that, Sir Charles. I'll confess to everything."

"There'll be no need for any of that," said Bainbridge.

"It's not just the bodies you intend to bury," said Newbury.

Bainbridge cocked a wan smile. "Indeed."

"But what will you tell them?" said Veronica. "The families? Mrs. Temple, who first came to ask for Sir Maurice's help?"

"We'll tell them the truth," said Bainbridge. "That a revenant had been stalking the graveyard and consuming the bodies of the recently deceased. That's all there was to it. Now the revenant has been...*dealt* with, and the matter is closed."

Baker was shaking. He began to stutter some words of thanks, but Bainbridge waved him quiet. "Come now, Reverend. There's a eulogy to be said. Let's do this properly."

Baker nodded, tears still trickling down his cheeks.

With a final glance at Newbury, Bainbridge pushed aside the door and led them out into the mist-laden night.

THE END

CREATOR BIOS

GEORGE MANN is the writer behind the *Dark Souls*, *Warhammer 40,000*, *Doctor Who: The Lost Dimension*, *Doctor Who: Supremacy of the Cybermen*, and *Doctor Who: The Eighth Doctor* comics, and is the author and creator of *Newbury & Hobbes*, as well as *Wychwood*, the *Tales of the Ghost* and numerous other novels and stories. He lives in Grantham with his wife and children..

DAN BOULTWOOD interweaves the suave decadence of David Niven, the sartorial elegance of Bertie Wooster and the streetwise cunning of a pre-War cockney gangster. He should have been born in 1921, in time to dodge the draft of the Second World War and become an unscrupulous spiv blackmarketeer. Instead, he was born in 1980. Too young to embrace New Romanticism, he chose to become a comic book artist instead. His work has graced such titles as *The Baker Street Irregulars*, *Hope Falls* and *Haggis & Quail*. His B-Movie-inspired *It Came!* is published by Titan Comics.

ROB STEEN is an experienced letterer whose skilled calligraphy has enlivened the works of many publishers, from Marvel comics such as *Wolverine and the X-Men* and *Fury: MAX*, DC titles such as *Arrowsmith* and *Astro City*, Valiant's *Harbinger* and *Bloodshot*. He has worked on Titan's *Warhammer 40,000*, *Rivers of London*, and *The Steel Prince*.